B

Understanding Company Strategy

An Introduction to Analysis and Implementation

Second Edition

Brian Houlden

BLACKWELL
Business

First published 1990
Reprinted 1991, 1992
First published in paperback 1993
Second edition published 1996

Blackwell Publishers Ltd
108 Cowley Road
Oxford OX4 1JF
UK

Blackwell Publishers Inc.
238 Main Street
Cambridge, Massachusetts 02142
USA

British Library Cataloguing in Publication Data

A CIP catalogue record for this book is available from the
British Library.

Library of Congress Cataloging-in-Publication Data

Houlden, Brian Thomas
Understanding company strategy : an introduction to analysis and
implementation / Brian Houlden. — 2nd ed.
p. cm.
Includes bibliographical references.
ISBN 0–631–20090–8 (alk. paper)
1. Strategic planning. I. Title.
HD30.28.H69 1996
658.4'012—dc20   96–6457
                                     CIP

ISBN 0–631–200908

Typeset in 11 on 13 pt Palatino
by Graphicraft Typesetters Ltd, Hong Kong
Printed in Great Britain by T. J. Press Ltd, Padstow, Cornwall.

This book is printed on acid-free paper

Page 9 - 66

Contents

Contents

Contents

Contents

Contents

Contents

Contents

Contents

Contents

Foreword

by Sir Adrian Cadbury

I enjoyed reading Brian Houlden's book on company strategy, because it sets the essential issues out clearly and it is written in straightforward English. The book is addressed to all those with a responsibility for planning the future of their part of a company or of the company as a whole. It will prove particularly useful to those who are coming to grips with issues of strategy for the first time. In addition to being intelligible to its business audience, *Understanding Company Strategy* has the merit of setting out how to develop a strategic plan from a standing start.

In the past, most small to medium-sized firms could rely on the growth of the industries of which they were a part to carry them forward. But the business world then was more predictable and discontinuities were less frequent. Every company now needs to give conscious thought to shaping its future in line with the way in which it predicts that its markets will evolve.

I agree with Brian Houlden on the importance of analysing not only the business environment within which the company has to operate, but also the likely actions of competitors. This is an aspect of strategic planning which most of us do less well than we should. The danger is that we draw up our plans on the basis of beating what our competitors are doing now, forgetting that they too are looking ahead. We have to devise strategies which will deliver a decisive advantage over what our competitors may have in mind. Competition is dynamic and our strategic thinking has to be dynamic as well.

Another aspect of strategy which is comprehensively dealt with in the book is the way in which the forward plans of a business unit – planning from the bottom up – need to be married with the top–down strategy of the board. The plans drawn up by the operating units will focus on the development of their existing businesses. The board has to decide whether those businesses fit its overall strategy for the company and, if they do not, how the company is to get from where it is now to where it wants to go. Both bottom–up and top–down planning are essential; the key lies in how they are brought together and in winning everyone's commitment to the outcome.

Brian Houlden brings out well the importance of distinguishing between strategic plans and forward budgets. Plans which are based on numbers projected into the future are worthless. Since the numbers will be wrong in any case, extended budgets of this kind remain untouched in desk drawers which is the best place for them. What matters is the thinking behind the numbers, which remains relevant however inaccurate the figures derived from it turn out to be. The fundamental questions are, which markets does the company intend to be in, what share of them can it achieve and how is it going to do so in the face of competitive reactions? Numbers can then be put against the plan which emerges, but the strategy itself has to be based on logical analysis of the business situation spiced with a dash of creativity.

I thought that the case studies were well chosen and interesting in their own right. It is heartening to find up-to-date British case studies in a business book and ones which reflect the author's own practical experience. The strength of the book lies in its practical, commonsense approach, which will commend itself to those who have the task of actually putting company strategies together, often for the first time.

I am sure that *Understanding Company Strategy* will find a well-deserved place on the bookshelves of practising managers who are concerned not only with the survival of their enterprises, but with their continued success in a tough competitive world.

Adrian Cadbury

Acknowledgements

I would like to thank the Institute of Directors for the considerable financial support which, over the years, has enabled me to concentrate on teaching and research into company strategy at the University of Warwick. I would also like to thank the various companies with whom I have worked, as a consultant or non-executive director or supervisor of student projects, and who have allowed me to describe in detail some of the features of the strategic issues which they have faced. Lastly, may I thank the many other companies and individuals not named, who have willingly shown me around their operations and discussed company strategy with me.

Introduction

What this Book is About

Good strategy choice is vital to company success. Two of the crucial abilities required of top executives and directors are the ability to think strategically and the ability to cause strategies to be implemented effectively. This is a basic and practical book, written for executives and directors who wish to develop these abilities with the aim of performing more effectively in the area of whole company strategy.

For those who already have a good basic understanding of company strategy, a few good books already exist; those that I recommend are listed in the references section. Likewise, for those who wish to develop their abilities in more depth in a particular functional strategy, be it marketing strategy, production strategy or any other single function, good books already exist and these too are included in the references section. However, and crucially, I know of no general book which starts from square one and is both practically oriented and readable. This book fills that gap.

For those executives in companies operating in only one area of business, whole company strategy is the same as whole business strategy. Here, determining business strategy involves looking at the business as a whole and the direction in which it is aiming for future success; this will require co-ordination of its functional strategies with the overall strategy. For those in more complex companies consisting of several businesses, whole company strategy includes the strategy of each of the individual businesses as well as the strategy of the group as a whole. This book addresses both types of operation.

1

Who this Book is For

The choice of company strategy is not something which can be safely ignored or handed over to either internal or external strategy consultants. Certainly, such advisers, and middle management, may be called on to assist with developing the groundwork; but top executives must themselves be able to think and act strategically and, if necessary, be competent to reject such advice.

For those directors and top executives heading up small companies, past experience has often been structured around one-year budgeting for the twelve months ahead, major capital decisions being made on an *ad hoc* basis and management handling of day-to-day problems being based on a 'fire-fighting' approach. Chief executives of such companies often tell me that although they do spend some time thinking about the longer term, such thinking is neither committed to paper nor subjected to thorough discussion with their colleagues. They consider that more time and more discipline need to be brought to bear on questions of company strategy; and they and their colleagues want a book which explains the relationship between strategy and day-to-day management in determining company success. Moreover, they want a book which looks not only at those companies which are performing well, but also at those companies which are not, and which do not have the funds to invest in long-term development. This book seeks to fulfil these needs.

Other executives work in companies, usually the larger ones, where company strategy is discussed at top executive and board levels. Often in senior functional posts, they feel the need to develop their understanding of company strategy, both to help them to contribute more to strategic thinking now and to prepare them for promotion to more senior posts later. They too seek a basic, practical book on company strategy.

My discussions with company strategic planners point yet again to the same need. Particularly in those groups which contain several largely autonomous subsidiaries, corporate strategic planners have said that the help they can give to the group would be greatly enhanced if senior executives in those subsidiaries were better able to diagnose and address the strategic choices which face them.

Chartered accounting firms require their recently qualified

accountants to develop a breadth of expertise beyond accounting itself. In their dealings with top executives, these accountants need to have a good understanding not only of marketing, production and other functions within a company, but also of company strategy itself. And a survey carried out for the British Institute of Management and published by them at the beginning of 1988 under the title *Profile of British Industry – The Manager's View*, revealed that three out of five managers felt that they required training in 'top management strategy'.

This book is therefore aimed at the following groups, in each of which there is a need to understand and think about whole company strategy and the actions required for its successful implementation:

- directors and top executives in small to medium-sized companies or in subsidiaries of larger groups;
- mid-career executives in medium-sized to large companies;
- young qualified accountants who will be dealing with top executives of companies;
- trainee management consultants;
- those in any of the above categories who are embarking on MBA or DMS programmes at university business schools or business management departments.

How Capability in Company Strategy can be Developed

It is not easy to develop strategic ability.

Several years ago, one company chief executive invited me to help develop the strategic abilities of his board of directors. This company had an annual turnover of some £45 million and was operating in five areas of the food services and catering industry. Its constituent businesses ranged from five-star hotel type catering right through to the very fast food catering required in large sports stadia. The board included directors responsible for each of the five businesses. My knowledge of their particular industry was limited; however, many of the ways of thinking about strategy are suited to a wide variety of businesses.

After a brief familiarization with the five specific businesses, it was agreed that my involvement should be in two stages. First I talked to the board collectively about strategy generally and pointed out some approaches which were likely to be of especial use to their businesses. This was followed by an 'action learning' approach. Each of the directors with responsibility for one of the businesses was asked to consider further the medium-term plan for his business, with a view to presenting that plan at a future board meeting. Accordingly, the agenda for subsequent board meetings contained a final item, which was for the board as a whole to discuss the proposed medium-term plan for one of its businesses. I attended the board meetings for this item on the agenda. Each director learnt about company strategy by revising his plans, responding to constructive criticism from his fellow directors and criticizing their plans in turn. My role was to contribute to the discussion as appropriate and to draw out the lessons which were being learnt.

This process continued for most of a year, after which I withdrew.

Some three years later the company sent to me for comment the written summary of the then medium-term plans for each of the businesses and for the group as a whole. It was clear from this that the strategic abilities of the directors had improved significantly. Moreover, the financial performance of the company had also noticeably improved, from poor to above average compared to its competitors. However, there remained areas where strategic abilities could be further improved; I pointed these out and gave advice both on the planning process and on some reading which might be of help.

I have described this example at some length to illustrate the following points:

- the ultimate purpose of company strategy is to improve a company's performance;
- a 'quick fix' is not possible: development of strategic ability takes considerable time and effort;
- perfection is not possible but improvement usually is;
- while reading and other forms of training can guide and speed up the development of strategic ability, actual experience is also essential.

This book therefore aims to contribute to the development of your strategic ability and the strategic capability of your company. Reading needs to be complemented by actual experience of making company strategy choices, taking action and seeing the results.

How this Book is Arranged

The book is divided into four parts, each of which should be read as a separate stage, leaving time between stages for reflection.

In chapters 1 and 2, which constitute part I, I explain in more detail what company strategy means, how it relates to day-to-day management, why it is important and what responsibilities for company strategy the chief executive, other executives and the board of directors carry.

Then, in part II, to start to develop your understanding, I focus on those companies, whether small or larger, which operate in only one business. This is the subject of chapters 3–5. Chapter 3 states what is meant by a clear and well-designed strategy for a business and develops the view that the success of a business depends on the way that it adapts itself to benefit from the opportunities and avoid the threats in its environment. Chapter 4 then presents a framework for analysing a business and its environment, with a view to locating and beginning to structure the strategic issues which it faces. Thus far, the approach is general to all businesses: from this point forward the issue or issues which face companies differ. Chapter 5 accordingly presents a series of actual companies and the strategic issues facing each of them.

By this stage you should have a better understanding of what company strategy is, at the single-business level; how to consider a particular situation; and the kind of issues which, either singly or together, can be important in different situations.

In part III of the book, covering chapters 6–8, this same sequence is used to consider strategy for those, usually larger, companies, which contain several businesses, including in some cases those groups which have a divisional structure between single businesses and group level.

Having developed your understanding of company strategy for both the single-business company and through to the large multi-business group, the book then moves in part IV to focus on the capability of a company, and of its senior executives, to address strategic issues, to make decisions and to implement those decisions effectively. As part of this theme, chapter 10 considers corporate strategic planning processes and the help they can give to overall company strategy. Chapter 11 looks at the contribution of internal or external strategy consultants and chapter 12 considers how the relationship between these consultants and the company can be managed so as to transfer the skills of analysing strategy situations to senior executives in the company.

The body of the book is intended to be read sequentially. For the reader who wishes to pursue particular topics further, there are four appendices and references for further reading. As articles tend to be more succinct than books, where possible these references are to short articles on specific topics.

In writing this book I have been forced to tread a very thin line. Any book for senior executives has to be as brief as is practicable. To be over-brief risks being unintelligible to many; to explain too much risks alienating those who already have some understanding of strategic thinking. I hope that those of you in this second category will find the structure easily understandable and therefore be able to skim quickly through those pages which are not of interest and move on to those which are.

The first edition of this book was published in 1990. Response to it was good and confirmed that it was largely meeting the needs of the particular audience described on pages 2 and 3. In this edition the main thrust of the changes has been to bring it up to date. For the company examples which have been retained it is important to convey the fact that the issues which a company faces usually change over time. The company is trying to steer a course which will be successful in spite of the dynamics it is facing; I have therefore described what has happened in the years since the first edition. I have also introduced some new examples. These focus on other issues which have become more important since the first edition, including the effects of management buyouts and the particular issues facing privatized utilities.

Just as a company's strategy cannot be static, so the field of strategic ability is developing over time. This edition therefore also reflects advances in understanding what good strategic ability involves.

6

PART I

SETTING THE SCENE

KEY POINTS

- What company strategy means
- Why it is important
- Who is responsible for it

Chapter 1

What is Company Strategy and Why is it Important?

1.1 Examples of Strategic Action

1.1.1 The Takeover Trail

Probably the most obvious type of strategic action is takeovers.

During most of the 1980s it may have appeared that companies like Beazer, Blue Arrow, Brent Walker, Bunzl, Coloroll, Hazlewood Foods, Hillsdown Holdings, Polly Peck, Ward White and Williams Holdings had found the way to success. Each had grown very fast with the early shareholders seeing substantial gains in the value of their holdings.

For example, over the period 1980–8 Hillsdown's turnover multiplied by 47 and its profits before tax by more than 200. Besides some organic growth, its main path of expansion was by acquisition and some diversification. During this period Hillsdown made some 50 takeovers, with the result that in 1989 it had significant

9

activities in poultry, eggs and animal feed; fresh meat and bacon; food processing and distribution; stationery and office equipment; furniture manufacture and plywood distribution; and, on a smaller scale, also in travel and property.

But where are all these companies now? All have had their difficulties. Some have continued as independent companies but have restructured and focused their businesses; they have lost their previous image as star performers. Over half ran into serious problems with the result that they were broken up, taken over or suffered other major changes in corporate governance and financial structure.

Perhaps the early successes of these companies were made possible by a rising stock market, when new shares could be issued at a good price and when interest rates were relatively low. Higher interest rates, a flat stock market or a recession are environments which such companies find very dangerous. Those which have come through the recession of the early 1990s acted early enough to avoid going under; they adopted new strategies aimed at reducing their gearing and refocusing their operations.

So expansion by a rapid series of takeovers is not the 'Midas touch'. For a few who get the timing and pricing right and who then stop the process, consolidate and refocus it may be. But it is a high-risk strategy not suited to many companies.

1.1.2 Diversification versus Concentration

At the time of producing this second edition, Trafalgar House had failed in its bid for Northern Electric, a diversification move, while Glaxo had succeeded with its bid for Wellcome, a company operating in the same area of business as itself. If the bid in the first case had been successful, would it have increased long-term success? And will the combination of Glaxo and Wellcome lead to better long-term success than what it would have been for either company alone?

To explore these questions a little further, it is helpful to look at a third example over a much longer period of time. This is Cadbury Schweppes, which has recently expanded its soft drinks business in the US by acquiring A & W Brands and Dr Pepper/Seven-Up.

Before their merger in 1969, Cadbury and Schweppes were two long-established and well-known companies heavily dependent on the UK market. Both had been diversifying; for example, in 1968 Schweppes bought Typhoo (tea). After the merger, this diversification continued with, for example, the purchase in 1972 of Jeyes (household products). But performance during the 1970s and early 1980s was disappointing, with profit/sales around 6%. In 1984 Cadbury Schweppes divested both Jeyes and Typhoo and concentrated on establishing itself as a leading world competitor in the two core businesses of chocolate and soft drinks. The takeovers of A & W Brands and Dr Pepper/Seven-Up are in line with this strategy.

Since 1984, when Cadbury Schweppes decided to pursue this strategy of focusing on becoming a world leader in two main areas of business, it has performed much better. Sales now exceed £4 billion p.a. and pre-tax profits are roughly 12% of sales.

With hindsight, why were Typhoo and Jeyes bought? And why did it take so long to divest them and improve performance? These moves show strategic decision-making in action, and show that it is not easy to make good strategic decisions.

1.1.3   Responding to a Changing Environment

Perhaps Cadbury Schweppes was slow to recognize that the environment in which it was operating was changing. Given Britain's entry into the European Community and a trend towards freer and wider international competition, to spread its resources thinly across too wide a variety of products would expose it to attack by companies operating globally and specializing in individual product areas.

During the 1980s and 1990s, Cadbury Schweppes has not been alone in transforming itself from a multi-product, mainly UK-oriented company into a more focused and less diverse company competing in wider international markets. Reed International, which had previously diversified into newspapers (the *Mirror*) and decorative products (Polycell, Crown paints and wallpaper, etc.), also divested these activities so as to concentrate more on its publishing and information operations. Early in 1993 this focus and thrust was further strengthened by its merger with Elsevier to form Reed Elsevier, now one of the world's leading publishing and information businesses. Similarly, when TI Group reviewed its performance and activities, it concluded that not only was it too dependent on the UK but also that its spread of activities was too diverse. As a result it divested its activities in the domestic consumer market, including bicycles (Raleigh) and domestic appliances (Creda). This enabled it to concentrate resources on becoming a global competitor in a few carefully selected specialist engineering areas where it already had good experience and performance. In other words, TI decided to be more selective and to build on its strengths. For example, it invested in buying other companies in both the mechanical seals and small diameter tubes businesses: and it is now the global leader in both of these areas.

1.1.4 What is the Best Strategy?

While some of the companies which I have described have been successful, others have appeared successful in the short term but this success has not been sustained. While some of those in the first set have succeeded by initial acquisition and diversification, most of those in the second set appear to be succeeding by concentrating. But this cannot be a general path to success; if it were, why is it that there are successful companies like Hanson, which operates in unrelated businesses such as brick production and tobacco?

For many companies, takeovers are not the path used for success; they have successfully grown by investing in the most promising of their existing businesses.

Clearly, the best strategy is not the same for all companies, not even at the same time and in the same industry. The best strategy for a company depends on that company's performance, its particular strengths and weaknesses, and the opportunities and threats in its particular environment. And even for that one company, the best strategy may well change over time.

1.2 What is Company Strategy?

Whatever the size or complexity of the company, the core of company strategy concerns *markets* and *products* or *services*. It is about choosing:

- where and how to compete;
- whom to appoint in top executive positions;

- how to organize the company and motivate all employees;
- how to allocate resources to yield the greatest overall success.

What this means in terms of specific decisions that need to be made depends in the first place on the type of company.

1.2.1   Different Structures, Different Strategies

Companies vary widely. Some are simple and consist of only one business; others are complex, with the group as a whole containing many businesses. GEC, for example, comprises more than 100 businesses. Within such a complex group, some of the businesses may be closely related, for example in terms of technology. Others may be largely autonomous, competing in entirely different areas in terms both of technology and of markets. Where a few businesses are closely related and the organizational structure attempts to bring them together to benefit from these relationships, this cluster is usually described as a division.

To distinguish between these different types and parts of companies, in the rest of this book I will be using the following terms and definitions:

Business strategy: the strategy of a single business, which may be either completely independent or part of a larger group of businesses.

Divisional strategy: the strategy across related businesses which are part of a larger group.

Group strategy: the strategy across several businesses which may or may not be related to each other and may or may not be clustered into divisions within the group.

Corporate strategy: the strategy of the whole company. For a single independent business, corporate strategy is the same as business strategy. In a more complex group, corporate strategy embraces business strategy for each of the individual businesses (and divisional strategy, if there are also divisions) as well as group strategy.

Whatever the complexity of the whole company, corporate strategy is concerned with the direction a company takes over time and with the use of its available resources. Such decisions must not be taken solely by one individual department within a business, nor by an individual business within a group. These decisions are corporate because there is competition for substantial resources, the allocation of which will significantly affect the performance of the company as a whole. Strategy decisions made by businesses (or divisions) within a group will be constrained by the overall decisions on strategy and allocation of resources made at the divisional or group level.

1.2.2 The Crucial Questions

Within these constraints, a single business is faced by the following kinds of strategic questions.

- Whether, while retaining its focus, the business should conserve its use of resources and retrench, or significantly increase the resources used and expand its activities. For example, if current capacity is a constraint on expansion, it could establish a second factory or, alternatively, cut out lower-margin products/customers.
- Whether the positioning of the business in relation to its products/services, markets and competitors should be changed – for example, by moving more up-market.
- Whether the level of resources invested in particular parts of the business, and the emphasis on using these resources, should be changed. For example:
  - whether to increase R&D expenditure to provide the basis for faster future growth;
  - whether to invest in the production activity, so as substantially to improve performance in terms of quality, productivity and delivery over the medium term (for example, over recent years this emphasis has been a significant factor in the vehicle industry);
  - whether to invest in the human resources side of the business, perhaps via a substantial training programme or substantial improvement in industrial relations.

Where a company consists of more than one business (with or without divisions) group strategy involves questions such as:

- whether to draw resources away from some businesses (or divisions) and allocate more to others;
- what functions should be performed centrally (e.g. R&D or management development), what powers should be delegated to businesses (or divisions) and what information will be required to check that performance is as planned.

1.3 The Importance of Company Strategy

1.3.1 Good Strategy and Good Management

It used to be said that it was more important to 'do the right things' than to 'do things right'. In other words, strategy was more important than the management of day-to-day operations.

This was probably true in the 1960s and 1970s, decades when the UK economy was expanding and competition in most sectors was not intense. Repositioning a company could move it into an activity where it was relatively easy to make profits. For example, during the UK property boom of this period, even poorly managed companies found it easy to make profits.

But since those times the world has become more turbulent and more competitive. While it is still true that a strategy which positions a company badly compared to its competitors can lead to its failure, it is also true that poor day-to-day management can have the same effect. Success will be achieved only by both good strategy and sound day-to-day management.

1.3.2 Strategy and Survival: an Example

During the 1980s, the UK clothing industry came under increasing pressure. Imports from low-labour-cost countries such as Hong Kong and South Korea threatened British companies operating at the high-volume/low-cost end of the market; while at the other end of the market, imports of high-quality clothing from European Community countries such as Germany also made inroads. Many UK clothing manufacturing companies therefore struggled to survive.

Those which were operating at the lower end of the market could not survive indefinitely solely by tightening up their day-to-day management even to the point of perfection itself. They had to choose from three alternative strategies:

- staying in the high-volume/low-cost end of the market, gaining volume and hence economies of scale, probably by taking over similar companies, combining this with a high level of automation to offset the disadvantages of relatively high labour costs;
- avoiding the threat from low-labour-cost countries by moving up-market or into a branded niche;
- pulling out of clothing manufacturing in the UK before the company became valueless, importing clothing from abroad, perhaps by having its own manufacturing overseas or importing from other manufacturers.

Many companies in this and other industries have failed because they neither foresaw the dangers ahead nor spotted the opportunities; and so they failed to change their strategies (Houlden and Spurrell, 1986). Strategy, clearly, is vital not only to a company's success, but to its very survival.

Chapter 2

Responsibility for Corporate Strategy

2.1 The Corporate Board and the Managing Director
2.2 Divisions and Subsidiary Businesses and Their Executives

2.1 The Corporate Board and the Managing Director

Within complex companies, much of the responsibility for divisional or business strategy often lies with the top executives at these levels. The degree of responsibility and accountability they face will depend on the degree of autonomy allowed, and the constraints imposed, by the level above. However, ultimate responsibility for corporate strategy always rests with the corporate board.

2.1.1 The Legal Obligations of Directors

Under UK law (Loose, 1987), a director of a company is accountable, both individually and jointly with the other directors, for the company's viability and future success. So a director's responsibility is fundamentally different from a manager's, for whereas a manager shares responsibility with others, each director is ultimately accountable for the whole company.

This accountability is to the company, not to the shareholders. If a majority of the shareholders disagrees with the decisions of the board of directors, those shareholders are not normally free to change that decision directly. So, for example, when the annual general meeting of the company is held and the directors are proposing the payment of a dividend, the shareholders have no powers there and then to raise the dividend. Similarly, the shareholders have no powers to order any specific action by the employees of the company. Their real power resides in their ability to remove the directors and replace them with others.

2.1.2 Competence and Competition

A company's chances of success depend heavily on both the quality of the board (Parker, 1978; Houlden and King, 1978) and senior management and on the company's competitive position; when faced with strong competition, a company will be more at risk if either its directors or its senior management are not of high quality.

2.1.3 The Main Roles of the Board

The board's main roles are:

* to direct the company;
* to appoint the (group) managing director/chief executive;
* to delegate appropriate powers for running the company;
* to monitor the performance of the company;
* to take corrective action where necessary.

Directing the company involves deciding the direction in which the company aims to go over the next few years. In other words, the board must decide corporate strategy; and each director must therefore possess strategic ability.

This does not mean that the board does all, or even any, of the preparation and thinking necessary to decide strategy. (In the smallest companies they may well do so – if it is done at all; such directors will have several roles, including that of day-to-day operational management.) In all but the smallest companies much of the preparation and initial thinking behind a corporate strategy proposal will have been done by senior management; however, delegation of this preparation does not mean that the board should abdicate its responsibilities for actually deciding on corporate strategy.

2.1.4 Strategy Proposals: Involvement and Detachment

I have supervised research into the formulation of two corporate strategy decisions in a large group embracing an airline, a chain of hotels, etc. In one case a proposal for a major investment was passed to the group corporate planner for appraisal before the main board decision. Subsequent observation showed that the board, having sought his advice, erred on the side of abdicating responsibility, taking the view: 'If the corporate planner thinks it is OK, it must be.' In another case in the same group, a different proposal for major expenditure was not put to the corporate planner. It was put to the board with the support of the chairman, whose approach was: 'I will see that it gets through.' The danger of such a commitment is that proposals may get 'steamrollered' through without full enough discussion. In this case, all except one of the directors were willing to go along with the chairman and move to the next item; but that one director considered that crucial evidence was missing and dug his heels in. When the extra information became available the proposal was rejected.

The board should not abdicate its responsibility for corporate strategy; and the chairman should not allow it to do so. While a chairman may well have initial views on a proposal, he also has the separate responsibility of chairing the board meetings. This involves ensuring that directors do not treat lightly their responsibility for corporate strategy. The purpose of board discussion is to appraise a proposal critically before reaching an agreed judgement on it. If the chairman can find a director willing to put a counter-argument before agreement is finally reached, this will help to stimulate debate and thus reduce the risk of wrong decisions.

2.1.5 The Composition of the Board

To be successful, a company needs leadership – a complex factor, involving enthusiasm and drive balanced with wisdom and good judgement. If the chairman is not also the managing director, the relationship between the chairman and the (group) managing director is crucial. The roles taken by the holders of these positions vary widely; what ultimately matters as far as corporate strategy is concerned is whether the pair work together effectively to decide and implement it.

A responsible board will not only pursue financial success, it will also behave in such a way that will neither cause serious concern nor put the company's longer-term survival at risk. The recent concern about the quality of corporate governance in some companies illustrates this point (Cadbury, 1992; Blackburn, 1994).

In some cases of publicly quoted companies there has been concern about the clarity and fairness of the accounts. Concern has also been expressed about some executive directors giving more attention to their own interests than to those of the company and its shareholders; the outcry about the level of total payments to some directors, and its lack of link to performance, is a reflection of this problem. All directors should remember that legally their responsibility is to the company and its future.

A responsible board will monitor both the implementation of corporate strategy and overall performance. It will be able to foresee and respond to both external pressures and the internal problems of the company itself. A board that is biased or deficient in professional skills can therefore put the survival of the company at risk. Each director should have common basic abilities (to understand balance sheets and profit and loss accounts, to recognize and assess a business opportunity, etc.). Beyond this, each director should also contribute one or more of the more specialized skills required to give the board as a whole the abilities it needs. For example, if a company's success is heavily dependent on its relationships with the government, then it is important for at least one of the board to have a good understanding of, and perhaps access to, the 'corridors of power'. Similarly, a company operating in high technology ought to have on the board at least one director with expertise in that technology.

The balance between executives and non-executives on the board is another important factor. Both have a part to play. Non-executive directors (sometimes referred to as part-time or independent directors) bring the benefit of external experiences to the board, and should also contribute the ability to look at the company's affairs more dispassionately. They are particularly well placed to keep an eye on the behaviour of the board and the perceived behaviour of the company. The balance between executive and non-executive directors varies from company to company, as indeed it should. Most publicly quoted British companies include a non-executive component on their boards of between 20% and 50%. A single non-executive on the board is unlikely to have sufficient impact to be effective; a minimum of two or three, depending on the size of the complete board, is generally regarded as necessary to provide adequate input. Conversely, a predominantly non-executive board would be in danger of becoming too detached from the running of the company and the implementation of strategy.

The role of the main board in determining corporate strategy is crucial. 'Bottom–up' corporate plans which are mainly aggregates of elements originating at lower levels are usually unsatisfactory in that they tend to target lower overall performance than those coming from the top down. Generally, too much emphasis from either direction is best avoided. The more effective corporate strategic planning processes start with the top giving guidelines within which individual divisions or businesses should plan, followed by feedback and iteration.

2.2 Divisions and Subsidiary Businesses and Their Executives

2.2.1 The Strategic Planning Needs of a Group

The larger and more complex a group of businesses, the greater its need of a corporate strategic planning process to assist the development and choice of corporate strategy. Chapters 10 and 11 therefore focus specifically on the value of corporate strategic planning processes and of strategic planning consultants, be they internal to the company or called in from outside. Senior executives, at business, division or group level, must have a sufficiently good understanding of strategy to be able to distinguish between helpful and harmful planning systems and between well-informed and dangerous advice from consultants.

2.2.2 The Need for Strategic Competence at Subsidiary Level

The degree of responsibility for its own success carried by a division or individual business depends on the degree of autonomy it enjoys. Subject to the constraints imposed by the level above, the current performance and future success of a division or individual business ultimately lies in the hands of the top executive of that unit and the other senior executives. Each level should be treated as a discrete company whose success depends on the ability of its executives. If you are an executive at one of these levels, to accept a strategy which is flawed or performance targets which are unattainable may put both the business's success and your own continued employment at risk. There is therefore a need for whole-company strategic ability at each of the main levels – business, division and group – as well as on the corporate board itself.

PART II

COMPANY STRATEGY FOR A SINGLE BUSINESS

KEY POINTS

- What is meant by business strategy?
- The importance of relating the business to its environment
- A general purpose framework for describing the situation of a business and for deciding its strategy
- Practical examples of various key issues which can occur in different companies and the approaches which can be used to address them

Chapter 3

Formulating Strategy: a Business and its Environment

A business is an operating unit which sells a distinct set of products or services to an identifiable group of customers and is in competition with a well-defined set of competitors. For the whole of part II of this book – that is, from this chapter up to and including chapter 5 – you should now focus your thoughts on a single business. This may be an independent company containing only one business, or it may be a business within a larger group. (Part III will consider the interaction between the business and the group (or division) above it.)

Some businesses produce a product, others provide a service; many combine a product with a service, such as technical advice to the customer, maintenance and spares service or the serving of food. Basic strategic thinking is common to all of these situations. In the rest of this book the word *product* should therefore be read to include service where appropriate.

Managing a business strategically is about thinking, deciding and acting strategically. It is a process which requires leadership if it is to be effective and translate into business success.

3.1 What is a Business Strategy?

A full statement of a selected business strategy is a *business plan* defining:

- what kind of business (in terms of structure, capabilities, focus in terms of products/services and markets, and performance) the company aims to be by a particular time in the future;
- the resources required to achieve this, and how they are going to be obtained;
- what the main steps are along the way;
- who is responsible for causing each of the various steps to occur;
- what the key signals, the 'milestones', are, which will show whether the strategy is on target, in terms of both actions and performance;
- what external factors need to be kept under review for indications that a change in strategy or plan may be required.

Added to this may be a broader statement of the longer-term view of the 'mission' of the company, such as 'to become the world leader in mechanical seals' or 'to become the leading multi-colour quality jobbing printing company in north-east England'.

3.2 'Crafting Strategy': How is it Done?

3.2.1 The Process

To arrive at such a statement of business strategy requires analysis, judgement and decision in the face of uncertainty by those responsible for the overall success of the company.

The importance of analysis lies in providing a better foundation for decision. Analysis takes time and effort; but good analysis will cut through the mass of detail and get to the core of the situation quickly.

The process of formulating a business strategy inevitably differs considerably among companies. These differences arise from the type and size of the business, its structure and its style of leadership. The process will also vary in the degree to which analysis is committed to paper. The effectiveness of the process will also vary among businesses, and it does not follow that a process recorded on paper will automatically be more effective than one contained entirely in the head of the chief executive. Nevertheless, in whatever form the process takes shape, if it is to be effective it is likely to contain the elements summarized in figure 3.1. For ease of understanding, these elements are presented in a rational sequence and it is this sequence which will form the basis for the more detailed discussion later in the book. It should, however, be appreciated that this description of the process is drastically simplified and takes no account of certain important factors outside the sequence presented. For example, there is usually a considerable time lag between recognizing the need for a strategy review and the improved performance which the action programme seeks. Therefore it is usually not beneficial to make frequent major changes in strategy. Major changes are likely to be interspersed with minor strategy 'tuning' in intervening years. Initially the understanding which comes from analysing the company and its environment may well be incomplete, with the result that modifications to the strategy are made as implementation is carried out and as a fuller insight into the company's competitive position develops. Similarly, the action programme may need modification to overcome difficulties encountered during implementation.

Henry Mintzberg (1988) has aptly described the process as 'crafting strategy'.

3.2.2 The Critical Importance of the Key (or 'Elephant') Issues

Each of the stages in this process is essential. One of the most critical to its success is the diagnosis of the key issues, or what I prefer to call the 'elephant' issues. For a single business often there

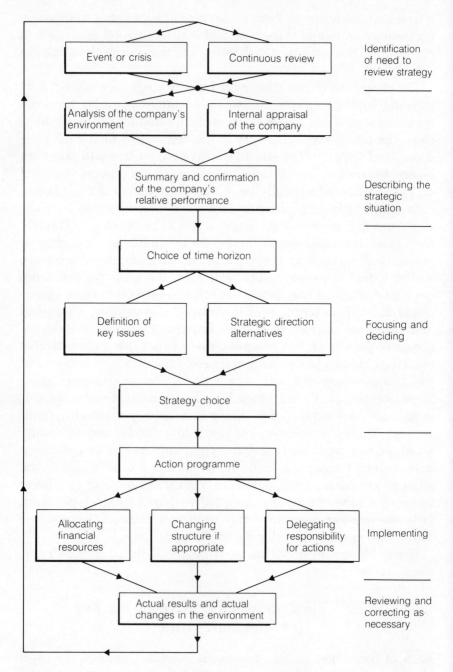

Figure 3.1 Elements of the process of choosing and implementing a business strategy.

is one, and rarely are there more than three, really important major issues which must be taken into account in deciding strategy. If one of these is not diagnosed, a false view is taken of the situation, with the result that the strategy chosen is most likely to be wrong.

Sometimes the elephant issues are pretty obvious. In other cases they are very difficult to diagnose (the 'elephants' are hidden in the undergrowth). Each elephant issue will normally fall within one of the categories listed earlier at the bottom of page 14 and the top of page 15. Often a full statement of an elephant issue is of the form: 'Whether or not to . . . and if so how to . . . and when to . . . ?'

The 'whether or not' is to do with the allocation or withdrawal of resources, the 'how' involves defining the actions for implementation (including where appropriate, changes in organization and information systems) and the 'when' is to do with whether or not action should be delayed as well as the timing of later actions.

A common failing in defining elephant issues is to leave out the 'whether' and to focus only on the 'how' and even defining that in terms of what one function of the business should do, when in fact almost any company strategy choice requires action by several of the functions.

3.3 Winners and Losers: How Businesses Evolve

Analysing business strategy is about explaining why some companies win and others lose. This means we must be able to explain what has actually happened in the past and what is likely to happen in the future. Hindsight is usually easier than prophecy; there are frequently several possible reasons for what has happened, all plausible and none necessarily correct. The real test of hindsight is whether an explanation of what is causing companies to win and lose helps us to forecast events in the face of the inevitable uncertainty which the future holds – including the appearance of factors which have not occurred before.

3.3.1 Adapting to the Environment

In the second half of the nineteenth century, Charles Darwin formulated and elaborated the theory of evolution of species. Put in simple terms, the theory stated that living forms either evolve in their changing environment to retain their vigour, or even become dominant; or, if they fail to adapt, sooner or later they will wither and perish. Since the 1960s a body of knowledge about the survival and success of businesses has been developed, which could in aggregate be described as a theory of evolution of businesses. Given a specific (though changing) environment, businesses possessing certain types of internal characteristics and pursuing certain strategies are more likely than others to survive and prosper.

3.3.2 The Life of a Business: Choice and Change

To develop your understanding of this picture, we will start here with a very simple foundation and then build up towards the greater complexity of real business situations.

Let us run through the evolution of a business in its simplest form: the single-business company. Bear in mind throughout this description that the business evolves in an environment that is not static but changing, sometimes turbulently, as are the opportunities open to the business within it.

We start with an area of business opportunity which is growing. An entrepreneur recognizes the opportunity and launches a new company to exploit it.

During the next period both this opportunity and the company grow relatively fast; but this attracts competitors who could be a future threat to the original company. By this stage the entrepreneur has recognized a different opportunity nearby and has begun to develop his company to enable it to take advantage of this new opportunity. Herein lie the seeds of the future choice he will have to make.

In the next stage, the original opportunity has reached its maximum and is likely to begin declining; competition has also intensified. In this situation, facing a mature market, the entrepreneur knows that margins will suffer and that he/she has only two options: he/she can either get his/her company out, or stay and fight. If he/she fights to the bitter end – even if the company wins over all its competitors – he/she knows that should the opportunity eventually totally disappear, so will his/her company. However, if he/she does decide to stay in the mature market and if the competitors withdraw, the company can sometimes make considerable profits before the market vanishes completely. If he/ she takes this path, he/she needs to find the best strategy to maximize the cash yield from this closure process; would it be better to sell the company?

Alternatively, the entrepreneur can pursue a different strategic course. This involves 'milking' funds from the company's activity in the mature market and using them to build up its activities in the new opportunity, perceived earlier, to the point where ultimately the whole company will be focused on that area. If this shift is managed effectively the company will continue its existence.

A successful company must change. It foresees changes in its environment and shifts its assets to be in phase with opportunities as they develop. It then tries to establish strong defensible positions in the chosen areas of opportunity before competition has had time to build up. The term 'assets' covers not only the kind recorded in the balance sheet, but also less tangible assets such as research knowledge, patents, purchasing power, management ability and the motivation and skills of all of its employees.

As this is a very simple description, it embraces virtually all business strategy situations. Inevitably, its simplicity limits its usefulness in analysing particular company situations, but there are a few important general points to be drawn from it before we move on to more detailed frameworks.

3.3.3 Learning to Learn: a Sense of History

To develop good strategic ability you need to develop a *sense of history*. In other words, you need to understand how the environment and the business itself have been changing over time, and why. You need to be able to look into the future, reviewing the various ways in which the environment might be changing and how the business will be affected by these changes unless actions are taken to alter its future strategic direction.

A company both feeds off its environment and is affected by it. It can learn from being faced with different environments, but not all companies learn quickly and effectively. The employees of companies which have successfully weathered a survival crisis, or an unwanted takeover bid, are usually subsequently much more aware of changes in the environment and more prompt in their actions to adjust to these changes.

31

By contrast, a company which has been in an easy environment for a long period can become 'flabby', complacent and unresponsive to changes in the environment. This has been one of the problems faced by those public utilities in the UK which have been privatized; major changes in organisation and in the way people think and behave have been essential. The need for change has been even greater for companies in the former Eastern Bloc. It is the responsibility of the top management of all companies to keep them in trim and 'on their toes'. Beware of having things too easy!

3.3.4 Being Prepared for Change

To have sufficent resources to move into a new activity requires a secure financial base and core activities with a strong positive cash flow. This in turn will have required tight management and effective learning in each evolutionary stage.

It takes time to move from one strategic focus to another. To be too late in developing a strong presence in a growing area of opportunity can easily result in having moved 'out of the frying pan and into the fire'. In other words, shifting a company's focus from an area in which it is established but where financial performance is declining into an area which is growing but where other companies are already well established, can be an even worse use of resources than staying put.

3.3.5 Keeping up with the Times

The world is littered with the debris of companies which collapsed because they failed to evolve. In the UK, many failed to see the deep recessions of the early 1980s and the early 1990s coming until it was too late. Others either failed or were taken over during the early 1990s, not because they did not respond quickly to the onset of the recession but because they had a longer-term strategy which had been out of phase with the environment for many years and the recession was the 'last straw'. With the economic boom of the late 1980s they were making statements like 'turnover has increased by 6% and profits by 2% – haven't we done well!' In reality, inflation was the cause of some of this growth and the rest reflected not an increase but a fall in market share. The true picture was 'we have lost market share and our profit margins have fallen – haven't we done badly!' Their masking of reality caused them to ignore the real decline and the underlying strategic threat. As a result they either collapsed or were taken over.

The environment is turbulent and unstable. To be successful, companies must understand its changes and change their own strategies accordingly.

3.4 The Purpose of a Business

3.4.1 The Need for Cohesion

A business is a combination of people, physical and other assets *with a purpose*. It will not stay viable for long if its purpose is obscure or if there are major forces within the business with diametrically opposed purposes. The collapse of partnerships is often due to the lack of clear agreement beforehand on what each partner is going to contribute, for what purpose, and what benefit each is seeking; and to the consequent lack of a common bond strong enough to survive the difficulties and choices that will arise. Any business must have both a *raison d'être* and a cement of common purpose, not just to hold it together but to give it momentum in its chosen direction. Without an agreed purpose, discussions about alternative strategies may well be a waste of time. If you do not know where you are trying to go, there is little point debating how to get there!

A business with a clear purpose and a well-chosen strategy also needs to motivate its employees behind that purpose, so that all their energies are directed towards the same goal.

3.4.2 Defining the Purpose

The purpose of a business, however, is not easy to define. Even for publicly quoted companies, the purpose is only rarely formally agreed and recorded. If asked about purpose, the senior executives of such companies would probably initially reply: 'profit, of course'. Further questions, such as 'do you mean short-term or long-term?', 'how about profit/sales and ROCE?', 'what about growth?' and 'how about earnings per share?', will often expose uncertainties about purpose. It is a good discipline for the senior executives of any business to clarify, and if possible eliminate, any disagreement on purpose.

In a small privately owned business the purpose is even less likely to have been agreed and recorded. Here too, when opportunities or crises arise, discussion of the firm's purpose should precede any strategic decision. For example, many such businesses exist to provide an income and job interest for members of the family. What should happen if one of them is not willing to pull his/her weight? What if an opportunity occurs which would enable the company to grow rapidly but which could result in the loss of controlling ownership, yet provide major personal capital gains? In such cases, is keeping ownership in the family a crucial part of the purpose, or a constraint which needs to be considered but which may be given up at the right price?

It will be appreciated that purpose is even more difficult to define in public sector businesses such as police, hospitals, etc. where profit is not among the applicable criteria. Such situations are not investigated in this book. Nevertheless, many of the principles behind the approaches described here are applicable and should form part of the basis for better management of those activities.

3.5 Vision, Mission, Strategy and Implementation

The term 'objectives' is used with such a variety of meanings by people discussing strategy that I try to avoid using it altogether.

Similar difficulties sometimes occur with the use of the terms 'vision' and 'mission', which some people tend to use with the same meaning. Neither is the same as 'purpose'.

I limit my use of the term 'vision' to those chief executives of leading companies who have a belief, usually based on past experiences, which strongly draws their view of strategy in a particular direction. With some, this may be a belief in success from leading in technology; with others, it may come from pursuing what they see as an important but unmet market opportunity; and with others it may, for example, be a belief that vertical integration is the way to succeed. Some companies are led by people with vision and will continue to be very successful; however, circumstances can arise when the past experience is no longer so relevant and when over-reliance on the vision leading strategy choice can be dangerous.

Many companies have what they describe as a 'mission statement'. Often this is a public relations statement either having little real substance or focusing entirely on how nicely the company says it aims to behave in relation to employees, the wider public and the physical environment. While such considerations are important, they are not the core of what a statement of mission is to strategists. To me, a company's mission statement can only be made after careful, more penetrative thought has been given to strategy and a choice has been made. A good mission statement is a short summary conveying to other employees, the press and the wider public, as appropriate, the product/market thrust of the company, its determination to be increasingly successful and how it aims to behave.

So, in contrast to vision, which may lead strategy analysis, strategy analysis cannot be led by a mission – a mission statement can only be successfully produced after strategy analysis.

No strategy is of real value unless it is implemented. This requires leadership, the careful planning of actions and co-ordination of all in the business (Hamel and Prahalad, 1980). A good mission statement can play a very effective part in helping all in the company to see how their individual actions contribute towards the whole.

3.6 The Strategic Horizon

How far ahead should you look at the business and its environment when considering strategy? The answer depends on several factors.

3.6.1 The Inherent Momentum of a Business

Any business, even quite a small one, is like a supertanker. Its culture, commitment and abilities give it a momentum carrying it in a particular direction. Without an overall strategy it is like a supertanker in a fog and without a rudder; its captain and senior officers cannot see far ahead and its future direction will be roughly a continuation of its present direction, until it hits the rocks or whatever other dangers are ahead! A business needs a well-considered strategy if it is to move ahead safely and purposefully.

3.6.2 Choosing Direction: Start with the Present

A business strategy is a choice of where to steer towards, some time ahead. If that involves a change of direction compared to the past, then significant positive effort is necessary to bring that change about. Just as with the supertanker, some time may elapse before the company responds to any change in steering. A major change in strategy usually requires a change in organizational structure as well as changes in the information and control systems, attitudes, training, personnel recruitment, etc.

Setting strategic direction also involves setting demanding targets, without which the business is likely to sink into complacency and poor performance. However, the future is uncertain and the business may be in a healthy or a vulnerable state. So, a necessary part of deciding business strategy is to consider the company *in the present*: its present strengths, its present performance and the present environment. A company which is financially weak has less freedom of choice than one which is financially strong, but more incentive to act!

3.6.3 The Future: Next Week, Next Year, Next Decade?

Then there is a need to look to the future. If the company is in an increasingly threatening environment, where its very survival is at risk, strategic thinking must be totally focused on the very short-term requirement of ensuring survival. In other words, the 'strategic horizon' will have to be very short term – in the direst cases perhaps even the next week or so. As the threat to survival is pushed away, and as the environment clears and offers more likelihood of good opportunities, so the horizon for strategic thinking can, and should, be extended to at least the medium term of three to five years ahead.

For example, many of the companies which had well-developed corporate planning processes before the deep recession of the early 1990s left their medium- and long-term plans to collect dust during the recession itself. They focused on a shorter time horizon, varying from perhaps six months to two years according to the effect the recession was having on performance. As the danger of serious damage or collapse receded and as the future became clearer and offered more promise again, so they pushed their strategic horizon back to three or more years ahead. However, in the changed environment after the recession many of their old long-term plans, though containing some good ideas, were found to be no longer adequate, as they failed to address key issues which had now emerged as critical to any strategy choice.

3.7 Success and its Measurement

3.7.1 Taking Stock

There is a tale about a visitor driving in the countryside who had lost his way. He stopped to ask one of the locals for directions. After a very complicated explanation of all the features along the way and the various turnings to take, the local man said, 'but if I was trying to get there, I wouldn't start from here.'

Where a company is trying to get to, and how likely it is to get there, are affected by where it starts from. If it has been, and is currently, performing badly, then it will neither have nor be able to attract the resources to enable it to pursue some of the strategies open to its more successful competitors. Besides its lack of financial strength, it will probably also lack the management abilities to pursue strategies open to some of its competitors. So the first stage of any strategic review must be aimed at answering two questions:

- Over recent years, how has our position in the environment been changing and how well have we been performing?
- What is our present position and performance?

3.7.2 How Much Room for Manoeuvre?

Most businesses have little freedom to change their focus in the short term. Even in the longer term some cannot make major changes in strategy without first strengthening their current financial performance and the abilities of their management. For example, a small poorly performing plant-hire company serving the construction industry is unlikely to possess the resources or the skills which would allow it to operate effectively in roadway construction or house-building. However, during the 1980s larger, more broadly based construction companies were able to shift their use of resources away from roadway and other public construction and into the more buoyant private housing and commercial building sectors. A company's success should not be measured solely in financial terms, ignoring restrictions on its flexibility.

3.7.3   The Importance of Relative Position

Success is also relative to actual competitors in the past and potential competitors in the future, across the full range of strategic directions the business could choose to pursue. During the UK property boom of the late 1980s, even the worst-managed companies could hardly fail to make 'good' profits. But when the boom was over, those at the 'bottom of the pack' were forced out of business. Similarly, during the depths of the 1990s recession, there were some sectors of business where all of the competitors were making a loss. Again, it was those at the top of the pack, generally, that survived.

3.7.4   The Picture over Time

A company's performance can vary considerably from one year to the next. So to get an idea of its success it is necessary to look at the accounts over a period of several years. I generally prefer to look at past figures over a period of five to ten years, not only to absorb particular accounting choices year by year but also to cover the performance through both boom and slump conditions. Taking one year with another, I can take a view on how well the company has been managed and whether its performance is improving compared to its competitors.

Figures over these extended periods will of course include inflation. It may be necessary to start with turnover figures and correct for inflation, particularly when trying to understand what has happened to volume of output and hence to the level of use of capacity. In those cases where volumes are not directly available, correction using the retail prices index gives only a very rough approximation; in most cases it will be necessary to be more precise than this. A better correction can be made by understanding the major components of cost, often labour and materials, and then, using national statistics (for labour in that industry and for that type of material), creating one's own index. Even so, any such correction must be treated with caution. For example, in times of severe recession profit margins will be cut, so any correction of sales figures over a period including some recession conditions using such an index will slightly overstate the unused capacity.

3.7.5   Which Indicators to Examine?

Success, then, is relative to competitors' performance; and the assessment of past and present success needs to be based on examination of figures over several years, making allowance for inflation where necessary. But what figures?

To measure success one is looking for indicators of two things: first, how well the *resources* put into the business have been producing current benefits; and secondly, how much the assets of the business have been *strengthened* to yield increasing benefits in the future. One is also interested in how much *risk* is involved in the business's operations.

Public companies: dividends, prices, earnings   With a company whose shares are available to the public, one is interested in the sequence of dividends paid over the years and the change in the level of the share price compared to prices in the sector generally. Using this basis, one would have to allow for the period over which the original investment in shares was made (and for any extra calls on shareholders since then) and for inflation. One must also take into account how much the company has been growing and the level of its borrowings. Earnings per share will give an indication, but the current figure can depend fairly heavily on success (or lack of it) in the company's earlier history. The change in earnings per share will give a better measure of the more recent rate of improvement in the company's performance. Dividends per share will also present difficulties of interpretation and, in any case, result from the company's choice of how much to pay out after the performance is known.

For publicly quoted companies, considerable caution should be exercised in using price/earnings ratios (P/E ratios). The earnings in such ratios are historical and refer back to the most recently published accounts. These cover a period (normally of a year) which finished between three and fifteen months previously. Conversely, the price is the market's view of the future prospects of the company. The P/E ratio is therefore an odd statistic looking to the future divided by the past. A high P/E ratio can therefore be a reflection of either low past earnings or expected good profits.

Profits and growth   Another way of trying to get a first feel of how successful a company has been, and is currently, is to look at profit margins and growth. It is possible for a company to increase its rate of growth by lowering its profit margins. This may be part of a strategy to dominate the market and to benefit later from economies of scale. Conversely, the company could cease to invest for the future and temporarily increase profit margins. Sooner or later, however, growth and profit margins have to be brought into balance.

A successful company is one which is consistently beating its competitors on both growth and profit margins; and of all the possible indicators of a company's performance, this is where I prefer to start. Taking care to make allowances when looking at the growth figures for any substantial calls on shareholders for extra funding, I start by looking at just three sets of figures (compared to those of key competitors, if available):

- growth – changes in turnover over the years;
- profit margins
    - profit-before-interest-and-tax / sales, known as 'return on sales' (ROS);
    - return on capital employed (ROCE);
- risk – the level of borrowing.

If a company is making losses, checks must then quickly be made as to whether or not it is facing a survival crisis. (Indeed, if your company is making an annual loss of some 2% or more on sales, its cash flow could well be negative and its life-blood ebbing away. The company could now be facing a survival crisis, and speed of action could be critical. Rather than continue reading this book sequentially, I suggest that you immediately turn to the section on survival and recovery on page 58.) If a company is beating its competitors on growth, ROS and ROCE then it is probably winning. A check on other measures, such as the rate of change in share price and dividends compared to competitors, will normally confirm this conclusion. If the two profit margin measures appear to point in different directions, then there is a need to look more deeply into the accounts to explain why this has occurred.

In normal times (neither of boom nor of deep recession), good growth, ROS of around 8–12% and ROCE of 20–25%, would give a first indication of a successful manufacturing company. (Lower levels of ROS would be expected in sectors where the value added for work done is proportionally less; for example, in buying and selling commodities.) However, this first indication should wherever possible be checked by comparison with the performance of key competitors.

Beyond the numbers There may well be other important evidence not apparent from all these figures. Besides the financial evidence, other, more subjective and qualitative factors need to be assessed before forming a view of how well a company has been, and is, doing, and how effective its management team is. For example:

- How old is the company's equipment?
- How about the effects of recent changes in the top executives?
- How about research developments which in the future may lead to significant growth and profits?
- What about a new and dangerous competitor which has recently entered the market?

The combination of careful analysis of financial information and an intelligent appraisal of other factors forms a good basis for relating the company to the choices likely to confront it in the future environment.

3.7.6 The Stock Market's Evaluation of Companies

Various studies have shown that share prices on the stock market are closely related to figures calculated on the basis of cash flow.

On page 39 I referred to measuring success by assessing, firstly, how well the resources put into a company have been producing current benefits and, secondly, how much the assets of the company have been strengthened to yield increasing benefits in the future. In terms of cash flow, this means determining what the present cash flow is (some of which may be paid out in dividends, while some may be reinvested in improving the company's future performance). It also means looking to the future and seeing how risk has been changed (e.g. by using some of the cash flow to reduce borrowings) and making a realistic forecast of (hopefully improved) cash flow in future years. Discounting future cash flows back to today, and combining them with present cash flows, gives a good indicator of the value of the company and hence the appropriate price of its shares.

3.8 Who are the Competitors?

3.8.1 Ways of Defining the Competition

A business's competitors may change over time; so may the position of the business compared to the competition generally. At any particular time the competitors of a business are defined in terms of *sphere* and *radius* of competition.

The *sphere of competition* is a precise definition of the type of business activity engaged in. For example, a specialist design-and-build construction company operating at the high-quality end of the commercial building construction business will be faced with various competitors. Some may be similar design-and-build companies; others will be more broadly based companies perhaps working with independent architects; and some of these will be parts of larger national groups. The sphere of competition in such an example needs careful thought. Probably in the past it has been high-quality commercial building construction with the customer dealing separately with the architect. Customer behaviour may, however, be changing towards a situation where the customer prefers to deal with one company which takes responsibility for both design and building. If this change is occurring then the sphere of competition is changing.

Radius of competition is the geographical distance over which a company should be capable of competing if it is efficient and the distance from which it can expect competition from competitors. In this particular example, radius of competition will probably depend on the size of the contracts involved. Relatively small jobs may only attract local companies or the local branches of larger national companies. Very large contracts may well attract competition from global construction companies.

In those cases where a business, whether it be producing a product or supplying a service, has more than one point of production/supply, it may be necessary to think of the radius of competition at two levels: the business as a whole, and each of the individual points of production/service. If, for example, a company is extracting sand at two points, one in Scotland and one in the south of England, because it is uneconomic to transport sand over long distances, that is for many purposes like operating two independent businesses. Conversely, a major supermarket chain will be treating the whole of the UK as the radius within which it must choose where to operate. It will be competing mainly against other major UK supermarket chains and therefore analysis will be most usefully based on the radius of competition for the company as a whole – that is, across the whole of the UK.

3.8.2 Changes in the Pattern of Competition

Neither the sphere nor the radius of competition is necessarily fixed. The radius of competition can well increase over time, particularly with changes in technology. For example, in the days of mechanical calculators competition in producing and selling these large and bulky machines was largely limited to national markets. With the development of pocket-sized electronic calculators, the economies of mass production and transport are such that competition is now virtually global. This transition to international competition has already affected many areas of business and will affect more. In some areas, however, because of the nature of customer requirements, or the method of production, or the product/service itself, or the cost of transport (compared to production costs), competition will always remain localized.

3.8.3 Pinpointing the Key Competitors

So, to define your business's key competitors you must answer the following questions:

- Exactly what business are we in (sphere of competition)?
- How far away are we able to compete, and from what distances

are competitors competing and likely to compete (radius of competition)?

- Are there likely to be changes which will alter either the sphere or the radius of competition over time (the future environment)?
- Which companies are, and are likely to be, the competitors within this sphere and radius of competition (pattern of competition)?
- Which competitors are winning at present and are others threatening to win in the future (key competitors)?

Chapter 4

Describing the Strategic Situation of a Business

By now you should have a broad understanding of what company strategy is, why it is important, how it relates to day-to-day management, who is ultimately responsible for it and where your own responsibility lies. You should also be aware of your need to develop your strategic ability, not only in your present post but also to assist your career as it develops. You should not only be thinking about your particular business's *performance* but also about its *capabilities*. And you should be ready to think much more deeply about the environment within which your business is trying to win and the need to understand the forces of competition.

You will recall that the framework set out in figure 3.1 began with parallel investigations into the business itself and into its environment. Chapter 3 outlined the principles and essential factors at stake; in this chapter we will look in closer detail at building up an accurate picture of a business's strategic position.

4.1   Getting a Full and Accurate Picture

It is not easy to analyse business strategy well; even those who are most experienced can make mistakes. Analysing a single-business company with the aim of choosing a business strategy is rather like looking from a helicopter at an iceberg in bad weather. The helicopter is necessary to afford a broad view enabling you to recognize the most important features: you need to be able to detach yourself from the detail. A business is like an iceberg in that while some of its features (those above the water) are fairly obvious, the others (below the water) are more difficult to see; and even when they can be made out the picture formed is rather fuzzy and can be inaccurate. Some features may not be visible at all. Also, as with an iceberg, looking at a business from one angle alone will usually give a false view of the whole (what shape is the eight-ninths under water?). And the whole process is undertaken in conditions resembling bad weather: the business environment is as complex, uncertain, turbulent and changing as the oceans.

Therefore, any attempt to describe a business and its environment must be based on looking at the situation from many different angles and gradually building up a coherent description which will command the confidence and consequently the support of the board. The larger the resources at risk, the greater the burden of accuracy borne by this description and the greater the effort that needs to go into building it up. This chapter presents ways of structuring the picture of the business in such a way as to serve these requirements of coherence and accuracy. Both of the frameworks outlined below encourage you to look at the business and its environment in various ways. The first framework, known as the TOWS (or SWOT) matrix, is more appropriate for smaller businesses or where a relatively quick analysis is needed. The second framework makes for a more complete description of the business. It carries less risk of an important factor being overlooked, so it is more often used for describing the situation of larger businesses where larger sums are at risk.

4.2 A Simple Framework: the TOWS (or SWOT) Matrix

The TOWS matrix (Threats, Opportunities, Weaknesses, Strengths) is the simplest form of presentation that is of practical value for describing a business and its environment. In chapter 3 we considered a very simplified picture of the company, its environment and some opportunities it might face: the TOWS matrix is a simple framework for taking that picture one stage further. It consists of a set of four boxes into which to put the answers to each of four questions: two about the environment and two about the business itself. The questions are:

- In the environment, what are the main (a) opportunities and (b) threats?
- For the company, what are its *distinctive* (a) strengths and (b) weaknesses *compared to its competitors?*

The answers to these questions are then laid out in the form shown in figure 4.1.

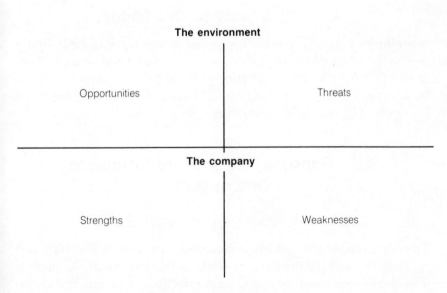

Figure 4.1 The TOWS matrix.

A poor strategy is usually the result of inadequate awareness of a company's environment. Strange as it may seem, there are some companies in the UK whose chief executives cannot name the company's two most important competitors! To ensure that appropriate effort is put into thinking about the environment, and particularly about the opportunities within it, I prefer to put the environment above the company in this matrix, hence the abbreviation TOWS. Others prefer to place the company at the top and therefore use the abbreviation SWOT.

If you would like to look at an example of the TOWS matrix in use, please see the Newprint (A) case in appendix A, which also comments on how to use the matrix effectively.

4.2.1 Matching Strengths and Opportunities

Essentially, analysing the company and its environment in this way helps to match the company's strengths with the environmental opportunities. The company needs certain strengths to enable it to pursue opportunities successfully. If it has weaknesses which will significantly lower its performance when pursuing a particular opportunity, the strategy must include actions to overcome these weaknesses.

4.2.2 One Business, One Matrix

Sometimes a company which appears at first sight to be a single business in fact consists of two or more related businesses. If so, to use the TOWS matrix effectively, the separate businesses must be analysed in separate matrices. This is in fact the case with the Newprint (A) example in appendix A.

4.3 Constructing a More Complete Description

4.3.1 Selecting Environmental Factors

The environment in which a business operates is complex but much of the complexity may be relatively unimportant. To analyse a business's strategic position most effectively one needs to have guidance on which of the many environmental factors are most likely to be significant. This section draws on the work of well-known strategic thinkers to construct a framework that focuses attention without oversimplifying.

Kenichi Ohmae (Ohmae, 1983), a leading strategist and, until recently, managing director of the Tokyo office of McKinsey and Company, stresses the importance of the *company, competitors* and *customers*. Michael Porter, a leading professor at Harvard Business School who is well known for his books and articles on corporate strategy and the phrase 'competitive advantage', adds *suppliers, new products* and *new competitors* to this list (Porter, 1979). The series of concentric circles shown in figure 4.2 summarizes these and other similar lines of thought, placing significant factors in a three-stage process of analysis.

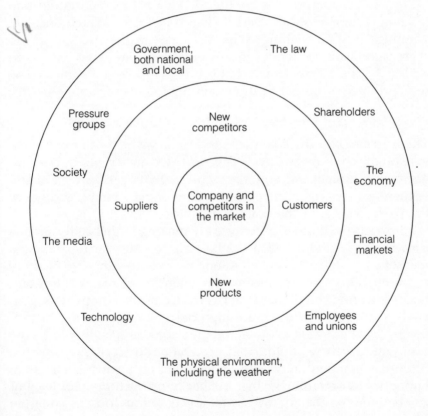

Figure 4.2 A more detailed framework for describing the strategic situation of a business.

4.3.2   The First Step: Understanding the Market and Competitors

At the heart of the analysis of business strategy must be an understanding of the market and of the competitors in that market. If this understanding is lacking or faulty, the rest of the analysis will rest on a false base; hence the position of this item in the innermost circle. Is the market a segment of a wider market? If so, what is known about that wider market? It could be that knowledge on this broader front would lead to consideration of a shift in focus of the business. It could be that the structure of market segments is going to change; therefore it is necessary to grasp the existence of that possibility. Is the market new, growing fast or declining? The nature of competition will be different at each of these stages.

How many competitors are there? What is the size distribution of competitors? How successful is each of them? Which ones are winning/most threatening? What strategies are they pursuing? Are there significant economies in this business from being big (economies of scale)? If so, from what source do these economies come (e.g. production mechanization/automation, distribution, etc.)?

4.3.3   The Second Step: Pressure Factors

The intermediate circle contains the factors which can exert pressure on the core competitive struggle. These are suppliers, customers, new products and new competitors. Extra pressure from any of these sources can reduce the freedom of manoeuvre, and hence the performance, of the main competitors.

For example, if the competitors are making large profit margins (say, over 15% ROS) and if the barriers to entry facing potential market entrants are relatively minor, new competitors are likely to come on the scene, increasing the intensity of competition and hence lowering the financial performance of the competitors generally. Conversely, if there are high barriers discouraging or preventing new entrants to the market (as, for example, would be the case with expensive automated production) then risk of pressure from new competitors would be less. Not only entry barriers are important in determining the number of competitors and level of competition: so also are the costs of exit. If exit costs in a market are low, the poorer performers are more likely to withdraw than in a market where exit costs are high.

Again, a competitor losing under existing competitive conditions may only be able to survive if it introduces a new product or service sufficient to undermine the existing stronger position of its competitors. In the early years of the semiconductor industry, the rate of innovation required to lead the changes from 4K to 64K RAM products was such that key executives frequently broke away from leading companies to set up new companies, using their acquired expertise and new-found freedom to change at a faster pace, enabling them to overtake many of the existing, more established, competitors such as the firms they had left. This freedom to innovate fast gave these companies a distinct competitive advantage.

4.3.4 Exploring the Relationships among Factors

Understanding the forces at work, not only in the centre circle and in the intermediate circle but also between the two, will assist the development of business strategy both for those companies which are winning and for those which are losing.

Before we move on to the outer circle of figure 4.2, the importance of the relationships among suppliers, competitors and customers in the intermediate circle needs to be stressed. For example, consider as competitors (in the centre circle) the suppliers of food to food stores in the UK. Over the last 15 years or so, the large national chains, such as Sainsbury, Tesco and Asda, have been shifting their emphasis to large superstores and have been becoming increasingly dominant. Consequently, they have been able to exert increasing pressure on food suppliers. The increased power of these customers has reduced the freedom of the food suppliers to make profits. Perhaps the rash of takeovers during the 1980s of small food suppliers (e.g. by Hillsdown Holdings, Hazlewood Foods, etc.) was a reaction aimed at redressing this balance. Could it be that the real battle in the food business will be over who controls the distribution channels?

- Is your arena of competition being increasingly dominated by a strong supplier or customer?
- How can you retain or develop a competitive advantage?

4.3.5   The Last Step: the Wider Environment

The outer circle in figure 4.2 describes the factors in the wider environment. For example, for a company heavily dependent on defence procurement, the government, both in its general policy-making and as a customer, will be a key factor in the environment. Another company might be faced with a strong and vigorous national trade union, which at certain times may be a very important factor in its environment; and so on.

It should be noted that the recent emphasis in the news media on the need to improve the quality of corporate governance has originated from concern by different groups focusing on different aspects of corporate governance. Concerns by shareholders and the financial markets were addressed by the work of the Cadbury Committee. Society, political parties and the trade unions have been focusing more on the salaries of, and large financial gains made by, some executive directors. Such pressures can lead in the longer term to changes in professional codes of behaviour and in the legal framework within which companies operate.

Over the time horizon at which you are looking, do you expect any changes to the importance and nature of the factors in this outer circle of figure 4.2?

4.3.6   Using the Whole Framework

Analysis of a company's environment should start with the centre circle and then move outwards to locate and describe those factors which are of most importance. For all other than monopoly situations, the centre circle will always be crucially important. Usually several of the factors in the intermediate circle will be important, and some, though fewer, of those in the outer circle; however, in any circle there may be a factor of vital importance: for example, government policy on defence for defence contractors, or for many companies the impact of the changes in the European Community.

Some academics refer to some of the factors in the environment, such as customers, suppliers, shareholders, employees and society generally, as 'stakeholders'. This implies to me that they are in some ways different from the other factors and have rights as part-owners, which they are not. I and others (e.g. Argenti, 1993) think that this is a dangerous way of distinguishing between, and

52

giving more weight to, some of the factors in the environment. Each factor must be considered on its own merits for the situation of a particular business. If a factor is important, assessment of the opportunities or threats which it brings must take into account the attitudes and power which those attempting to represent that factor may have.

4.4 Reviewing Performance: Asking the Right Questions

On the basis of our understanding of the competitive environment, what we are seeking to do is to explain the company's recent and current performance in terms of its abilities and actions. If the company has been performing badly compared to its competitors, is this because it is positioned badly or because it has internal weaknesses which need to be overcome? If the company has been performing better than its competitors, we need to be able to recognize not only the key factors which have led to this success but also any significant weaknesses which could lower its performance in the future. As for a detective trying to find the source of a crime, this requires starting from a variety of directions and then, according to what is found, deciding progressively where to probe in greater depth. The effective strategist will be able to focus on the important factors quickly. The main starting points are:

- using one's own eyes and ears;
- detailed accounts over the years;
- the top management and the organizational structure;
- marketing;
- production and distribution;
- the source of ideas for new products/services.

Observation An effective strategist will have trained his/her eyes and ears to pick up clues which will help to indicate some of the main features of a company. For example, when looking around the works he/she will quickly notice the level of activity, old machinery, large quantities of work in progress, muddled layouts, large quantities of scrap, etc. He/she will also be able to encourage others to talk freely in a way which will assist diagnosis. He/she will be a good listener and pick up the points to pursue.

Examining the accounts   The accounts will have to be looked at several times during the analysis. Initially the strategist will be interested in trends in sales and profit margins over several years. Correcting for inflation or significant increases in material costs, what has been happening to volume? If volume has fallen in a declining market, what has this meant for capacity utilization and what has happened to manning levels? If volume has been increasing rapidly, when and in what steps has new capacity been added? What is known about the effects on sales and profit margins of the new products which have been added to the range (and about discontinued products)? If there has been a period of disappointing performance followed by a distinct improvement, is there evidence to support the view that this has resulted from a change in the top management (such as a dynamic new managing director)? These and many other questions need to be considered both at the outset and later if the maximum value is to be obtained from the accounts.

Management and organization   How strong is the management of the company? Is the board well balanced and effective? What are the major changes which have been made over the last few years, both to the structure and in the top appointments, and with what results? If it is a family business and the chairman is also the managing director, what are the risks to the company if he should become unfit or retire soon? Is there clarity in the role of the various departments, or confusion, duplication and passing of the buck when troubles arise?

Sales and marketing   What is the pattern of sales by customer segments, and who are the main customers? Is this changing? If one customer takes a large proportion of the output, how vulnerable does this make the company? Where is the marketing effort mainly aimed? How are prices set? What about recent and planned new products? What other opportunities are there for future growth? In the company's present markets, what are the 'order-winning criteria'? In other words, what are the relative weights of price, quality, delivery speed and delivery reliability in determining whether an order is taken or not? This will have a major impact on the most appropriate production activity, in terms of its equipment, layout, flexibility, control systems, design capability, etc.

Production and distribution   In production, the interest is in the matching of the function to the needs of the market. If low cost is the key to success in this market, what has been happening to productivity and what plans are there for further improvement? Are the accounting data obscuring reality because the cost of purchasing the machines has already been written off? With what degree of change in product variety, variation in sales levels for different products, etc. has production had to cope? What part does production play in determining business strategy?

Within distribution the questions that need to be asked include: How well do delivery patterns meet customer needs? Can the efficiency of providing this delivery service be improved by changes in the location of stores, in the size, type and number of vehicles, in the quality of management of the distribution activity and in how they are motivated and held accountable? Should the whole operation be subcontracted? And so on.

These are some of the many questions which need to be asked if the main reasons for the company's recent performance are to be understood and the strengths and weaknesses for future development of the business clearly defined. This process of concentrated thought about both the company itself and its environment will have thrown up some of the strategic issues which need to be addressed, as well as some of the strategic directions which may be worth pursuing in future years. If you wish to understand more fully how this process of describing a business and its environment is carried out and how the important issues are diagnosed, please now turn to appendix B, which takes you through the development of the analysis in an actual situation.

This is as far as discussing business strategy in general can usefully be taken. Businesses vary widely, as do the important issues which their chosen strategy must address. So from here we will move on to some typical and actual company situations.

Chapter 5

Key Issues and Strategy Choice in Various Actual Situations

5.1   Introduction

5.1.1   The Examples Chosen for this Chapter

It is not always easy to decide how many businesses there really are in a company. In a complex group the existence of formal subsidiaries may give some indication, but even so some of these subsidiaries may each cover several activities which should initially be considered as separate businesses. Given our present concern in this part of the book with the single-business company, I have

56

avoided this uncertainty by choosing for my examples in this chapter mainly small, often privately owned companies, which in most cases are neither large enough nor complex enough to warrant being treated as more than one business for the purposes of analysis here.

Except for Thermalite, all of these are companies with which I have been personally involved, whether as a non-executive director, strategy consultant, student project supervisor or just a friend of the owner. The choice of these particular businesses does not imply either effective or ineffective management.

5.1.2 Highlighting the Key Issues in Strategy Choice

The description of the business and its environment, as set out in the previous chapter, is an essential foundation to be laid before deciding what the key issues are which a chosen strategy for your company must address.

There are normally several issues in any situation, but only a few of these will be of key importance (the 'elephant' issues) in thinking about and choosing between alternative strategies. Across businesses, the variety of such key issues is very wide indeed. This chapter aims to explain a few of the more common situations, how they can be addressed conceptually and the choice of strategic direction they suggest. To do this it looks at a selection of actual company situations, chosen to highlight different types of issue and their handling. Your own company may face just these issues or others: the key question you must tackle is which of them is of most importance to your company. You must also identify any other issues that are important and which of the concepts for addressing the various issues are of value to you.

5.1.3 From Survival to Diversification

Because survival crises are not uncommon for single businesses, and because a crisis by its very nature requires urgent attention, this is the first situation to be addressed.

We will then go on to look at other situations where a survival crisis is not imminent, where the strategic horizon is further ahead and where there is a choice to be made of alternative strategic directions. Of these, the most commonly encountered is where the business is positioned compared to its competitors in such a way that it should be able to perform well but is performing only moderately. It needs to 'learn' how to improve its performance and to build 'layers of advantage' so that over time it becomes more permanently successful. Two companies are given as examples: Grass Concrete Ltd and Thermalite Ltd.

We then move on to the situation of a business whose future on its existing focus looks bleak, and where there is therefore a need to change the focus. The company chosen is Hancock and Lane Ltd.

Finally, we look at situations where a business has the opportunity to advance faster by opening up related areas of business beyond its core: to diversify. One example, Elkay and Conblock, involves diversification close to the existing business, where innovation is important; the other, Allan H. Williams Ltd, involves a more conglomerate type of diversification into areas further afield.

Inevitably, with the need in each case to describe the company and the issues before considering the choice of strategy, this chapter is the longest in the book. You will find working through it both easier and more beneficial if you pause after reading about each company to reflect on what has been said and ask yourself whether your company contains any of the features involved. If so, some of the concepts presented may also be helpful to you.

5.2 Survival and Recovery

Each of the companies which features in this section is facing not two or three key issues but just one critical issue, namely:

- Is the business facing a survival crisis? If so, what is its cause and what actions must be taken in the immediate future to avoid collapse?

5.2.1 Recognizing a Crisis Early: the Need for Vigilance

Looking through the literature on company strategy you might be forgiven for incorrectly inferring that survival crises rarely occur. Some books on company strategy do not mention them at all, while most of those which do discuss survival only include it rather late and apparently as a minor afterthought. Survival crises or near-crises are in fact much more common certainly than the literature conveys and probably more than most managers expect ('It can't happen here'). John Argenti (1975), Stuart Slatter (1984), Hugh O'Neill (1986) and Bill Houston (1989) are some of the few writers who have attempted to redress this imbalance in the literature.

If you are in charge of a business which is an independent company and which is making losses, are you really certain that the bank manager will not call in the overdraft later today? If your business is making losses and is part of a larger group, are you really certain that the group is not about to tell you of a decision to close your company down or to sell it off cheaply?

That survival crises, including crises of ownership, occur more often than most managers expect is well illustrated by the fact that during the second half of 1989, when the first edition of this book was being drafted, two of the companies that featured in this book experienced crises to different degrees. The aluminium window-frame business of Allan H. Williams was put into administrative receivership and was bought by a large construction group; and Jaguar was taken over by Ford. Since the first edition, three other companies have had changes of ownership.

To those involved, most real survival crises for individual businesses creep up unexpectedly, are pretty sudden and result in collapse within a few weeks unless drastic action is taken. In this situation the time horizon for strategic action is days or weeks rather than months or years.

To fail to recognize a survival crisis when it is occurring means complete collapse. It is better to err on the side of suspecting a crisis even when a slide in performance has not yet reached crisis proportions. What, then, are the first signs of impending crisis?

5.2.2 Example: a Printing Company on the Brink

Survival crises can occur at any time but are more common during recessions. They are not a new phenomenon of the recession of the 1990s; even those that occurred then had similar characteristics to others in the recession of the early 1980s. Survival crises have an effect on the top executives concerned, in that if they learn from having pulled their company through, they will then be more alive to the danger before the next recession and should then be able to reduce its impact on the company. To see this longer-term impact, I have chosen a company whose survival crisis occurred in the 1980s. I am then able to tell you how it pulled through and how it then coped with the major recession of the early 1990s.

Although a company which has been underperforming compared to its competitors over recent years will have lower financial resources with which to withstand a survival crisis, this does not mean that survival crises cannot arise in companies which have been performing well. One example of an apparently successful firm hit by crisis involves the company Newprint, described in appendix A and used in chapter 4 to illustrate the TOWS matrix. The Newprint (B) case of appendix A includes a detailed description of the company some four years after the first case, at a time when the company was heading for a survival crisis.

Briefly, the situation was as follows.

Newprint is a printing company. Over the years it had been growing at a rate above the average in a slowly growing market. In the late 1970s it had considerably increased its capacity; it had moved into a larger factory and introduced double-shift working. Figure 5.1 shows why a crisis had arisen.

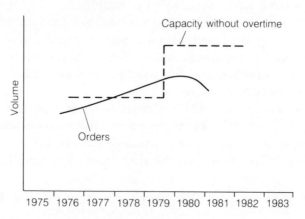

Figure 5.1   The crisis in Newprint (B).

Whereas the company's capacity and overhead costs had been increasing in the expectation of an expanding market, suddenly its sales had turned downwards. That downturn probably occurred

60

some three months before the time of the case; but no significant action had occurred to deal with this issue. Why not?

Lack of alertness, lack of information   The simple answer is that a failure on the part of top executives to realize that a survival crisis was approaching was combined with an unwillingness to admit the threat and to do anything about it. The only recorded total picture of what was happening in the market was that given by sales figures in the monthly accounts; and this information only reflected the actual position in the market some two months earlier.

Costs are incurred unnecessarily if there is a delay in responding to a market downturn. Conversely, sales volume can be lost in a market upturn if there is delay in providing the extra capacity. So sensors of what is *currently* happening in the marketplace are essential. Foresight of what is going to happen is even more helpful!

The need for urgent and correct action   Faced with a survival crisis, a company does not have a choice of strategic directions. It must do everything to project itself straight out of the 'swamp' before it is sucked under.

A full analysis of the situation and a description of the actions taken in this particular case are given in appendix B. Since the cause of Newprint's problems was overcapacity and the associated high costs, the company reduced its capacity quickly and survived.

Survive and succeed: the learning experience   During the 1980s the market in which Newprint operates strengthened. It earned good profit margins up to the start of the recession of the early 1990s. The market then weakened until about 1993, after which there was a fairly steady recovery. Over this second recession, Newprint suffered less severely than it had in the recession of the early 1980s. Over the ten years, turnover roughly trebled; after allowing for inflation, this represents roughly a doubling in volume and a good improvement in productivity. Why was performance better than up to and over the previous recession?

Clearly the top executives did learn from their experiences of the recession of the early 1980s. Generally, management is tighter. During the period of boom, changes in manning were made in small steps; as the recession of the early 1990s developed, numbers employed were reduced more promptly. Similarly, investments in equipment were more carefully phased; the largest single investment was not made approaching or during the recession but in 1993, when the medium-term prospects were better.

In these and other ways the directors of Newprint learned from their experience of the recession of the early 1980s to the benefit of the company. Any manager must try to learn from all of his/her experiences. A manager who has never been through a survival crisis will have missed an experience which may be essential to developing these capabilities.

5.2.3 Factors Affecting Survival Chances in Recession

The survival crisis which Newprint (B) faced in the early 1980s was an emergency brought on by the severity of the recession itself and its effect on the market. Many companies, of course, went under during the severe recessions of both the early 1980s and the early 1990s. Some entered a recession at a stage when they were so weak financially that, even though they reacted quickly, the damage caused by a few months of losses was enough to cause collapse.

Others were larger and had more 'fat' off which they could live, and struggled on for over a year before they too failed. The example of Weston Hydraulics Ltd in appendix B is of a company which, if it had been independent, would have collapsed early in the recession. It was faced with a long decline in its market starting well before the general recession and continuing into the mid-1980s. After the impact of the recession of the early 1980s, in 1984 it suffered a second crisis when its major customer went into receivership. More recently it had to cope with the recession of the early 1990s.

5.2.4 Why and How do Companies Fail?

The causes of company collapse are several.

Misjudged new starts Some companies have only a short and not very successful life. These 'damp squibs' fail mainly because of a lack of proper planning before the company is launched.

Following the increased emphasis in UK government policy on enterprise and encouraging the development of new businesses, many good books (Dewhurst and Burns, 1983; Hill, 1987; Waterworth, 1988) have been published on launching new businesses and developing their performance. The questions to be asked of any entrepreneur before launch are:

- Is there a market need?
- Do you really know the product/service required?
- Can you produce it efficiently?
- Do you have the managerial abilities necessary (energy, determination, marketing ability, production ability, financial ability, etc.)?
- Do you have a realistic medium-term plan to viability (this plan needs to bring the above elements together and to form the basis for control and review of the business)? Cash flow is particularly important.
- Do you have the necessary financial resources?

A serious gap anywhere in this 'jigsaw' which needs to be put together means that there is not a whole viable business. Any gap will be a weakness which, if not quickly corrected, is liable to cause poor performance and early failure.

Vulnerability to external shocks   For established companies, the risk of complete collapse depends on two factors, one internal and one external:

- the severity of the impact which caused the crisis;
- the size of the company and its financial reserves, reflected in its level of borrowings.

A company with no net borrowings and a cash mountain could withstand a severe impact, or several impacts over a period of years, each of which would weaken it, before it became finally so weak that the next impact caused it to collapse.
  Examples of such impacts are:

- sudden severe downturn in the total market, as in Newprint (B);

- sudden loss of market share (e.g. the start of a price war, entry of a new product or new competitor);
- loss of a major customer;
- major loss arising from debtor collapse;
- loss on a major order/contract;
- failure of a new product on which the future of the business has been staked;
- loss of financial control (e.g. sudden build-up of debtors, raw material stock, work in progress, etc.);
- a major realignment of exchange rates or change in import controls.

Over-commitment to rapid growth For well-established businesses which pursue a period of rapid growth, an additional cause of failure is over-commitment to a growth which does not materialize. Illustrations of this phenomenon are skateboards and home computers in the toys business. Most toy and games companies have a variety of products at different stages of their lives on the market. The future of a company depends on the continuing flow of successful new toys or games. Ideas need to be well sieved and each new launch needs to be well planned. Good management will keep to a minimum the number of toys or games launched which turn out to have not been worthwhile. Only a few products (e.g. Monopoly) do well and stay profitable for long periods of time. Most others have a short life. Occasionally a toy or games company finds a real winner which has a meteoric rise and then disappears like a 'shooting star'. Any toy or games company finding such a potential winner faces the issue of how far to chase it.

For a small company this is rather like being on a 'snakes and ladders' board. It may go up a ladder, but it might also run into a snake which can not only destroy the gain, just made, but may even lower it to a position worse than before it went up the ladder. Opportunities for rapid growth may well provide the funds necessary to expand a company's capacity (equipment, etc.) but if this path is taken it must be quickly followed by broadening the company's base to reduce its vulnerability to that particular market, product or customer.

If a company pursues such an opportunity half-heartedly it may make little or no profit, for it will lack the volume necessary to get costs per item down. If it commits itself to the maximum growth in the market, sooner or later the market may well collapse and take the company with it. In the early stages of home computers, this is the dilemma which Dragon faced before it failed.

5.2.5 The Behaviour of Senior Executives during a Survival Crisis

A survival crisis occurs because a major danger has not been foreseen and appropriate avoiding action taken. So when it does develop, sooner or later, it comes as a frightening surprise.

As the earlier examples have illustrated, delay in realizing that a crisis is looming can be caused by lack of signals from the environment. Whether this is the case or not, many executives either fail to see whatever signals are available or refuse to face up to them.

Symptoms of evasion   This unwillingness to face up to reality shows in various forms. One example is the survival crisis of a long-established ballroom dancing school, run in rented premises. The owner of the business, an expert teacher of ballroom dancing, had become very interested in local council work and had become a councillor. This interest began to take too much of his time and attention, with the result that the business suffered and performance declined. He fell behind on quarterly payments of rent. He also knew that a five-year review of the level of rent was due and that, after a period of high inflation, this would almost certainly mean a substantial increase in future rent payments. He bought a new car which the business could not afford. He decided to take an expensive holiday in Miami and, to cap it all, he decided to pay off all his creditors before leaving! Inevitably when he returned he ran straight into a crisis. In his subconscious he was worried about the rent due and the future increase; the stress he was under led to the other aberrations of the car, the holiday and the creditor actions; these were a form of escapism.

More mundane manifestations of the same behaviour are the creative accounting and wishful thinking ('it will come right again, it always does') so common during survival crises.

The need for realism   In the Weston case in appendix B, a management demoralized by five years of losses was still not facing

65

up to reality. For the current year it had again produced an optimistic budget, which had had to be revised downwards before the second half of the year. In a survival crisis, realism, erring if necessary on the side of caution, is essential. A strategy which is likely to mean survival even if some other unforeseen difficulties arise is better than one based on unfounded optimism.

The dangers of stress   Once faced, a crisis requires a concentration of attention and effort. This itself brings dangers of which you should be aware. The top executives will have to work faster and for longer hours. They will be under stress. Because stress causes the body's control mechanisms to operate, those managers less able to cope may oscillate in their behaviour between depression and levity. There will also be a tendency to 'clutch at straws'. There may be a temporary belief that a single action has been found which will put things right, when in most cases a series of actions in a concerted campaign is necessary.

Benefiting from a survival crisis   Experience does not automatically result in learning. But provided that in the long term a manager's health is not impaired, severe shocks which are brought under control are more likely to provide learning experiences than minor events. So a survival crisis is a rapid learning time for most of those who have been through it, particularly if, when the crisis is over, they think through the lessons and record them for the future should the threat of another crisis arise.

5.2.6   Strategies for Survival and Recovery

Shortening the strategic horizon   In a real survival crisis for a single business, all spending for benefits months or years ahead must immediately be stopped (or deferred until the crisis has been overcome). The focus must be 100% on stemming the haemorrhage of cash from the business and getting cash flow positive as quickly as possible. The detail of what to do will depend on the causes of the crisis.

Addressing the immediate cause   Attention must first be focused on the event which precipitated the crisis. Was it a one-off event such as the collapse of a major customer debtor? Before this, was performance satisfactory? If so, then, except for avoiding such a degree of dependence on another customer in the future, the longer-term strategy may well be sound. In the short term, some combination of squeezing cash out of the business and seeking short-term extra funding must be found to see the company through.

If the cause has not passed but is still a continuing problem – for example, excess capacity in a collapsed market – then the core of the corrective action must be to offset the cause directly, for example by cutting capacity and associated direct and overhead costs.

However, if the survival crisis has been developing over several years, and if only a small event has precipitated it, then the main cause has been there for a long time and is more deep-seated. A change in the top management was probably called for a few years ago. Without both such a change now and the injection of new funds it may well be too late to rescue the business.

Core and back-up action   What is needed first, in all cases, is rapid recognition of the core action needed.

This core action may in some cases take time to have effect; and by itself it may not be sufficient to stop the cash loss. Around this core action, then, other specific action must be taken:

- to cut expenditure and bring in sufficient cash to prevent collapse in the short term;
- to improve the position further by other steps which may need a little time to take effect.

Examples of emergency actions to be considered include:

- reduction in price of standard products in stock to increase sales and lower stocks;
- increased efforts to reduce debtors;
- stopping all recruitment and training;
- stopping all development;
- generally cutting budgets line by line, either to the level needed for a conservative estimate of sales or zero for those items, such as entertainment, which are of debatable value in the short term and which ought to be the subject of individual case-by-case approval;

- selling off assets not clearly making a sufficient contribution (e.g. excess cars, land, property, etc.).

Attempting to generate cash by extending credit terms can be dangerous, because creditors may suspect a possible collapse and could well demand even earlier payment. Generating cash from the sale of assets in a hurry can result in lower cash generation than selling at a more leisurely pace but if that is the only way of avoiding collapse it has to be done.

A short-term plan of response   All these survival measures should be pulled together into a short-term plan – three months, perhaps – clearly focused on turning round the cash flow quickly. Once the first draft of this plan has been drawn up, consideration can then be given to whether some actions should be speeded up and others given more time to yield more cash. The whole plan should be briefly summarized in terms of statements of actions to be performed by named individuals, and a statement of cash flow, week by week. Should short-term external funding be necessary to see the company through, the confidence which can be placed in this plan will be crucial to securing these funds.

Towards recovery – adjusting priorities   Once the immediate crisis is relieved, the strategic horizon can be gradually lengthened. Planning at this stage requires a well-judged balance between improving day-to-day management as necessary as well as deciding on the longer-term direction in which the company aims to go, together with settling on the first steps in this direction and when they will be possible. As time passes, this balance should be adjusted: in other words, the relative proportions of attention devoted to day-to-day management action for today's performance, and strategic actions to improve future performance, can begin to move towards a more healthy mix of the two.

If a business which is part of a larger group is in a survival crisis there can be a tendency not to act as quickly as the situation requires. Lack of awareness or lack of action by group staff, and complacency, inability or fear of the business itself being closed, can lead unnecessarily to considerable loss of group financial resources.

5.3 A Business Requiring no Change in Focus but Underperforming

5.3.1 The Continuing Quest for Improvement

Many businesses, while correctly positioned in growing markets and having good market shares, are not producing the financial performance of which they should be capable. Why is this?

Since the time when they established their present positions, things have changed. Competitors have developed their capabilities and have now established significant advantages: they are innovating more rapidly, raising productivity faster, have achieved higher levels of quality, and so on. These changes leave the business with competitive disadvantages: hence its underperformance.

To be successful, a business must be continually seeking improvement. It must seek to learn from its own experiences and from comparison with its competitors. It must also look to the future environment and consider what new advantages it can establish which will help it to be more successful.

How effective is each part of the business and how does each compare with that of competitors? For example, if success depends to a high degree on the quality of the design activity, how effective is the design function in terms of its costs and speed of service, and in terms of the market's reaction to the designs produced? Similarly, if the key to success in a market is being the lowest-cost producer, how can that position be best achieved and an advantage established over competitors?

Learning is particularly important with any new product or service. The most important thing one knows about a new product is that one knows very little. In other words, doing something new involves moving outside one's own experience to a greater or lesser extent. Therefore any plan before launch is bound to contain errors. The company which learns most rapidly after the launch, and takes the necessary action, will have a competitive advantage and as a result perform better. Time can be spent and experiences can occur without learning necessarily resulting: it is necessary to be alert, imaginative and observant.

5.3.2 Example: Grass Concrete – Learning after the Launch

The main issues addressed in this example are:

• how to improve marketing;
• how to improve the cost and speed of delivery;
• what opportunities exist outside the UK?

Grass Concrete Ltd was launched in 1971 based on a new patented product with an associated customer advisory service. The patent was for placing in the final position a patterned former (which happens to be made of plastic) into which concrete is poured, so that when the concrete has set the former can be removed by a process of burning, leaving a pattern of holes. These holes are filled with soil in which grass seed is then sown. The result is a surface with the strength of concrete but the appearance of grass.

This product, sold under the brand name 'Grasscrete', has been used in many situations both in the UK and overseas, where the combination of strength and appearance is needed to preserve the environment. For example, the external surface of the Bradwell Dam near Milton Keynes is surfaced with it, to preserve the appearance of the dam wall in an area of natural beauty. Steeper parts of the embankment of the M25 are lined with Grasscrete. Without this lining, in heavy rain the soil would slip down onto the motorway.

Before the product launch it was decided that the company should not manufacture the plastic formers but instead buy them from a company with plastic-moulding capabilities. The company was therefore to be focused on marketing the formers and the process of using them, including advice on the choice of seed and at the site. An advertising programme was prepared and salesmen appointed.

Initial advantages The company started with a competitive advantage arising from possession of the patent, which prevented competitors forming this type of surface *in situ*. The only way other companies could compete was by pre-casting patterned concrete blocks at a place away from site. This was suitable for some types of applications but was only competitive for small areas. For large areas, forming the surface *in situ* was much cheaper.

Two disadvantages, shortly to be explained, developed in marketing and in the supply of the plastic formers.

Early indicators neglected The result of this combination of advantages and disadvantages was that some two years after the launch of the company, it was making losses large enough to put its survival at risk. Why? And what could be done?

The main reason is that it had not consciously forced itself to learn quickly from its early experiences.

For example, the order book contained information on the types of construction jobs which were yielding most orders, particularly large orders. There were a few very large orders, but there were also many very small orders. The 'profit' on some of these small orders was less than the travelling costs of the salesman going to get it, even excluding the cost of his time! So it should have been clear earlier that the pre-launch plan needed revision in terms of the number of salesmen needed; there should be fewer, and they should only pursue potentially large orders. For these the company had a distinct advantage and making a visit to convert an interest into an order was well worthwhile. To generate smaller orders the main weapon had to be advertising in trade publications and the mailing of publicity material, with enquiries being handled by telephone and correspondence.

Similarly, review of the pattern of demand and of the price, delivery and quality of the plastic formers led to a change in the supplier and the contract involved. As a result, quality was improved, stocks were maintained by the supplier to ensure speedy delivery, and the cost of the formers was significantly reduced.

Resurgence and maturity Having overcome these disadvantages, Grass Concrete had a distinct advantage over its competitors. It then used its improving financial strength and these advantages to establish the use of Grasscrete overseas, where the use of the patents was licensed. During this patent-protected period Grass Concrete became a very successful small company with good profit margins and a strong, well-developed market position both in the UK and overseas.

However, it was inevitable that the patents would become time-

71

expired and that the company would have to address this issue to remain successful. Profit margins would be under pressure and royalties from abroad would drop significantly.

Income from abroad is now down to about 5% of total income. The company has refocused its activities on the UK. It has recently secured the exclusive UK licence for a product called Betaflor. This is a patented walling system based on specially designed inter-locking pressed concrete blocks. Its uses are for steep retaining walls and vertical walls in applications such as landscape remod-elling, planters and rockeries, canal and stream embankments, secondary sea defence and acoustic walls. As a result, Grass Con-crete is able to improve its efficiency by marketing both the Grasscrete and Betaflor ranges.

The result of this change in strategy and focus back on the UK is that during the recession of the early 1990s the turnover of Grass Concrete fell by about 15% but has now recovered to its pre-recession level. With the addition of income from the Betaflor license, turnover in the current year is expected to increase to over £4 million with reasonable profit margins and good cash flow.

Overview of Grass Concrete's history Looking back over the total life of Grass Concrete Ltd, it is clear that, except for the delay in learning that the initial launch plan needed significant change, the company has been well managed. It faced up to the elephant issue arising from the fact that Grasscrete could not profitably sustain a larger company; a turnover of some £2 or 3 million p.a. in the UK was the best level with appropriately low fixed costs. It also faced up to the issue of the then approaching expiry of its patents. It coped well with the recession of the early 1990s and, with the addition of the Betaflor range, now has a secure position with the prospect of some growth over at least the next few years.

Rodney Walker, its Chairman and controlling shareholder, has not wasted the good cash flow from the company; it has been used to purchase and develop other small businesses. The experience he gained in running Grass Concrete has enabled him to broaden both his business and his charitable work. Besides various com-pany directorships, his other activities include chairmanships of the Sports Council of Great Britain, the Rugby Football League, the Bradford Hospitals Trust and the NHS Trust Federation.

The history of Grass Concrete Ltd is a good example of effective learning from experience, avoidance of growth for growth's sake and using this learning not only for an enjoyable career but also giving back some of this learning to the benefit of society.

The lesson from Grass Concrete to other companies just starting up is that any plan for a company's launch must include a date for early review, and if necessary, revision, of the remainder of the plan.

5.3.3 Example: Thermalite's Changes in Ownership

A brief history   Thermalite manufactures high-quality aerated concrete insulation blocks. The focus of this example is the period from 1983 to 1986 when Thermalite was an independent single-business company.

Before 1983, for many years Thermalite was a manufacturing subsidiary of John Laing plc, a large publicly quoted company whose main activities are in building and civil engineering. While such blocks are used in building construction, the core skills of John Laing are not in manufacturing operations but in managing large construction projects. Over the years up to 1983, the turnover of Thermalite had increased to some £27 million p.a. with only average profit margins.

In June 1983 an earlier managing director of Thermalite, together with an existing manager and other experienced managers from outside the company, purchased Thermalite in what is best described as a mixture of a management buy-out (MBO or buy-out for short) and a management buy-in (MBI), with a small element of employee share ownership created after the purchase.

An MBO has been defined (Wright et al., 1990) as:

> Essentially, a buy-out occurs when the ownership of a firm is transferred to a new set of shareholders among whom the incumbent management are a significant element, usually having been key to initiating the deal. The firm becomes a private independent company, with outside funding normally in the form of a mixture of equity, provided by various development capital firms, and debt provided by banks.

During the 1980s and to date there have been some 5,400 buy-outs in the UK. It is therefore important to consider in this book how such a change in ownership affects performance and strategy.

Management buy-ins are less common than buy-outs. As the name implies, a management buy-in occurs when the ownership of a firm is taken over by a new set of shareholders led by a manager or managers with good previous business experience but not in the particular company concerned.

Over the period to April 1986, the new team increased the turnover of Thermalite to some £49 million p.a. and improved its profit margins. It was sold to Marley plc and as a result those who took part in the MBO/MBI saw their original investments multiply almost threefold.

Buy-outs in general   To understand why performance improved but a trade sale occurred later, you need to understand how buy-outs affect motivations and performance (Houlden, 1990, 1994). Buy-out companies vary widely. Most, but not all, were underperforming before the buy-out; indeed some come from receivership. Others occur as part of a privatization or as a result of a family wishing to sell a family-controlled company. However, the largest block of buy-outs is from situations like the Thermalite example, where a group sells a subsidiary to its management, the subsidiary usually being an underperformer and often not part of the core activity of the group.

It is difficult for any group in this situation to improve the subsidiary's performance. If the group gets more involved, it may not have the experience needed and in any case may be diverting attention from its core businesses, which themselves might start to deteriorate. If it gives the subsidiary more autonomy and accountability, it has difficulty in causing sufficient motivation and risk/reward to secure good performance.

For a group, selling a business to its managers can remove a problem as well as yielding much-needed cash. From the managers leading the buy-out it requires the investment of a significant enough part of their personal resources to act as a 'stick and carrot' to their motivation. If they fail, they lose a lot of their hard-won personal resources. If they succeed, they may well later make a significant capital gain as well as having a job they enjoy up to the time when they decide to cash in.

By eight years after buy-out, roughly 40% of all buy-outs have exited. A few have gone into receivership, and most of the rest have either been floated on the Stock Exchange or, like Thermalite, been sold via a trade sale. Looking only at those companies which at the different stages are still owned by the managers who led the buy-out, on average, compared to the period before the buy-out, performance improves for the first three years after buy-out but then slowly declines at least up to 10 years after the buy-out. Why is this?

In the first few years after buy-out, the pressure on the management, both from themselves and from the investing institutions, is usually to make a significant short-term improvement in performance, including improvement in cash flow. For most of the institutions, their investment in buy-outs is aimed at significant capital gain within some three to four years; few of the institutions who invest in buy-outs are investing in these companies for the long term of 10 years or more.

With these pressures, it is not surprising that, on average, a buy-out improves performance in the first few years, although of course a few do not achieve this improvement.

But why does this improvement turn to slow decline after about three years?

This is partly explained by the early flotations and trade sales. Some of the better performing companies, many of which were performing better than other buy-out companies even before the buy-out itself, have therefore left the sample. But this does not appear to be the full explanation. My view is that the rest of this slow decline is due to two factors:

- The hopes and worries which those leading the buy-out experienced during the first few years after buy-out have given way to some complacency.
- The strategies aimed at improving performance in the short term have not been replaced by the appropriate balance between shorter-term actions and new investments to give more thrust to the company for better longer-term performance.

Reflections on Thermalite during the MBO/MBI phase   The team leading Thermalite over the period 1983–6 did significantly improve its performance; this is consistent with the pattern for buy-outs generally. They were fortunate in benefiting from the Thatcher/ Lawson boom in private house-building but also they were motivated to take short-term actions to quickly improve performance.

Unlike some other buy-outs, they also started to invest in developing the company for the longer term. For example, they took the decision to make a major investment in a new state-of-the-art plant at Newbury, the final commissioning of which occurred just after the acquisition of Thermalite by Marley.

Marley's ownership of Thermalite In the year of the trade sale to Marley, turnover jumped by over 15% and profit/sales by about 50%. This was the result mainly of achieving peak selling prices just prior to the onset of the recession. After the acquisition, Marley appointed a new Managing Director of Thermalite – John Castle. He retained only the previous Finance Director and recruited new expertise in sales, marketing and technology, and reorganized production to create a compact, well-balanced and thrustful board.

Looking now at the period to date, inevitably the recession of the early 1990s impacted on Thermalite's performance, as it did on the Building Materials Division of Marley within which Thermalite was later located. Thermalite has retained and strengthened its leadership in its segment of the market. Faced with the decline in demand due to the recession, it has closed its older, less efficient plants and improved both productivity and quality. Inevitably, margins deteriorated, but they are recovering. Thermalite is now well placed to give good margins again as the level of new house-building increases.

This improvement in Thermalite's competitive position up to, during and after the 1990s recession has been the result of not only addressing the short-term issues of dealing with the recession itself but also addressing medium- to longer-term issues. Soon after the takeover by Marley, a review was undertaken of the market positioning, pricing, selling effort and production costs of each of the products in the range, with a view to maintaining margins on commodity products and introducing differentiated products. The development and introduction of new blocks and the continuing investments to improve productivity clearly show the management's commitment to not only good day-to-day efficiency, but also to addressing the medium- to longer-term issues which will determine the longer-term success of the company.

General lessons on strategy for buy-out (and buy-in) companies
Before entering into a buy-out, managers must draw up a realistic

plan. This should include some assessment of whether in the medium term there should be a flotation or trade sale or whether it is the kind of business which will best perform in the long term by staying independent. This early view will also be influenced by the ages and motivations of the managers leading the buy-out. In some cases the desire to avoid redundancy can tempt an MBO team to go ahead at a price which can lead to collapse of the company. Realism is essential.

After the buy-out, normally the focus must be on short-term improvements and cash flow. (There are a few exceptions to this. One is an MBO of a fledgeling pharmaceutical company. For this type of company, a buy-out is a 'sink or swim' period. The main focus must be on quickly developing the new product, probably to the stage of early marketing on a limited geographical basis. Such a company may then be sold to a multinational pharmaceutical company able to convert this early limited success to greater success by securing global approvals and sales.)

However, once these actions have begun to yield sustainable improvements in performance, perhaps after a year or two into the buy-out, there is a need to give more weight to medium- to longer-term strategy considerations. A more positive view needs to be taken of whether exit within the next year or two or long-term independence is practicable and preferred. Once that view has been taken, the strategy issues become more obvious. If an exit is intended, the two main questions are how to prepare the company so that it will command the highest price and when the exit should be attempted; this will depend on general conditions in the economy and the level of the stock market. However, if longer-term independence is envisaged, the main issue is what investments behind what strategic direction will most improve competitiveness and performance over the longer term.

Ownership change does affect strategy choice.

5.3.4 Lack of Co-ordination between Marketing and Production

A different cause of underperformance in a company which needs no change in focus is a lack of strategic co-ordination between the activities of the marketing and production departments.

In boosting a company with sluggish performance, it is often fruitful to give marketing additional backing, particularly if this is associated with bringing in a dynamic marketing executive from another company. This should lead to more ideas and better growth. But a company strategy determined entirely by a marketing thrust can cause trouble. Why?

The reason lies in the relationship between the marketing and production functions. In many companies the production function is not strategically led but runs mainly on a day-to-day operational basis. In the past such companies will have changed only slowly. Production has taken the stance: 'tell us what you want and we will produce it: if we find that we need additional equipment we will come back later for authority.' In today's more turbulent and competitive environment, there are companies where this attitude by production is causing the company to decline.

Imagine what happens when marketing is given a leading role but insufficient thought is given to the production implications of new initiatives. Marketing is steadily increasing its demands. It is requiring greater and greater variety of products at lower and lower costs with quicker and quicker delivery, perhaps with better and better quality added for good measure! Top production management is spending all of its time 'fire-fighting' today's problems; delivery times are getting longer and costs are not being reduced. Certainly production, like any other department, will perform more efficiently under some pressure, but excessive pressure can be counterproductive (Houlden and Woodcock, 1989).

In these circumstances the top production executive must create time to think and act strategically. He/she must point out that, for instance, high-volume, low-cost objectives require different equipment, different skills, different works layout and different management processes from high-quality, low-volume specials. It is impossible to produce all kinds of order and meet all kinds of objectives simultaneously. He/she must get back into a company strategy meeting and ensure that the production implications of marketing initiatives are thoroughly explored *before* company strategy is decided.

One of the problems here is the different strategic horizons of production and marketing. A high proportion of the capital investment of many companies is in the production activity. Once these investments have been made, the company is committed to a type of activity for several years ahead. As technology is constantly advancing, any major capital investment decision must be taken after considering how that technology is changing and whether it would be better to delay purchase for a year or two. Marketing decisions can be changed more easily and at less cost.

Production strategy, and technology in fields where it is changing, must play their part alongside marketing strategy in deciding company strategy (Hill, 1983).

In service companies, a similar problem may occur. Their 'production' activities are usually referred to as 'operations' – hence the term 'operations management'. With their often relatively high investment in IT hardware and software, a major change in market focus can well cause high costs and take considerable time to implement. These factors must be taken into account before a change in business strategy is made.

5.3.5 Example: Marketing and Production at Cross Purposes

Take a company in the business of converting coils of narrow metal strip into sections, for a variety of purposes. Over several years it struggled to make reasonable profits. Throughout this period the company had tried to increase its productivity by developing for its own use cold rolling machines which would run much faster than those of its competitors. Thus it had a strength in machine development. Again, its marketing staff were energetic and came up with many ideas for new products; as a result it had a strong order book. So why was the company not making good profits?

Because production strategy and marketing strategy were in conflict. The production strategy was aimed at producing long runs at low cost. The marketing strategy was aimed at a large number of customers and their various requirements, and the order book therefore contained a high proportion of small orders. As a result the machines were spending a large proportion of time on being changed over to specifications for the next order.

What was needed was a review of the potential market and a choice of company strategy between:

- the high-volume, low-cost segment, which would take advantage of the company's skills in machine development but would

79

require marketing to focus its efforts and pricing mainly on getting larger orders;
- specials, which would not require a change in marketing strategy but would require the company to concentrate its production effort on developing machines and systems to allow quick set-up times.

To be effective, departmental strategies must be compatible with each other and consistent with the overall business strategy. Poor performance caused by lack of internal consistency between departmental strategies, in line with the overall strategy, is quite a common failing (Stone and Heany, 1984).

5.4 A Business Facing Deteriorating Performance and Requiring a Major Change in Strategic Focus

5.4.1 The Product Life Cycle

There are times when, no matter how well a business is run from its present position and focus, the future looks bleak. For example, it may have a low market share in a business area where there are substantial economies of scale and where other much larger competitors are bound to win in the long term. Or the total market may be declining, putting the future of the business at risk.

The factors that determine these events are:

- the life cycle of individual products (or services);
- the renewal of that type of presence in the market by the introduction of replacement products; and
- whether the company has only one product or several.

Figure 5.2 gives a simple summary of the *product life cycle*. Before any product is launched, costs are incurred. These costs comprise various types of expenditure: product development, market research, investment in production facilities, etc. After the product is launched, these costs continue in the form of sales promotion, production, and so on. Income from sales initially grows slowly but then accelerates before flattening as the product reaches its full

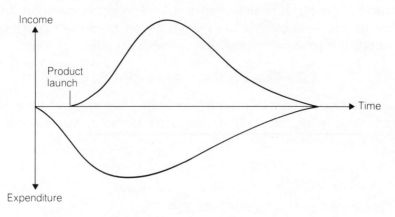

Figure 5.2 The product life cycle.

potential in the market. Thereafter it will sooner or later decline as other products, including perhaps a 'mark two' product from the original producer, take over.

In the later stages of the life cycle, the company aims to keep the product viable on the market longer by improving production costs, product quality, delivery and reliability. It may also extend the life cycle of the existing product by relatively low-cost 'face lifts' rather than complete replacement by a new product.

The need for new products Nevertheless, faced with the potential decline in its sales, to maintain and improve its performance a company must be continually developing replacement or entirely new products.

With the continuing advances in technology, costs of developing new products are increasing. The rate of innovation is also tending to increase in most areas of business. Therefore, not only are product life cycles tending to shorten on the horizontal axis in figure 5.2, but the area under the cost curve is tending to increase. To be successful under these conditions, timing and finding a larger market become critical factors. No longer can development be allowed to proceed at a leisurely pace. Time lost is markets missed. If the new product cannot be developed and launched on time, it is better to keep the present product going for longer and to develop a still more advanced product for introduction later. And with ever higher costs for development of new products, more

81

careful selection of which products to develop is essential. Each product needs to be able to generate larger sales than previously – hence the need for a push into wider markets.

5.4.2 The Business Area Life Pattern

For a particular type of product, including the renewal through a mark two, mark three, etc. series, there is also a *business area life pattern* as illustrated in figure 5.3.

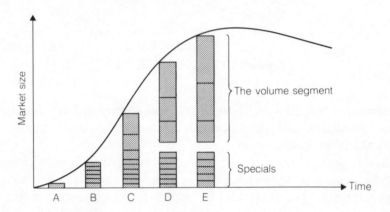

Figure 5.3   A business area life pattern.

At stage A someone has recognized a need and has started a company to gain from meeting that need. At stage B, other companies, represented in the diagram by the individual boxes in the column, have entered the growing market. At stage C, one (the largest) of the competitors has learnt how to succeed and grow and has begun to find economies of scale. This has begun to threaten others, who must either copy this initiative or find other ways of being successful. This threat increases, with the result that while there may still be new entrants to this market, others are withdrawing, collapsing or being taken over.

At stage D the business area may well be dividing into separate competition *segments*. One will be the high-volume, low-cost segment in which customers are prepared to accept one of a small range of standard products/services in return for low cost. This standardization permits economies of scale by the producer (e.g. a dedicated production line). Another segment will be for those

82

(usually fewer) customers requiring higher quality and prepared to pay a higher price or even who wish to have a personalized product with features solely for them. For these lower volumes, different production facilities may be required, both to produce the lower volumes (e.g. one-off or batch production as against continuous production) and to meet the customer needs at this level, where design, quality, reliability and delivery are more important than price.

Successful market segmentation: 'standards' and 'specials'
Understanding the order in which different groups of customers rank their preferences for price, design, quality, delivery, reliability, after-sales service (the 'order winning criteria') is important to successful market segmentation and to tailoring your company's production facilities to exploiting the market to the full. For example, the repairer of a critical component of expensive electrical equipment has correctly identified and focused on a segment within the electrical component business. This company carries sufficient capacity to guarantee repair and return with 24 hours; this quick turn-round attracts a higher price. The company is more successful than its competitors.

Variations on the basic pattern Most business areas divide into at least these two segments of 'standards' (high volume at low cost) and 'specials'. But it is important to check whether more than two segments exist. An additional segment may occur, for example in locations isolated by geography, where the volume of demand and the costs of transport are such that delivery from a distant plant producing in high volume is not competitive. The example of Weston Hydraulics in appendix B is of a business area which has three segments.

Business areas are by no means uniform in their development. Some may not divide into segments at all; or, if they do, the number of segments may change over the life of the business area.

Competition within a segment While there will be some competition between segments in an attempt to lure more customers from one segment to another, the main competition will be within segments. It will intensify as the competitors learn how to compete, and will be most intense when the market matures. At that point, stage E in figure 5.3, few if any new competitors will be entering the business area because profit margins will be declining and it will have lost its attraction. The weaker companies will be disappearing (by collapse, takeover and withdrawal). In the longer term the number of companies remaining in the high-volume, low-cost segment will depend on a number of factors, including the magnitude of the economies of scale, the investment costs of getting to high volumes, the cost of withdrawal from the segment (known as *exit barriers*), monopoly controls, etc.

Choice of position   These changes in a business area present strategic issues to the competitors within it. As the area develops further, some of the companies which initially chose to compete in the volume segment will realize that they are losing and that they will have to decide whether to try to transfer to the specials segment. There will be companies which are less aware of developments and which do not make a choice between competing more vigorously in the volume segment or getting into specials. This 'caught on the fence' position will leave them vulnerable to more effective competitors from both segments. This is an issue currently facing some of the Europe-based car manufacturers; and in the service sector, with the freeing of the UK financial markets, the medium-sized building societies, among others, are confronting the same problem.

Once the business area has passed through maturity, demand may have settled at a plateau at such a low level that it is no longer economic for a company to specialize in either the standards or the specials segment. Reverting to equipment which is fairly effective at making products for both types of customer may be more appropriate.

Profit margins and growth opportunities tend to differ between the segments. Usually, specials offer higher profit margins, but the market tends to be smaller. Sometimes the volume segment takes over the whole market. In other areas of business the volume segment may become very dominant, only for new specials segments to develop and to recover more of the market. For example, this happened during the 1980s in the UK in the bread business, where fresh crusty bread and wholemeal bread had a resurgence in popularity.

5.4.3 Example: Narrowboat Builder Faces Loss of Core Market

The issue which this example illustrates is:

* to what new focus should the company shift its resources and abilities, when faced with a future serious decline in its core business?

In its earlier history Hancock and Lane Ltd chose to enter the market for narrowboats when the volume segment could develop. Later, after several years of considerable success, the company decided to withdraw entirely from this business area when the market declined and the advantages of volume production disappeared.

Britain's canals were originally built for the transport of industrial goods, but this traffic has declined to near zero. Since World War II, the canals have become an important part of the leisure industry. A quiet holiday meandering along the canals, away from the bustle of city life, has become popular.

Hancock and Lane was started 30 years ago by two agricultural engineers, Paul Hancock and Tony Lane. Soon after completing their studies at a technical college, they decided to build a steel narrowboat for leisure use on the canals.

The genesis of the business: a market opportunity Then they saw their chance. With interest in holidays on the canals swelling rapidly, the canal authorities were substantially increasing the number of licences for narrowboats to operate on the waterways. Before this time, the narrowboat building business consisted of small companies at the canal side, building boats one by one; their owners were often sole traders, who did not wish for much other than a basic living and to get away from the 'rat race'. Paul and Tony saw the opportunity for economies of scale and production in all weathers, in a factory properly equipped with overhead cranes, etc. In other words, they recognized the opportunity to split the market into volume and one-off segments and in the volume segment to standardize on a few standard narrowboat structures, with the detailed interiors to suit individual customer requirements.

They were successful. Over the period to 1980 they developed the company to an output of some 150 narrowboats per year and a turnover of £1.3 million p.a. Profits before tax were about 15% of sales. The company had become the market leader with a 30% share of the total leisure narrowboat market. During this time the model range was updated to stay in the lead, both in appearance and in the technologies of fittings and instruments.

Preparation for market decline Well before 1980, when UK demand for new narrowboats peaked, the company foresaw a decline in the market. The country's canals were getting full and the number of new licences being issued was going to fall. Steel narrowboats have long lives, and repair and refurbishment come before any consideration of replacement. Therefore, orders for new narrowboats, either for new owners or as replacements, were unlikely.

Considering a new focus Paul and Tony therefore began to assess alternatives. Figure 5.4 maps out the possibilities reviewed by

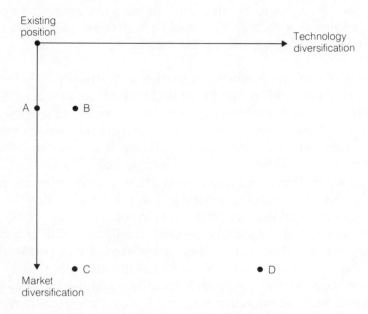

Figure 5.4   The product/market diversification mix.

means of a product/market matrix. They began by looking at steel-boat building markets in which their abilities and facilities could be used effectively. For example, they employed consultants to carry out assessments of possible leisure developments on the French canals, steel-hulled boats for dock and coastal work, etc. None of these, however, offered the opportunity they were seeking. This first move in the consideration of alternatives is indicated by point A on figure 5.4: they were seeking to use their existing technology skills and some of their existing marketing skills in a slightly different market. Perhaps the dock and coastal vessels business would have required a small development of their technological skills (point B), but that was not a major problem. They also briefly considered other possibilities (e.g. the manufacture and lease of floating homes) which might draw on some of their existing abilities.

This search led Paul and Tony to the conclusion that they must plan to withdraw entirely from the narrowboat business, even though they were the market leader. There was no sense in staying with it until they were forced to withdraw; the water's edge narrowboat builders would be willing to continue in business on very low overheads and with very low margins. But should they sell up completely and take early retirement? They were too young and vigorous to do that. So what else could they consider?

Maximizing experience gained   The further away from existing abilities a diversification is chosen, the less the value of experience already possessed and the greater the risks involved, particularly if other competitors are well established. One alternative considered in this case was to open a garden centre: they had a property appropriately located on a busy roundabout. With the national increase in leisure, they had seen new garden centres prospering in other parts of the country. Should they get into this business area (point D in figure 5.4)? They had only a few of the skills which would be needed; and a detailed analysis of population density, competition, etc. showed them that besides the risk due to lack of experience, the level of turnover from this one site (or a nearby alternative site) would not be large enough to occupy and interest both of them. There was also the expectation that larger retail groups would become a greater threat to competition in this market. So this option, too, was rejected.

An appropriate option   During the period when the narrowboat business had been expanding, a new and larger factory had become necessary. Paul and Tony had employed a construction company to manage the whole job but had supplied the steelwork for the structure themselves, using their buying power and the cutting and welding facilities from their narrowboat business. So they had already developed some of the abilities necessary for erecting steel structured factory units. This gave them the idea for the right new venture. With the growth of new businesses and the development of industrial estates in the East Midlands and Home Counties, they decided to go into the factory construction business, selling some and leasing others, including their existing factories.

They knew they were taking a risk. They were financially strong and willing to risk some of their resources. They are now a successful company in this new business area.

Over the years since this change of focus, Tony Lane and Paul Hancock have been successful. A site they originally bought at Daventry is now fully developed and the factories successfully let or sold. Work on a second site at Rugby is now under way.

The future   Paul Hancock and Tony Lane are now in their mid-50s. Financially, both are so secure that if they wish to retire after completing work on the Rugby site they can do so. But my betting is that they will then still be pretty active, whether that be in factory construction or something else which attracts them; they are successful entrepreneurs determined to also enjoy life.

Changing tack successfully   This example illustrates the importance, in this type of changing environment, of:

- retaining an entrepreneurial flair;
- generating and being open to ideas;
- being able to recognize opportunities when they arise (*windows of opportunity*);
- being able to foresee threats;
- being willing to face up to facts and if necessary to pull out before decline occurs;
- being quick to act once a choice has been made.

Hancock and Lane would have run into a survival crisis had its directors not foreseen the decline in the market. This foresight allowed them the time to consider thoroughly many alternatives before making the successful choice of the company's future direction.

5.5 Diversification beyond a Single Business

5.5.1 The Need for Forethought

When a company has become well established in a single business, one issue it needs to address is whether its future success would be increased if it were to use some of the funds it is creating to develop other businesses.

Diversification is a step into the unknown which may be successful or may seriously weaken the business, even send it into a survival crisis. It is all too easy to jump in with too little thought, a course followed sometimes by luck but more often by disappointment (Porter, 1987).

5.5.2 Why Diversify?

There are many reasons why a single-business company may wish to consider diversifying. These include:

- to replace a dying core business;
- as a first stage in a search for additional growth opportunities;
- to broaden the company's base and reduce the risk of being entirely dependent on one business sector;
- during a recession, temporarily to use existing resources more fully;
- to strengthen the technology base for future developments;
- to provide a smaller but related business in which future top management can develop their general management abilities;
- to protect raw material supply;
- to protect customer outlets;
- to benefit from synergy by having a larger turnover on which some activities can be run jointly (e.g. joint purchasing or R&D).

Diversification can be effected by gradual growth away from the core or by takeover of an existing company. Since the former is more likely to be practicable with a single-business and typically smaller company, the discussion of takeovers and of divestment will be delayed until discussion of group strategy in part III.

No diversification should be initiated until its purpose has been defined, alternative ways of meeting this aim have been compared and action plans have been drawn up to check that the purpose is likely to be achieved. For example, a desire to protect customer outlets, which might be achieved by entering the outlet level itself, may often obscure excessive costs and uncompetitiveness in the core business; correcting this lack of competitiveness may remove the problem.

If the diversification is to be by organic growth away from the core, then the same questions need to be answered as for starting a new business: whether all of the necessary components such as a market need, a product, marketing ability, production ability and general management ability are available, and whether a plan for the diversification over the next year or two is in place.

5.5.3 Planning Diversification

Any plan for diversification should contain provision for a thorough review some six to twelve months after the programme has been started. Is the plan still right or is there now a better plan? Is the diversification achieving the performance specified in the plan? If not, what action is needed to bring performance up to plan, or is there a need to revise the plan itself?

It is often the case that the purpose of a diversification will also define the action which should follow later. Consider, for example, a company which is performing well in a new growth environment and which wishes also to broaden its base for the future. It may have eliminated some alternatives but then be unsure which of, say, four others is best. They all look promising. So it decides to start diversifying in four directions. This is really a decision to search by actually trying each option; so within the first year a thorough review should be carried out, to decide which of the four offers the best future prospects and whether all or most of the others should be stopped. Continuing with all four could mean that the best was starved of resources and the worst could run into continuing losses.

If a diversification is outstandingly successful (for example, the Vodafone development by Racal), this may well raise the question whether it offers sufficient growth potential to consider making it the new core of the future company, taking over from its original business. This longer-term change in the core of a set of related businesses is considered further under group strategy in part III.

5.5.4 Example: Window Frames to Aluminium Pressings

A privately owned company, Allan H. Williams Ltd, manufacturer of quality aluminium window frames for the construction of prestige office buildings, illustrates some of the opportunities and dangers of diversification. The issues which this company was seeking to address were:

- How should growth be increased?
- How should a family member's career be developed?
- Is diversification a way of meeting either of the above issues and, if so, in what direction should diversification occur?

In 1979 this company considered various possibilities for diversifying beyond its core business.

Motives for diversifying With the development of new methods of building construction, it had already extended its core business to cover the manufacture of aluminium curtain-walling (the aluminium panels which in some buildings are hung from the building frame to complete the external surface between the windows). At that time, building construction was recovering from a minor trough in demand, but little growth was expected in the market over the next few years. UK exports were at a low level and not expected to recover sufficiently to offer the rate of growth being sought. So one of the motivations for considering diversification in this case was to increase profitable growth.

A second factor causing an interest in diversification was that one of the members of the family which had a controlling interest in the company was employed in it; he had reached the stage of both management training and experience in this and other companies when his further development required that he be given the chance to run a small business on his own.

The possibilities   The alternatives which were considered over a period of a year or so included:

- manufacture and sale of domestic DIY double glazing;
- manufacture of aluminium pressings;
- wholesaling of glass;
- manufacture of in-fill panels for curtain-walling.

All of these were related to the core business.

Selecting a route   Using the product/market matrix shown in figure 5.4, at first sight it might have seemed obvious that DIY double glazing was the option closest to existing experience and therefore the one to be chosen. However, after careful thought it was obvious that this alternative should be rejected. The main reasons were:

- the DIY market was coming to maturity and contained strong, well-established competitors;
- the company did not have the production capability required;
- the company did not have the skills required in door-to-door selling;
- entering the DIY double glazing market could harm the company's image in its core business.

By 1979 the DIY double glazing area of business had developed over a period of some 20 years. It was approaching maturity with companies like Everest and Anglia in a dominant position, enjoying substantial economies of scale in production. This was not the time for a new entrant into this market. If Allan H. Williams had wished to take this path, the time to do so would have been at least ten years earlier, when others were also learning.

The company's skills were in design to meet customer requirements and in manufacturing in small batches to high quality standards. Its equipment, labour skills, production procedures and controls were all attuned to the needs of that segment of the market. The DIY double glazing market requires a few standard window sections produced in volume at low cost on automated equipment, with different labour skills, procedures and controls.

The marketing skills of Allan H. Williams lay in dealing with architects and building contractors engaged on large contracts. Managing a large sales force selling from door to door to domestic buyers requires entirely different marketing skills.

The company decided to enter the aluminium pressings business. It was a successful diversification.

Advantages of the chosen option   The advantages which Allan H. Williams possessed were:

- the company was buying-in a significant quantity of aluminium pressings, which it could transfer to a new company;
- it knew the aluminium pressings business from a customer's point of view.

While the company had no skills in managing an aluminium pressings business, it did know who the most effective managing directors in action were. If it were to enter this new business area it had to be able to entice one of these away from his existing employer.

New aluminium presses are expensive, but at that time there was a lot of excess capacity, so almost-new presses could be bought relatively cheaply. Small new industrial premises were also easily available at fairly low rental levels.

Strategy for diversification   The strategy chosen was based on the following actions:

- set up a separate company with a capacity some 25% greater than Allan H. Williams's total aluminium pressings requirement;
- appoint a quality managing director, whose employment package would include a minority shareholding in this new business;
- buy two near-new aluminium presses;
- rent a modern industrial unit of a size to allow some future expansion;
- initially put all of Allan H. Williams's requirements into this new company, but make plans for the company to be autonomous within one year.

The new company has performed well ever since its establishment. The payback period on the original investment was good.

Further diversification   However, while this choice did meet Allan H. Williams's desire for additional growth, it did not offer the opportunity for a member of the family to manage the business. (It will be noticed that an important element of the diversification plan was to appoint a managing director of proven ability in that role and in that business.) So could either of the other two alternatives offer further growth combined with meeting this additional objective?

Getting into the glass wholesaling business was an interesting possibility. The company not only manufactured aluminium window frames but also 'fixed' (i.e. installed) them on site and, to do this, bought large quantities of window glass. The company could therefore channel its requirements to any such wholesaling business. Glass wholesaling was a business area with good performance and reasonable prospects.

However, it would have been almost impossible to enter this market from scratch. This is because the large wholesalers are well established and can buy glass at a significantly lower price than a small stockholder can. Buying an existing wholesaler would require a substantial investment and would not be the environment in which to develop the general management skills of the family member; again, an experienced managing director from the glass wholesaling business would have to be recruited as part of any plan. So this alternative was rejected.

The in-fill panels business presented a different prospect. In-fill panels were a fairly recent development alongside that of curtain walling. The companies operating in this business area were fairly small and prices were high. Starting from scratch was a possibility which would allow time for learning at a relatively low risk. If successful, it would provide additional growth to the firm as a whole as well as a cheaper source of supply to Allan H. Williams, thus giving it a competitive advantage in its curtain-walling business.

A decision was made to go ahead. The pre-launch plan included the recruitment of someone with the necessary technical expertise. An advanced moulding press and associated equipment were bought and the company started in a small factory unit with some half-a-dozen employees. After some minor difficulties, both on the technical side and in developing a set of regular customers, it is now a successful autonomous business, small but growing steadily.

The importance of autonomy in conserving management time
The initial stages of the aluminium pressings and in-fill panels businesses required the attention of the top management of Allan H. Williams. If this had continued to be the case, too much top-level attention could have been drawn away from the core business, leading to poorer performance there. Requiring the two businesses to become autonomous quickly avoided this.

Collapse of the original core business While these diversifications into the aluminium pressings and in-fill panels businesses were successful, unfortunately the window frame and curtain-walling business suffered in the late 1980s and, finally, in late 1989, went into receivership. Why was this? During the mid-1980s it increased its turnover partly by taking on larger individual contracts. A study by an external consultant just before its demise concluded that control had suffered and recommended how controls should be changed to meet the needs of these much larger contracts. This elephant strategic issue had been developing for a few years but had not been diagnosed until too late – hence the company's collapse.

5.5.5 Broad or Focused Growth during Diversification: an Analogy

Many companies, as they develop, increase the variety of their products or services, either in terms of the range of sizes or in terms of variety of design. The strategic issue is whether this development should be left free or controlled, across a broad base or more tightly focused.

Analogies are not the real thing and therefore cannot sensibly be taken too far. However, they can help to convey understanding. Before giving a practical example of this issue, therefore, I want to introduce the analogy which I have found useful in explaining this type of question to senior executives. The analogy is with a fruit tree – say, an apple tree.

Consider an apple tree in ordinary ground, neither swampy nor rich in all the mineral and organic matter which it requires. It can be left free to grow indefinitely. In this case, its shape and size will depend entirely on the environment which it has experienced. Its rate of growth will depend on the soil and the weather, particularly over the years of its early development. Its shape will depend on the weather (e.g. prevailing winds) and on the proximity of other trees (competitors) or obstacles, which may restrict the amount of sunshine it gets. It will develop an increasing number of side-shoots, with the result that its energy for growth will be widely dispersed; the many branches will begin to restrict one another's growth. Unrestrained growth will lead to most of the tree's energy going into branch and leaf (turnover) growth rather than flowers and apples (profits); and those apples that are borne will tend to be small.

A wise grower, then, will prune to concentrate growth on a well-balanced future tree structure. He will discourage growth for growth's sake and formation of excessive side-shoots. He will prune to encourage the bearing of a substantial crop of good-sized, high-quality apples. He will also spray periodically to kill pests and disease (excess material waste, overmanning, etc.). If the soil is lacking in quality, he will not randomly feed large quantities of ill-chosen fertilizers (throwing cash at the problem) but will carefully check the soil and select which fertilizers to use (investing in selected opportunities). As a result he will develop a well-structured tree which, over time, grows well and bears an increasing crop of quality apples.

Similarly, to be successful, a company needs careful choice of the longer-term shape towards which it is being directed; and, as it grows, it needs careful stimulus, combined with elimination of those products which make little contribution to profits. Controlled growth with controlled variety is necessary but, as with different types of apple trees, the degree of control required will vary from time to time and from company to company. Remember:

- diversification needs to be selective;
- the focus of an initial step in diversifying a business must be carefully chosen;
- further exploratory diversification needs subsequent review so that resources are concentrated on the developments showing greatest promise.

5.5.6 Example: Diversification and Rationalization in Electrical Components and Assemblies

In this example, the focus is first on two companies, Elkay and Conblock, in 1989. At that time, Elkay Electrical Manufacturing

96

Co. Ltd and Conblock Electrical Ltd were two closely related companies with a significant degree of common ownership. Taken together, they produced and supplied electrical components and assemblies. Their total joint turnover was some £6 million per year.

During the early 1990s, Conblock sold its assets and liabilities to Elkay and in May 1994 the whole company was sold to Smiths Industries plc. The second focus is therefore on 1994, the events leading up to the sale to Smiths and what has happened in the short period since then.

As will be seen later, the issue which the directors of the two companies tried to address in 1989 re-emerged as a more critical issue in the events leading up to the sale to Smiths Industries in 1994. For this reason the situation as seen in 1989 will be described at some length after looking briefly at the earlier history of the two companies.

History before 1989   The original company was Elkay, a service company whose origins lay in importing electrical components in bulk and selling them in smaller quantities to electrical companies and smaller wholesalers. Since those earlier days it had developed. It introduced some of its own components, such as timers, nylon cable glands, intruder alarms and smoke sensors. For some of these it sub-contracted the whole of the manufacturing process; for others it sub-contracted the manufacture of the parts but did its own assembly. In the late 1970s it decided to move more positively into the manufacture of components and assemblies – hence the setting up of Conblock, the associated manufacturing company.

Elkay and Conblock in 1989   In 1989 Elkay was still a bulk buyer of electrical components and assemblies, which it warehoused and then sold in smaller quantities to:

* manufacturers of domestic electrical appliances and lighting equipment;
* electrical wholesalers;
* area electricity boards and other significant users of electrical components and assemblies.

It was buying from its associated company, Conblock, from other UK manufacturers and from overseas suppliers.

Conblock's main production focus was the manufacture of connector blocks. It manufactured standard connector blocks for sale direct to some independent customers as well as for sale to Elkay. It also had a strong design capability for producing special connector blocks suited to the particular needs of individual electrical equipment manufacturers. It had an assembly section for its own products and for those previously assembled by Elkay.

Taken together, the two companies were doing well. From 1981 to 1988 turnover increased from £1.8 million to £5.8 million p.a. with good profit margins. Therefore, while there were parts of the two companies where performance could be, and was being, improved, the main strategic issue facing them was:

- where to focus the use of resources for future growth and success and how and when to implement any changes necessary.

The direction chosen would determine the way in which the relationship between the two companies should change over time. In 1989 Elkay was buying some components and assemblies from Conblock but on others it was free to choose between supply from Conblock or from other suppliers, often overseas.

Conblock could have further expanded its manufacturing facilities to meet all of Elkay's needs; if that happened then Elkay would be absorbed into Conblock as its marketing department. Alternatively, Elkay and Conblock could have become much more autonomous, Elkay being free to buy from wherever it liked. A third alternative would have been to concentrate more resources on developing Elkay.

The choice between these three future directions was heavily dependent on the best future strategy for Conblock. Conblock had two main strengths: its core manufacturing capability for producing connector blocks, both standards and specials, and its design capability for designing specials.

The question addressed in 1989 was, bearing in mind the opening up of the European Community market in 1992, what should be the balance between standard and special connector block manufacture in Conblock? The alternatives were:

- aim to become the European leader in volume production of standard connector blocks, with specials as a secondary activity;
- pursue both activities with equal vigour, possibly splitting Conblock into two separate companies later;
- put the main emphasis on developing the specials side of the company, with production of standards a secondary activity.

This choice would have had major implications for the future purchase of manufacturing equipment, the direction of sales effort and the emphasis on developing the design activity. Making this choice required an understanding of competition. With imports of standard connector blocks from countries such as Austria already quite common, the radius of competition for this type of product is certainly as wide as Europe. How fast was that market growing? How strong were the competitors in that business compared to Conblock/Elkay? For specials, was the radius of competition bound to be less? How large was the potential market within that distance? How strong was Conblock compared with any competitors within that radius? How could more leads for specials be generated? Could Conblock improve its selection of which specials to develop, etc? Coming down to a more detailed level, in both Elkay and Conblock we meet the issue of how large the range of products in the catalogue should be. For example, Elkay in 1989 more than doubled its catalogue listings. How could the process of deciding what products to add and what products to remove from the catalogues be improved? Should cash generated by Elkay be used in Conblock, thus assisting faster growth of Conblock but restricting the growth of Elkay?

These are some of the many questions which were being considered, in the process of guiding the overall future of the two companies. Unrestrained growth in all directions would have led to a fall in profit margins and a shortage of funds for promising activities. In fact the directors did not make a clear strategy choice in 1989. Expansion continued, diversification increased and more investments were made in Conblock. However the recession of the early 1990s was approaching!

The sale of Elkay to Smiths Industries in 1994   As the recession developed, overall performance deteriorated. Turnover and margins declined, particularly in Conblock, where the problem focused on its sales in volume of standard connector blocks. This was the 'commodity' part of its business. In this type of business, market dominance and economies of scale are important to long-term success. In a recession the strongest competitors will protect their heavier investments and will be able to drop prices from a higher profit margin to maintain their volume throughput. The result was that companies like Conblock were forced into losses on standard connector blocks with a smaller knock-on effect on the demand for specials.

Clearly, there was a big question mark about the future of Conblock and there were also many smaller issues to address. But more urgent than these medium-term issues was the need to deal with what could become a survival crisis. (At this point, if you have forgotten, you should look back to section 5.2, 'Survival and Recovery'.)

Emergency actions were taken to improve the cash position in the short term. Actions included the closure of Conblock as a separate company, a cut in stocks of about £^{1}/$_2$ million and a reduction in the number employed; for example, administrative staffing was cut by 20.

Once these and other emergency actions had been taken, more analysis was undertaken to check the overall strategy and to determine the way forward. By this time in the history of these companies, some of the relatives of the two directors who had led the companies in the earlier years were in more senior positions, including directorships. A divergence of views on the best way forward was developing. On the one hand, there were those who felt that as the effects of recession receded, fairly general expansion should be continued. Others argued for a more focused strategy, preferring better profit margins with slower growth to higher sales growth.

The differences between shareholding directors on the best way forward increased. As a result it was agreed that a change in ownership was necessary. An MBO by some of the directors was considered. The only path which all could agree was the sale of the whole activity to another company, hence the sale to Smiths Industries in 1994.

During this period of soul-searching, a number of conclusions emerged, with the result that further actions were taken. These included rationalization of the activities of Conblock. Connector blocks are made of plastic containing metallic parts for the electrical connection. The company had invested in special presses to make these metal parts in-house. However, its expertise was not in metal pressing and its volumes were insufficient to give low-cost production. So these presses were sold at a good price, yielding much-needed cash, and costs were reduced by buying-in these metal parts.

The company shifted towards greater focus. For example, one of Elkay's most profitable and promising product areas was cable glands. This activity was given more resources to expand.

Recent performance as part of Smiths Industries   The Managing Director of Elkay, Bruce Fraser, has continued as the Managing Director of the company, within the Industrial Division of Smiths Industries. The focused strategy has been given more support. As a result, there has been some increase in turnover but the main change has been a considerable further increase in cash flow and in profit margins, which are now well above 10% of sales.

Looking back, it is now apparent that the problems described above started from about 1984. They were caused by the development of Conblock as a separate company and the greater difficulty of separating winners from losers as expansion continued and variety increased.

In this type of company, correct 'pruning of the apple tree' throughout its life is a continuing and core 'elephant' issue.

Having worked through this chapter, you should now have a good understanding of what strategy for a single business involves, and how the performance of the business affects not only the time horizon but also the number of options available. You should understand the general framework for describing the strategic situation for a single business, and how simple or detailed that thinking needs to be to get at the key factors and how they relate to one another. With experience you will find it possible to speed up that process. From the variety of situations described, you should have broadened your understanding to include some of the concepts required to tackle particular situations. Some combination of these concepts may be helpful in your particular company.

You should also be more aware of the nature of strategic issues and particularly the key, or elephant, issues, at the single business level. Often these elephants will be difficult to diagnose (hidden by the 'undergrowth'). Some will emerge for only a short period and if dealt with will not return. Others may recur from time to time, while yet others, like the one described for Elkay and Conblock, are a permanent feature of the business itself and must be reviewed from time to time.

PART III

COMPANY STRATEGY FOR A MULTI-BUSINESS GROUP

KEY POINTS

- What is the group part of group strategy?
- Increasingly global competition
- What has happened to the concept of 'synergy'?
- 'Value chains' and group 'cement'
- R&D and its management in corporate strategy
- A framework for describing the situation of a group and deciding its strategy
- Practical examples of various key issues which can occur in different groups, and the approaches which can be used to address them

Chapter 6

A Group and its Environment

This chapter and the two which follow it take you on to look at larger and more complex companies which contain several businesses: in other words, to group strategy. Some of the concerns and concepts examined in part II with respect to single businesses are also applicable – sometimes with modification – to whole divisions or groups; however, in the interests of conciseness, they will not be repeated in this part of the book. Similarly, as you read through part III, you will find concepts and situations described, some of which, again suitably adapted, may also be of value in certain business strategy situations.

Before we consider a framework for group strategy in chapter 7, there are several key concepts which need to be grasped. These are the subject of the present chapter, and include:

- economies and diseconomies of scale;
- synergy;
- value chains;

- company 'cement';
- the place of technology in group strategy.

6.1 The Nature of a Group

6.1.1 Size and Diversity

Not all single-business companies are small. For example, up to its takeover by Ford in 1989, Jaguar, with a turnover of some £1 billion p.a., was essentially involved in a single business area but with marketing activities in selected countries on a global basis. It could have been organized either as just one company or as a group with a core company producing and selling cars in the UK, plus associated fairly autonomous companies buying cars from this core company and selling them in particular overseas territories. Conversely, not all companies operating in more than one area of business are large and broken down into separate subsidiary companies. Elkay and Conblock, discussed in section 5.5.6 above, and Newprint (A), discussed in appendix A, illustrate this. Thus the split between this part and part II of the book is somewhat arbitrary. However, it will be easier to understand the situations described here if you do now think in terms of larger and more complex groups each containing several businesses.

Several of the concepts discussed earlier do apply directly to larger and more complex groups: such groups, of course, contain individual businesses and therefore strategic analysis for a group must include the analysis of its constituent businesses. In short, you already have a foundation on which to build, but you now need to extend the approach to address the additional questions raised by the nature of large and more complex groups.

6.1.2 Different Types of Group

Groups may be divided into several broad types, each with its own particular strategic features. They include the following:

- a group of several unrelated businesses, perhaps including service and produce subsidiaries – in other words, a true conglomerate;
- a group with several divisions (or 'business groups') and closely related subsidiary companies within each division (e.g. Hanson);
- a group containing businesses all closely related to each other:

for example, a group strongly dependent on one technological area (e.g. IBM or Rolls Royce);

- a vertically integrated group involved in all or most of the different stages from raw material supply through the various stages of production (such as component production and assembly) to sale of the complete product or service to the ultimate user, as well as perhaps sale of some of the output part of the way along this sequence.

6.1.3 Factors Shared by all Types of Group

Common to all of these situations are the following features:

- The turnover of the whole group is such that anything less than the best corporate strategy decisions results in large financial penalties. Therefore considerably more effort should be, and normally is, put into strategy analysis than would be appropriate in small businesses.
- Faced with increasingly global competition (Gluck, 1982) periodic reshaping of groups is common, not only by organic change but also by takeovers, divestments, strategic alliances, joint ventures, transnational mergers, etc.
- Because these companies are larger and complex and often operating in various countries throughout the world, the choices of the key personnel, organizational structure, degree of delegation, the information systems, methods of communication and motivation, training and career development, are critical to the overall strategy and the success of the group (Reinton and Foote, 1988).

The central question needing to be addressed is:

- On the assumption that individual subsidiary businesses have alternative strategies which they could pursue, what are the additional concepts (or extensions of concepts) which can help in consideration of overall strategy at division or group levels?

6.2 Economies and Diseconomies of Scale

Most companies that grow large do so to benefit from *economies of scale*. These economies can come from many sources.

6.2.1 The Benefits of Technological Progress

Some economies of scale are made possible by advances in science and technology, such as the following:

- new product design, the product often being more compact and able to satisfy more customer needs better;
- improved production equipment and processes, from hand methods through mechanization to automation;
- faster and cheaper transport;
- improved office equipment and processes, such as word processors, computer manipulation and display of data;
- improved communications.

A group, with its larger financial resources, can help its component businesses to gain these economies.

6.2.2 Increased Power and Joint Functions

Other economies of scale arise from increased bargaining power, for example in purchasing. Yet others arise from the shared use of activities across businesses, such as:

- joint R&D;
- joint distribution;
- joint marketing;
- joint treasury functions.

6.2.3 Recognizing Diseconomies of Scale

However, when a company increases its capacity and produces more of a given product or service, it does not automatically follow that the cost per unit of output will reduce. There may be no natural gain in producing more, or any gain may be more than wiped out by *diseconomies*. For example, a company publishing a regional newspaper may be able to improve the production cost per newspaper by printing more copies, but may have to incur additional costs of distribution over a wider radius if it wishes to increase its sales; and these extra costs may more than offset the production benefits.

Similarly, two businesses in the same group might see potential benefit in joint purchasing of their input material. But such joint purchasing could carry with it disadvantages for each of the two, such as:

- the need for extra staff;
- a loss of separate control of the quality of the material;
- a loss of separate control of the time of delivery of the material;
- further costs in moving the delivered material from the point of receipt;
- a loss in accountability and motivation, and therefore in performance.

Effective strategy analysis recognizes the potential economies of scale, defines how they can be achieved, recognizes the dangers of diseconomies and works out how they can be avoided or minimized.

6.2.4 The Effects of Scale in Different Contexts

The degree to which the potential for economies of scale exists varies between areas of business and over time in the same business. Consider, for example, in the retail trade, why it is that food supply is dominated by the major supermarket chains, many shoe shops are owned by one group and yet independent flower shops (goods perish quickly?) and sports goods shops (variety of sources of supply?) are still able to flourish.

Diseconomies of scale always exist but may be relatively insignificant across a certain range of sizes of business. However, these diseconomies may well become very significant above a certain size of business and prevent further development of the business in its existing form. An example of this is the wire spring industry.

What is the crucial size?   A wire spring company does not make standard springs but manufactures in batches to the particular requirements of the customer as to type of metal, strength, diameter of coil, length and shape of the ends, etc. As a result, there are some economies of scale in manufacture up to a certain level of capacity. However, as the volume of operation increases, so does the difficulty of scheduling and controlling production across so many individual orders. There is a stage at which maintaining efficient production requires additional, separate production facilities and management. For these, a new location, perhaps nearer to some of the customers, is probably preferable, the second factory being treated as a separate profit centre or subsidiary company.

If you would like to pursue this example further, please see the case of Steel Springs Ltd in appendix C. That case is a good example of the following issue:

- Should the three wire spring companies in the group be completely merged or should they remain largely autonomous? If they should remain largely autonomous and responsible for their own profitability (across production and marketing), are there any activities which should be run as a group or joint service (e.g. export marketing, purchasing)? If so, exactly how should this joint activity be operated and held accountable – as a group service charged as an overhead or as a separate profit centre which will only continue to exist if it proves its worth?

6.3 Synergy, Value Chains and Company 'Cement'

Synergy, value chains and company 'cement' are three particularly important concepts for the group strategist.

One of the features of management literature is the periodic development of concepts or techniques, usually of some merit, each of which for a time becomes the current 'buzzword', arousing a lot of attention and some action. Some business people reject the idea out of hand. Others take it up with enthusiasm but with insufficient thought or preparation, and then drop it like a hot potato. Wiser executives act more responsibly. They see some merit in the idea, explore its usefulness and how it can be adapted to meet their situation and then, after appropriate trial, arrange for it to take its right place alongside existing processes. Examples of such concepts and techniques are management by objectives, the various mathematical techniques and synergy.

6.3.1 Synergy

Synergy is defined in the dictionary as 'combined effect that exceeds the sum of individual effects'. Synergy in business is said to be generated when 3 + 2 = 6, in other words, when two or more actions have a greater effect when they are co-ordinated than when they are kept separate.

Synergy was a 1970s buzzword that has more recently been somewhat discredited. Some companies took over others, merging the two activities in the hope of synergistic benefits that in the event did not materialize. Too much faith had been placed in the *concept*, rather than putting effort into penetrative thinking as to precisely what synergies were possible and then following this up by specific actions to reap particular benefits (Campbell, 1995).

6.3.2 Adding Value: Value Chains

The disillusionment with synergy has led to the use by Professor Michael Porter of Harvard Business School, and others, of the concepts of 'adding value' and 'value chains' (Porter, 1985).

A business or a group of businesses benefits from meeting customer needs. To do this they use resources to develop products or services. Profit is the difference between (a) the sale price and (b) the total of the input cost of any material purchased plus the resources used to bring these products or services to the market. Each part of the business should add value by its activities. The greater the added value compared to the cost, the greater the ultimate profit. Thus, a company with a more effective purchasing activity than that of its competitors will have a competitive advantage in purchasing: for the same quality and quantity of material input, its starting costs will be lower and therefore the value added by the purchasing activity will be greater. Each department of a company, and each part of each department, is part of a chain of adding value to the product or service. Production can improve productivity, quality and delivery. Marketing can present the product or service in such a way as to strengthen demand and bring in sales in greater volumes and/or at higher prices than competitors' products or services, and so on (Copeland, Koller and Murrin, 1989).

This concept of a chain of added values extends across businesses in the same group. For example, joint distribution may yield the benefits of lower costs or more frequent delivery. In other words, adding value overlaps with the achievement of economies of scale.

The concept also extends into understanding how a company's

actions affect the costs and benefits to a customer. For example, an understanding between supplier and user of the effects on each of them of different delivery patterns can suggest better stockholding patterns and more appropriate delivery quantities and frequencies. 'Just-in-Time' manufacturing has developed from a deeper understanding of the value chains across companies.

The value chain concept therefore has advantages over the synergy concept in that it forces more focused thinking as to exactly where benefits can be gained, and includes benefits spanning across businesses and across suppliers, producers and customers.

6.3.3 Company Cement

Now think back to the examples referred to earlier (section 1.1.1) of companies such as Hillsdown Holdings, Beazer, Bunzl, Williams Holdings and Coloroll, all of which grew very rapidly, mainly by taking over other companies, in the 1980s. Obviously, these companies developed very strong capabilities in choosing, and putting a value on, takeover targets; also in the process of takeover itself and producing good performances from each company taken over in the years immediately after acquisition.

However, if such groups were to continue to be successful, having grown to considerable sizes, they also had to have:

- the structures, systems, styles, staff, etc. necessary for the effective direction and management of a large group;
- relationships between subsidiaries which reap the value-chain advantages.

These factors make up what I describe as *company cement*. There is no purpose in creating large buildings with good quality bricks but poor cement; sooner or later storms will expose their weaknesses and cause the buildings to collapse. Groups with this 'company cement' will have evolved to the stage where they will remain highly competitive and be able to cope with major changes in their environments.

Examples of companies which pursued such rapid growth policies in the 1970s and have now proved that they have developed the necessary 'cementing' abilities are Hanson and BTR. Of others which tried to take this path to growth in the 1980s, some have failed and others still need to find a way which will lead to long-term success.

6.4 Technology Choice, Ideas and Management of R&D

Most companies are involved with science or technology in some way or other. Many make use of technology developed by others; others are in businesses where the future success of the company depends on its own efforts to develop the technology of its products or services and/or their production and delivery.

6.4.1 The Need for Balance between Technology and Marketing

For all these companies, *technology choice*, taking its place alongside marketing strategy, is a necessary part of company strategy choice (Wilder, 1985). Whether technology or marketing plays the major part depends on the type of business involved. (As a very rough distinction, technology is often a more important factor in selling to industrial customers than it is in sales to domestic customers.) So, while this section focuses on science and technology rather than marketing, the importance of getting the appropriate balance between the two in deciding on and pursuing company strategy should be kept in mind.

Science has been defined as:

knowledge ascertained by observation and experiment, critically tested, systematized and brought under general principles

and technology as:

the practice of any or all of the applied sciences that have practical value and/or industrial use. (Macdonald, 1972)

6.4.2 Technology Choice and Company Size

For some small companies, technology choice and even direct investment in R&D is critical to success. Often, however, for small companies technology choice is less important and the technology that is used is mainly selected by following the lead of others. To consider technology choice more thoroughly, therefore, you need to start by considering those companies, typically larger ones, where technology is a critical element and which need to invest in R&D to generate the products on which future success will depend. Once that situation has been understood, it is then easier to consider how smaller companies can position themselves, so as to benefit from the advance of technology, without being at a competitive disadvantage compared to much larger companies.

6.4.3 Formulating a Technology Strategy

A large company whose success is heavily dependent on technology can be a single-business company, a division of a larger group or a group with several businesses all dependent on the same technology. To maintain its current performance and assure its future success, such a company needs to have not only a technology capability but also a company strategy containing a strong thread of technology strategy. This technology strategy will contain answers to the following questions:

- Exactly what is the technology within which the company is currently operating?
- Looking perhaps ten or more years ahead, what are the likely general developments in that technology, and are other technologies going to become important? This question requires thought about how the needs of existing customers might be better met, as well as how developing the technology might lead to different products and customers.
- Across the whole range of the company's effort in science and technology, what should be the investment in the following:
  - defensive work to extend the life cycle of existing products, including
    quality control and improvement;
    design modification;
  - offensive R&D to develop new products, including
    basic research;
    applied R&D;
    design?

What is known which will assist in developing answers to these questions?

The costs of R&D   An R&D activity may not be the cheapest, and normally should not be the sole, source of ideas for new products. Other ideas may well come from the customers, marketing, designers, looking at the products of competitors, other independent researchers (e.g. university staff, research associations), research publications, studying new patents, etc. So an effective technology strategy involves a choice of where to position resources in relation to these various alternatives and how best to organize selection and pursuit of these idea channels.

As science and technology advance to higher levels they split into more and more specializations, each requiring an in-depth knowledge. A technology strategy involves choosing which of several roads to take at each of the junctions encountered as the company progresses. Such decisions, once made, can be expensive to alter, in terms both of the time and the cost involved in catching up with others.

There is evidence to show that pursuing advances in science and technology is becoming more expensive for businesses, even after eliminating the effect of inflation on cost figures. The simplest areas of science and technology have been fully explored and largely exploited; it is now more difficult to find and develop new areas, and therefore, fairly generally, the cost of achieving individual research objectives is high. The effect on product life-cycle patterns is to increase the proportional costs of research and development. Not only is the cost area under the line on the life-cycle curve tending to get larger, it swells sooner and more markedly, indicating the greater time pressure on product development. This arises from increased competition and faster innovation by others. The effect is as shown in figure 6.1, where the dotted line is the past form of the life cycle and the solid line the new form that it is taking.

Whereas in the past a programme of research and development took several years, and the effect of being a year later than planned was relatively minor, such lateness can now cause a substantial, if not total, loss of market share and a major reversal in company performance. Similarly, whereas in the 1950s and 1960s R&D in many companies was loosely managed and lacked any clear direction, no company can now afford to allow such inefficiency. The direction and management of R&D is under the spotlight.

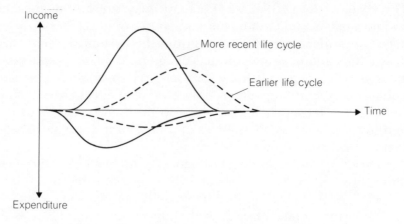

Figure 6.1 The changing shape of the product life cycle.

Placing R&D in a company context   Investment in R&D involves substantial sums. The company's future may well depend on the output of new products arising from R&D success. So R&D strategy is an essential and fundamental part of company strategy and, indeed, may well provide its cutting edge. This raises the questions:

• How much should a company spend on R&D?
• How should the activity be related to the rest of the company?
• How should the R&D staff be managed?

R&D expenditure varies widely between different sectors of industry. In sectors like timber, cement, clothing and footwear manufacture, expenditure on R&D may be less than 1% of turnover, whereas in pharmaceuticals, computers and aircraft manufacture it may be 10% or more. The higher levels of spending are in industries where technology is advancing fast and where the total market is expanding. The level of expenditure in any company will be based on:

• how strong financially the company is;
• what the levels of research have been in the past;
• how effective the R&D activity is in terms of the new products which have resulted per £ spent on research;

116

- the rate of spending and of new product launches by its competitors;
- the degree to which it can gainfully increase its future growth by investing in more R&D now;
- what opportunities it is well placed to pursue.

Balancing long-term and short-term research   The balance between longer-term basic research and shorter-term development work is critical. Without basic research knowledge, whether this be from within the company or from outside sources, the scope for developing new products in the future will contract. With too much basic research, the company may generate some knowledge from which it does not have the development and production capacities to reap the benefits. Development costs can well amount to ten times the basic research costs and production costs a further ten times that.

Centralized R&D, if not well managed, can become too remote from the company's needs. The researchers can develop more interest in conducting basic research and publishing articles than in developing successful products and processes of practical value to the company. If the funding of such R&D is entirely as a group or divisional overhead, this can only worsen the situation. Conversely, if the whole of R&D funding is based on contracts from the subsidiaries, this will tip the balance too strongly towards short-term projects to defend existing products or to bring on only the easily developed new products, with the result that the long-term success of the company is endangered. Funding on this basis can also lead to instability in the staffing of the R&D activity.

As with so many management situations, there is a need for balance somewhere between the two extremes. Centralized R&D should have some long-term funding to ensure continuity in long-term and basic research; this funding is rightfully the responsibility of the division or group as a whole. Subsidiary companies should be invited to comment once a year on the proposed R&D plan. But they should also be free to contract for some of the work in R&D. In this way they will have some influence on the overall programme and, at least for shorter-term work, they will be able to put pressure on completion within agreed time and cost limits.

Communication with functional departments   In many companies a major cause of lack of value from R&D is poor communication between R&D and the production and marketing departments of subsidiary companies. Involvement of these 'customers' at set stages throughout individual projects will help to keep the work on a useful track and help to ensure that transfer to production is effected more smoothly. A glance at the visitors' book at research laboratories (and the travelling claims of its staff) will soon indicate whether this liaison is occurring.

Chapter 7

Describing the Strategic Situation of a Group

Having now grafted on to your understanding of the concepts necessary for considering strategic issues for individual businesses some of the general concepts for looking at a group as a whole, we look in this chapter at a framework for describing the strategic situation of a group. In chapter 8 we then go on to consider examples of group strategy situations, on a pattern similar to that followed in part II.

I assume in this chapter that information as described in chapters 3–5 is available on the strategies open to individual businesses within a group and on the effect on each business of reduction or increase in the financial resources available. (If the group also contains divisions, it is also assumed that similar information is available on each division; divisional strategy will be discussed later.)

7.1 Group Strategy and Group *Raison d'être*

The concern of this chapter is how the existence of a group affects strategy choice for individual businesses and how the group as a whole can yield a better performance than the sum of what would occur if the group did not exist and if each of the businesses was completely independent. For without this benefit from the activities at group level, what justification is there in terms of competitiveness for the group to exist?

By analysing its individual businesses (or divisions), the group will have an overall view of how it is likely to perform in the future, if it makes no changes in the allocation of resources among businesses (or divisions) and if it leaves the organizational structure unchanged. It will also have information on the competitive position and prospects of each business (or division), including information on those parts of the group enjoying opportunities for successful growth, those which are in mature markets and those which are in declining markets. In some cases it may take the view that some of its businesses ought to be doing better and is considering what action to take to bring this about. It may also have information on opportunities outside existing activities.

7.1.1 The Group Environment

Group staff have a particular responsibility to look at the environment facing the group as a whole.

- How is the environment changing and how is it likely to change in the future?
- How well is the group performing compared to roughly similar groups?
- What strategies do they appear to be pursuing?
- Are there growth areas in which the group does not have an existing presence but which it could enter to its advantage,

either by organic growth or by takeover of existing businesses?
• Are several of our businesses competing with similar businesses in other different types of group from which they seem to be gaining greater competitive advantage than do our businesses?

These and related questions should lead a group to conclude either that the broad strategy of the group is about right and that only small modifications are needed, or that a significant shift in the overall emphasis of group strategy is warranted.

This chapter is concerned with situations in which it is necessary to consider making a significant shift in group strategy.

7.1.2 What is Involved in Changing Group Strategy?

A decision to change group strategy involves two closely related decisions:

• whether to change the allocation of resources between the parts of the group, including buying and selling businesses as appropriate – in other words, reshaping and rebalancing the group as a whole;
• what the structure of the group is to be: appointing the top executive of each of the units (division or business) at the level immediately below group level and deciding how these top executives are to be motivated and how they will relate to group executives.

For example, if a group consists of several businesses, all in some way related to each other in terms of products, technology or markets, an important decision is whether these businesses should operate independently or whether synergies should be sought from certain types of relationship: joint R&D, the sale of one's output to another, joint distribution, etc. The group may set up divisions to embrace related businesses in the hope of generating substantial synergy. But synergy does not flow automatically; effort has to be put into its generation. Also, against any advantages must be set some inevitable disadvantages arising from the introduction of an extra level of management. Extra overhead costs will be incurred and decisions may take longer to reach. Motivation within the individual businesses may suffer, resulting in poorer performance.

So, any analysis of a group must not only recognize the alternative strategies open to individual businesses in isolation, it must also recognize the relationships possible between businesses and the level of synergy which might be generated with the help of appropriate organizational arrangements: and the concomitant disadvantages of such arrangements.

To recognize the main potential synergies and how they might effectively be gained without incurring other serious disadvantages requires penetrative and creative thinking combined with wisdom and good judgement. For example, take a group with three divisions at present, which might benefit from a reorganization of two of these divisions into three others, making a new structure of four divisions in all. Clearly, analysis of this situation requires considerable thought.

In some cases, the group may take the view that, although the businesses it embraces and the organization structure do not need changing, there is a general underperformance. It may then have to consider replacing the chief executive with someone with more drive, determination to weed out inefficiencies, enthusiasm to pursue opportunities and leadership abilities to motivate others behind this thrust.

In other words, at group level most strategic issues involve complex interactions between resources for product/market alternatives, human resources and their melding into an effective organization.

7.1.3   Taking Stock of the Group Theme

Groups differ widely. A choice of a broad *group theme* is a choice of a set of businesses in which to compete and how best to compete in them, particularly in terms of the type of organization best suited to the situation. Success will not come to a group that does not yield benefits greater than the cost of keeping it in existence; nor will it, if another type of group with a different theme has greater advantages.

Given that the business environment is always changing, including changes in opportunities and in the behaviour of competitors, any group must periodically review its performance and the main issues which it faces, with a view to deciding whether its present direction needs minor modification or a significant change. Therefore, any framework for considering group strategy must involve taking stock of the existing theme, its advantages and disadvantages and whether it can be strengthened, for example, by divestment and purchase of businesses. For future success, the framework must also include consideration of whether a different theme would be preferable.

As there are many types of group, so there are many different types of theme. To illustrate how this review of group strategy can be approached, just a few of these themes will be selected for examination in the rest of this chapter. The types of group we will look at are:

- those comprising unrelated businesses;
- those comprising closely related businesses;
- those comprising loosely related businesses;
- those comprising sets of businesses which are closely related internally but with few if any relationships between the different sets;
- those groups of any of the above types but which are underperforming even though they contain the right businesses.

7.2 A Group of Unrelated Businesses

The success of a group composed of unrelated businesses – a *business conglomerate* – depends not only on the types of businesses involved and how they are managed but also (as for other types of group) on the quality and skills of the group executives.

7.2.1 Skills of Group and of Business Executives

In this type of group, given the wide range of markets and technologies in which the various businesses are involved, it is unlikely that group executives will develop in-depth understanding of these functions in each business; instead, they will probably have to rely mainly on taking a broad view and the use of financial criteria. The number of executives at group level is likely to be very low – say, below 50, even for a group with a turnover of several billion pounds per year.

Much will therefore depend on the quality of the managers of the individual businesses and the success of group executives in stimulating effective management by the managing directors of those businesses. The group will need to develop skills in buying and selling businesses as appropriate.

7.2.2 Competitive Strengths and Weaknesses

A group of varied businesses does have the advantage that it is less vulnerable to a temporary decline in the market for one of its businesses than an independent business would be. But businesses in such a group will be at a disadvantage if they operate in areas where competitors have significant advantages. For example, they would be at a serious disadvantage if they were to try to compete with other businesses operating within groups from which they could gain substantial synergy. In most cases, therefore, high technology is ruled out; so are areas where there are major economies of scale from operating on a global basis and areas where vertical integration, joint distribution, etc. are important.

7.2.3 Strategy Options for Conglomerates

It may well be the case that, to remain viable in the longer term, business conglomerates have to choose one of four options:

- operating in business areas where the radius of competition is not wide and is not likely to change significantly, where the level of technology is relatively low and where synergies with other businesses are limited;
- becoming more expert in buying ailing low-technology companies cheaply, turning them round, reinvigorating them and then selling them at a good profit;
- remaining a kind of conglomerate, not of individual businesses but by focusing on a few sets of related businesses;
- ceasing being a conglomerate of individual businesses, possibly by choosing a product/market focus and building a future based on a more closely related set of businesses and therefore selling and buying businesses to pursue this new strategy.

7.3 A Group of Closely Related Businesses

Groups which seek to gain substantially from the relationships among the businesses they embrace vary in the factor which binds them together.

7.3.1 Factors Binding the Constituent Companies Together

Some groups are based on ownership of a secure and low-cost source of raw material supply, reaping the benefits through to all stages of sale of the products and by-products. They consider that a gap in ownership at any stage in the sequence could lead, at particular times, to other companies developing sufficient power to reduce the group's profitability / growth. This choice of *vertical integration* is to be seen, for example, in groups based on oil, timber and cattle.

Other groups are built around a common technology. Such groups need to keep the definition of that technology under review as it develops. They may find, for example, that their technology is beginning to split and that the group either needs to choose one narrower focus or to split into divisions, each with a different technological focus.

Related functions may also provide the synergy which binds the companies together; for example, a food retailing group may have a centralized warehousing and distribution system for different store chains operating under different types of stockholding policies for individual stores.

7.3.2 The Role of Group Executives

Top executives at group level in these concerns will have an advantage over those in a business conglomerate, in that there is greater cohesion among their experiences in relation to the individual businesses. They should therefore benefit from increased understanding of the technology used and the various markets at stake. They should also develop a well-rounded understanding of the sector as a whole within which these businesses, and other businesses not in the group, are competing. This should strengthen the content of communications between the group and the individual businesses. It should also assist the group in taking a more balanced view of its relative position in its environment.

Groups of this kind seek to gain advantage not only over competing individual businesses but also over other groups with a similar central theme. They must therefore not only manage well on a day-to-day basis but must also generate substantial synergy to produce benefits that more than offset the costs of running the larger organization. However, they must avoid the temptation to also perform at group level activities aimed at synergies which in practice turn out to be less than the cost of reaping them. This will probably involve having a larger core of group staff than for a business conglomerate with a similar turnover, but not as large as many such groups currently have; some 250 is often the limit for even large groups.

7.3.3   A Flexible Approach towards Strategy

Because opportunities and threats are continually changing, for this type of group there is no fixed optimum set of businesses and relationships among them.

For example, there will be times when opportunities are rapidly opening up. In this environment, when the group will be diversifying so as to search out and secure more 'territory', some businesses within the group will need more freedom to behave entrepreneurially and to chase opportunities hard without worrying about gaining from relationships with the rest of the group. At other times, when the environment is more threatening, the group may concentrate itself. This alternation between diversification and concentration has been likened to the movement of a concertina.

Similarly, when one or a small set of the businesses within a group find a major opportunity, which it or they might have difficulty in pursuing without additional resources, the group may sell certain of its more peripheral activities in order to concentrate its resources behind a major thrust.

Yet again, there may be times when synergy opportunities are being missed because there is a gap in the set of businesses within the group. Starting up a new business or taking over an existing one then needs to be considered.

So this type of group needs to keep under review various group strategy issues, including:

- What is the factor which cements the group together and how can the group be best organized to reap significant benefit from it?
- Should particular businesses within the group be given greater freedom to expand fast, even at the expense of loss of synergy with the rest of the group?
- Should other businesses be required to manage with less resources and generate funds for use elsewhere in the group?
- Should the overall balance between diversification and concentration of businesses be changed?
- Are there businesses which should be sold, started up or bought?
- Are some of the businesses competing in global markets but lacking the necessary market share to be successful? If so, how about forming a strategic alliance between that business and a similar business within a competing group faced with the same issue?
- Do the organizational structure, information systems, senior executives, training, etc. (Waterman, Peters and Phillips, 1980) need to be changed to pursue the new group strategy?

7.3.4 Beware Blurring of Accountability

In any group of this type, the chief danger which has to be guarded against is the obscuring of accountability for performance. If the organization and individual objectives are not clearly understood, it is all too easy for group staff levels to increase to unreasonable levels, motivation to deteriorate, buck-passing to occur and performance to slip.

7.4   A Group of Loosely Related Businesses

7.4.1   Is Synergy Possible?

A group of businesses which are seen as neither strongly related nor independent can be an unstable state. This type of group can exist in one of two situations. It may be operating in a sector where strong relationships and considerable synergy are possible. If so, it must tidy up its set of businesses and seek also to benefit from these synergies, if its longer-term performance is not to suffer relative to competing groups.

Alternatively, it may be operating in a sector where significant synergies are not possible. For example, over recent years this appears to have been the case in several parts of the mechanical engineering and electrical engineering sectors, particularly the sub-sectors producing certain types of components. Many of the groups operating in these sectors found that they were too diversified in their products and too centralized in their decision-making to cope with the deep recession of the early 1980s. Those groups which were not strongly integrated were better able to foresee dangers and, with independent actions by the top executives of the individual businesses, were better able to respond with the necessary speed.

During that recession, more groups of this type shifted their emphasis towards decentralization and the shorter-term clear accountability of individual businesses.

7.4.2 Alternative Benefits to Synergy

When the impact of that recession began to lessen, these groups reviewed their portfolios, looked to the longer term and tended to move in the direction of a more narrowly focused set of businesses and higher-technology products aimed at increasing turnover by going for global markets, rather than the previous wide diversity of businesses in a more restricted market based on the UK and limited exports.

It could be said that these groups have exchanged economies of scale in production plus synergies between markets for the previous advantages of concentrating geographically across a greater number of only loosely related businesses.

7.4.3 The Emergence of Business Groups

Other groups, having learnt that their previous centralization in pursuit of synergy was not successful, and having cut their costs and left individual businesses to fight their own battles during the recession, have since begun to develop what are beginning to be described as *business groups* within the group as a whole. These are sets of businesses, usually only two or three, which together form a unit too small to be described as a division and more closely related in technology or markets; they are expected to yield pro-portionately more synergy than could be obtained across a wider set of businesses. As a result, some of these parent groups contain both largely autonomous individual businesses and small 'business groups'.

7.4.4 Growth, Synergy or Decomposition?

The strategy issues which need to be addressed by groups of loosely related businesses include the following:

- Where are the best opportunities for successful growth? What would be the likely results of pursuing a strategy to focus on them?
- Are there any significant potential synergies between any of the more promising businesses? How can this synergy be reaped and towards what future would this lead the group?
- If neither attractive growth nor synergy opportunities exist, is the group of businesses so large that performance will deteriorate compared to its competitors and, if so, should the group not be broken down into smaller separate groups of the type described earlier as business conglomerates?

7.5 A Group Containing Sets of Closely Related Businesses

This type of group is usually large, with tiers of management at the group, division and individual business levels. It seeks to benefit from gaining significant synergy within divisions and delegating heavily to them, while at the same time avoiding overall group performance depending too heavily on the fortunes of a single industrial sector.

7.5.1 Beyond Divisional Structure: Business Groups

Again, as with the type of group discussed in section 7.4, there has been a move towards 'business groups'. Disappointingly low synergy gains from the previous divisional organization, along with experience of the stultifying effect it had on entrepreneurial vigour at individual business level, have led some of these groups to reconsider their previous choice of organizational structure. Instead of up to, say, six divisions reporting to group level, some now have a combination of fewer divisions and a larger number of business groups doing so.

7.5.2 The Need for Organizational Change

Perhaps the most significant point to emerge from this and the preceding example of business groups is that, because the environment changes, *group organization also needs to be changed periodically*. Divisions or business groups should only be introduced between group and individual businesses if they are going to produce synergy not just equal to but in excess of their total cost – that cost including the demotivating effect they can have at the business level. A static structure may be a sign of inefficiency. A structure which contains a mixture of largely autonomous businesses, business groups and divisions, and which changes from time to time, may well be a sign of health.

7.5.3 Group Roles: Managing and Reviewing a Complex Structure

In these large organizations, group head office will provide some central skills, such as those needed for buying and selling businesses. In view of the variety of technologies and markets involved, the group will rely heavily on divisions, business groups and businesses for the understanding of competition at sector and segment levels. It will set the tone of performance expected by the exercise of its functions of *delegation*, *stimulation* and *control*:

- by the financial criteria it uses;
- by the activity of its treasury function;
- by the evidence in the form of plans it requires from the divisions;
- by the way it rewards performance of top executives at divisional and business levels.

The group will also need to address issues such as:

- Which of the divisions or business groups offers the best opportunity for additional investment?
- Is the future path of any of the existing divisions (or business groups) such that joining two divisions (or business groups)

or splitting an existing division (or business group) would be beneficial?

• Are there attractive opportunities for taking over other large groups? If so, which parts should then be divested and should an extra division (or business group) be set up or the parts allocated to existing divisions (or business groups)?

• Should any of the existing divisions (or business groups) be sold/spun off?

7.6 Underperforming Groups – Another Cause

In sections 7.2 to 7.5 we have looked at different types of groups defined by the types of products/markets of the businesses they contain. It has been argued that by sharpening the thinking on exactly what types of business in what type of organizational structure and with what type of role performed by the parent group, performance can be improved.

However, in some cases this focus alone will not yield the performance which should be achievable. Day-to-day management may be lax, with excess manning, little focus from the top on efficiency and a serious lack of motivation at business level and below.

This kind of situation not only raises questions about the quality of the board and the leadership abilities of the chief executive, it also gives rise to consideration of creating a leaner organization in which decision-making is pushed down to the lowest possible level (known as 'empowerment'). Many groups are finding that they can perform much better by devolving power below individual business level to a relatively large number of profit centres (and cost centres, where appropriate).

Chapter 8

Key Issues in Various Group Strategy Situations

This chapter looks at situations that have been described in publicly available material for various large groups. These examples have been chosen to illustrate a few of the issues that larger and more complex groups may face. You will see how, in the groups' responses to these issues, review and change of corporate strategy has been accompanied by change in organization.

8.1 Being Privatized: Facing up to Increasing Competition in the UK

8.1.1 Overview of UK Privatizations

During the 1980s, the UK led the way in privatizing many activities which were previously in the public sector. British Airways, BP and British Telecom stand out as commercially successful global competitors.

For some other activities privatized, any competition has been more local, and the pressures to perform have come from either the threat of takeover or the decisions by the regulator of that particular industry. The result has been that the levels of efficiency in the use of resources vary widely, with some being well respected and others, such as the regional electricity companies, the water companies and British Gas still, being criticized for poor service or lack of performance.

Because the number of these companies in the UK is now significant, it is appropriate to look at one such company in more detail in this section. The company chosen is Powergen plc; it has been chosen because, in contrast to many of the other companies privatized, it quickly responded to the move from the public to the private sector.

8.1.2 Privatization of Electricity in the UK

Privatization of Powergen occurred in 1991. Prior to this, electricity generation and transmission was the responsibility of the CEGB (the Central Electricity Generating Board) and distribution and sale was the responsibility of the Area Electricity Boards, all within the public sector. This mammoth activity was broken up in a series of privatizations, leaving only nuclear electricity generation, with its associated risks and uncertainties, in the public sector.

The electricity industry in Scotland was privatized, leaving the vertically integrated structure of Hydro Electric and Scottish Power intact.

In England and Wales, generation from fossil fuels was split into two companies: National Power, the larger, and Powergen. Other than direct sale of electricity to major industrial users, the sale

133

of electricity was divided into separate companies, the regional electricity companies. Between the generating companies and the regional electricity companies is National Grid plc, with responsibility for the national electricity grid and the passage of electricity through it. Besides the normal laws affecting any company, these privatized electricity companies operate within an environment regulated in the UK by the Office of Electricity Regulation ('Offer') headed by the Regulator. He/she has responsibilities to protect the public interest in areas such as encouraging efficiency, limiting price rises, encouraging competition, pollution levels, etc.

8.1.3 Powergen at Privatization

Before its break-up and privatization, the CEGB had excess electricity-generating capacity and hence high fixed costs, its fuel input was mainly coal from UK sources at above world prices and it was under pressure to reduce environmental pollution. Its culture was based on engineering excellence with a 'cost plus' approach to pricing. It had a complex structure very dependent on committee-based decisions and as a result had relatively high staffing.

With privatization, the market was being changed from a monopoly to one which was competitive and unique, with the result that no previous experience was available for guidance.

8.1.4 The Move by Hanson

Not surprisingly, a year or so before privatization the culture was very different to that which would be needed if Powergen were to thrive on the stock market after privatization. In many other privatizations, this 'culture drag' has been a serious obstacle to improving efficiency.

However, in this case Hanson Group plc made a bid to the government to take over the whole of the Powergen activities. This caused considerable concern within the staff of Powergen and did more than anything else to encourage the leadership thrust for an early major change in its attitude and culture after flotation as a public company. It stirred the management to produce a plan for flotation based on significant actions to improve performance. Powergen plc was floated early in 1991.

8.1.5 The Issues

Clearly, Powergen was facing many issues as well as considerable uncertainties. But most of these issues were within one overall elephant issue. The company's shares were to be on the stock market, it did not want to be taken over. It had to find ways of rapidly improving its profitability and its prospects for the longer term. So an overriding elephant issue was, roughly:

- Which plants and other activities to close or severely curtail, how to change culture to focus on commercial efficiency, how to reorganize so as to be most effective, how to cut costs all round and when to take all of the actions required so as to bring about a major improvement in overall performance which can then be sustained.

Once that issue had been addressed, other important but less major issues were seen. These were to do with the medium- and longer-term development of the company, covering not only investments to improve its core business of electricity generation but also whether it should diversify and, if so, into what types of activity.

8.1.6 Actions and Results

The strategy for achieving the major cultural changes was based on devolving decision-making to the lowest practical level, focusing on the value of sales, developing commercial and management skills, identifying discrete business units as profit/cost centres and creating an internal market for service providers, such as information system support. There are now over 50 profit/cost centres. In today's buzzwords, there has been a major change in terms of 'delayering' and 'empowerment'. Whereas just before privatization over 9,000 were employed by Powergen, by March 1995 this had reduced to around 3,700. Compared to 21 power stations before privatization, there are now 14. Investments have been made to improve their efficiency and to replace some of the original stations by combined cycle gas turbine stations. Over the period 1990–4, sales were reduced from £2.6 billion to £2.3 billion per year. Productivity was increased by about 70%. As a result, profits after tax increased from £201 million to £345 million.

During this period, some diversification moves were made. Powergen has acquired stakes in the development of a range of upstream gas assets. Overseas, it is involved in building and/or operating several electricity generation plants. Kinetica Ltd, a joint venture with Conoco, was formed to market gas downstream and to construct gas transport pipelines.

8.1.7 Issues for the Future

While some of the future can be foreseen, much is bound to be uncertain. How will regulation change? What strategic moves will National Power make? How will the recent flotation of National Grid and the takeovers of some of the regional electricity companies affect Powergen? How fast will it be possible to improve the efficiency of electricity generation from the various sources of power? What further opportunities will there be for diversification?

Nevertheless, as with many of the privatized companies, some of the main issues for the future are still clear. The first will be to do with what resources to allocate to the core business versus the various diversifications. For the core UK business of electricity generation, this leads to the continuing business strategy issue of how best to continue its success, particularly in terms of reducing the overall cost per unit of output, and achieve the world's best practice. For the diversifications, there will be the need to learn what type of diversification will lead to the greatest success and hence how to allocate resources between competing opportunities.

8.2 Facing up to Increasingly Global Competition

8.2.1 Responding to the European Challenge

In my view, one of the most damaging strategic mistakes made by British governments was the delay in joining the European Community. Not only did it allow those stronger nations which joined at the start to shape the Community's role, organization and procedures, such as the Common Agricultural Policy: it also allowed companies then in the Community time to develop strengths in this wider market before UK companies could attempt to do so. Let me explain.

End of a cosy home market: the change in 1992 Before the UK joined the Community, competition in the UK market was generally not intense. Leading competitors were often in the cosy position of each offering products across a wide range to a fairly stable set of customers. The potential economies of scale in production from attempting to dominate the UK market for selected products within the range were simply not sufficiently attractive. However, once the radius of competition shifts on to a European or, indeed, a global scale, in many cases these economies are worth going for; and there are competitors who recognize these opportunities and will go for them.

When the Community was created, European companies became more selective in some areas of business, aiming to win in some segments while withdrawing from others. By the time the UK joined the Community, this process had already reached the stage where certain European companies had already captured much of the 'high ground' and could not easily be dislodged. Exposed to fiercer competition by entry into the Community, some UK companies then found themselves under attack, across various parts of their product range, from different companies benefiting from economies of scale on particular products. With most of their strengths in the domestic market negated, such British companies had to decide quickly which products to defend in that market and how to build a bridgehead for establishing a future position in the Community market as a whole. This process was particularly difficult in, for example, certain areas of engineering.

However, in other areas, as a result of non-tariff barriers to trade (such as differences in quality standards, public sector procurement, etc.) freeing of trade did not progress so far. With the completion of the internal market in 1992, the Community environment changed for many more companies: they needed new strategies to address these new threats and to gain from the opportunities offered by this larger market (Friberg, 1988; Mitchell, 1989). They could no longer be 'all things to all men' but needed carefully to select the patch of high ground which they aimed to win.

Beyond Europe In those sectors where barriers to trade are fewer and economies of scale are substantial, competition has already become global, the weaker companies have disappeared and there are clear global winners. The tensions between the USA and the

Community in the area of aircraft manufacture arose from European attempts to restrain the world dominance of Boeing while developing a strong Community-based competitor. Any company operating in areas of business where there are sufficient economies of scale to reward those companies which choose to operate on a European or global basis, must address this issue.

8.2.2 In Pursuit of Global Dominance

Tackling the major areas in sequence In most of those industries where global leadership is a feasible aim, the sequence of moves to the winning position depends on the company's position in the three main trading areas: Europe, the Americas and the Far East. If a UK company is to become a global leader it must usually first establish its leadership in the European Community; if it cannot win there, it is unlikely to have the financial strength necessary or to have found and developed the capability to win elsewhere. Global leadership requires that a company is not only the leader in its home continent but also one of the leaders in the other two major trading areas of the world (Ohmae, 1985).

The need to move quickly Those concerned with developing corporate strategy in companies operating in areas for which there are significant potential economies of scale to be had from operating on a European or global basis are faced with an opportunity which, if not addressed quickly, could become a threat. Any such company, if not already number one or two in the global market, probably needs to aim to get into that position quickly. The questions it must urgently ask are:

- How strong is the company financially?
- In each of these potentially global areas of business, how strongly is it currently performing in the UK, in the Community and in the rest of the world?
- In which businesses does it have a good starting position from which it may go on to win on a global scale?
- How would its position be changed by joint ventures/corporate alliances/trans-European mergers?

8.2.3 Strategies for Competing Globally

For those companies which choose to operate in global businesses, company strategy must be designed specifically for the global environment (Hamel and Prahalad, 1986). Among the many questions which need to be answered are:

- What is the likely future pattern of global competition?
- Which are likely to be the main competitors (including new alliances)?
- Where are the main markets; how fast are they likely to grow?
- How far is it wise to standardize the product range?
- Where are the greatest risks associated with political instability?
- Bearing in mind transport costs, delivery times, etc., how many production points are needed and how can output flexibility be achieved to be able to respond to labour relations, exchange rates and other fluctuations?
- In the longer term, what is likely to happen to exchange rates?
- What are, and what is likely in the future to happen to, labour costs and productivity in each possible plant location?
- How should the company be organized (e.g. on a territorial or product basis)?
- How much delegation and control is appropriate? With new technology and its effect on communications and information-gathering, what systems should be used?

Abroad is different! Environmental differences between countries – commercial, political, cultural, etc. – are much greater than the differences which will be faced by a smaller company operating solely within a domestic market. Attempting to operate in overseas countries as one operates at home is bound to lead to unpleasant shocks. These differences have to be fully understood if a truly European or global strategy is to be successful.

8.2.4 Example: Jaguar

The vehicle industry The vehicle industry is one of the clearest examples of the progressive change in the nature of competition, from UK-only to Europe-wide and on to fully global competition. After World War II, vehicle companies faced competition mainly from other relatively small domestic companies. In the UK, names like Austin, Morris, Vauxhall, Standard, Hillman, Wolseley, Rootes and Ford (UK) reflected this mainly domestic competition. Gradually, however, competition intensified and the radius of competition increased. The weaker competitors collapsed or were taken over and larger competitors from overseas, with greater financial and technological strengths, were able to make big inroads. Some, like Chrysler, overstretched themselves and had to pull back, but others, like Volkswagen, Fiat and Renault, made more secure advances. In the 1970s and 1980s, the greatest impact came from the leading Japanese manufacturers such as Toyota, Honda and Nissan, who first achieved penetration with exports from Japan and later established manufacturing plants in the UK and elsewhere. This process of globalization and rationalization of the number of companies will continue for many years. There are still too many independent Europe-based car manufacturing companies with insufficient strength to stand up to increasingly strong global competitors.

This process of increasingly global competition started at the high volume/low price end of the market, where standardization, automation and economies of scale would have their greatest effect. It then progressed to the higher value luxury end of the market, with the result that even companies like Ferrari, Jaguar, Porsche, Lotus, Aston Martin and Rolls-Royce came under increased pressure.

The effect of new models   Any company operating in the global car market cannot afford to stand still. It must improve at least to the standard of the average of its competitors if it is not to decline and ultimately fail. Figure 8.1 gives a picture of what this means for introducing new models of a car in a particular segment of the market (Ashley, 1995).

The average car on the market has a particular level of appeal to potential customers. Over time, this average level of appeal of cars on the market increases. Let us refer to one particular company's model as being in the Mark I phase. If Mark I is below the average line, it will be losing compared to its competitors. To start winning, it must introduce a new, and better, model, Mark II. If Mark II takes it to well above the average line, it will win for longer than if Mark II is only marginally better than the average line at the time Mark II is introduced.

140

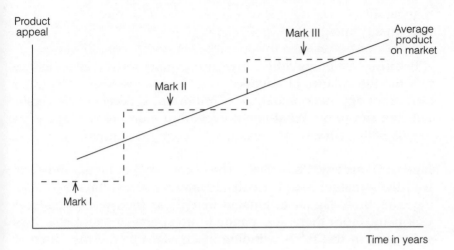

Figure 8.1   The product appeal of new models over time.

But developing a new model is expensive and there is a choice of whether to go for frequent small advances or fewer, larger advances. Larger advances are more risky but offer the possibility of greater benefits.

Whatever the choice of how large a step up to make from Mark I to Mark II, and from Mark II to Mark III, there is still the need to be effective in terms of costs and times taken up in product development. A particular model brought on to the market a year early means a longer period of winning. Costs wasted in development result in lower profits.

Before moving on to look at Jaguar, it is important to understand what customer appeal for cars as discussed above really means. A customer decides to buy one car rather than another because he/she perceives that in total it offers better value. In forming this view a customer looks at all or many factors from a list which includes:

- price;
- visual appeal;
- the feeling of quality;
- technical specification, including fuel consumption, acceleration, accessories, colour etc.;
- regular maintenance cost and frequency and the proximity of appropriate dealer premises;

141

- reliability;
- company image.

Because customers differ, any car company must take a view as to what the balance of advance should be across these and other factors for any new model. How important is acceleration versus fuel consumption? What about expenditure on better suspension versus better corrosion resistance or having a sunroof, etc.?

Jaguar: Overview, 1922–1995   The experiences of Jaguar illustrate well the strategic issues which car manufacturers have been facing over time. Jaguar originated in 1922 as the Swallow Sidecar Company. From there, it expanded into sports cars and was very successful in the 1950s, winning at Le Mans at the first attempt followed by several other victories. In 1966 it was merged with BMC and in 1968 became part of the larger British Leyland. It was demerged and floated on the Stock Exchange in 1984.

Figure 8.2 summarizes Jaguar's sales over the period 1974–94.

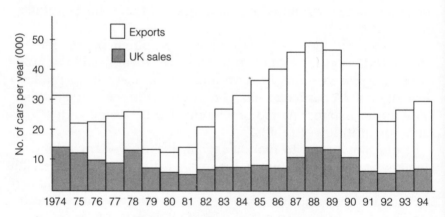

Figure 8.2   Jaguar: sales, 1974–1994.

Over this period, why did sales slip twice? Certainly the recessions of the early 1980s and early 1990s played their part. And what were the actions which led to the company's survival and recovery in the 1980s before being hit by the recession of the early 1990s? And what does the period after the 1989 takeover by Ford tell us about strategy in this industry?

142

Jaguar, 1974–89   Jaguar operates in the luxury segment of the car industry. Its main competitors are Mercedes, BMW and Porsche. In the 1960s and 1970s it had been losing competitiveness primarily because it had been falling behind these competitors in its engineering and manufacturing operations. Quality and productivity had not improved as they should have done. As a result, customers were turning elsewhere for more reliable cars offering better value for money.

So in April 1980, under its then new Chairman, John (now Sir John) Egan (now Chairman of BAA), Jaguar began its revival programme. Resolute action was taken to reduce costs and increase efficiency, while close attention was paid to achieving high quality consistent with rising production.

In 1980, productivity had averaged 1.3 cars per man per annum. By 1988 had been raised to roughly 4 cars per man. An example of the significant improvement in quality was the fact that in 1988, after a long period of absence, a Jaguar won the famous Le Mans 24-Hour Race.

Backing up this thrust was a marketing strategy involving top-quality customer service and a concentration on the main overseas markets in addition to the UK, particularly the USA, Germany and Japan.

During 1987, a new XJ6 saloon range was successfully launched. In spite of a downturn in the US market for luxury cars, Jaguar improved its market share.

Ford paid £8.50 per share for Jaguar in 1989. Five years earlier, in 1984, when Jaguar was floated as a separate company, the shares had been priced at £1.65 each, so the shareholders were well pleased with their gains. Had it been floated too cheaply? Did Ford pay too much? Even allowing for these uncertainties, my view is that between 1984 and 1989 the company did improve its position relative to its competitors.

Even before the takeover by Ford, there were some causes for concern. The fall in the value of the US dollar, and the approach of the recession in the US, meant that total sales of luxury cars there were declining. Some of its major competitors suffered badly, but the appeal of the new Jaguar XJ6 meant that Jaguar sales there fell less.

Jaguar, 1989–1995   Before focusing in particular on the Jaguar part of Ford in 1989, I will briefly describe the state of the whole car industry globally in that year, the position of Ford and other US-based multinationals at that time, the major issues they faced and what they were beginning to do. I will then focus on Jaguar, the issues which that part of Ford was facing, what Ford and Jaguar did to improve Jaguar's longer-term performance and the results to date.

In the world environment, the USA was entering a recession which on a world basis might have been shallow but turned out to be very deep and more severe than the recession of the early 1980s. The UK tends to be behind the USA but by 1990 was already entering recession; other countries in Europe, and even Japan, were to feel the effects of the world recession later. So even for the most successful car manufacturers, such as Toyota, Honda and Nissan, difficult times were approaching.

Of the three major US-based car manufacturers, Chrysler had already suffered. Being smaller and more able to change quickly, it was showing signs of coping with the recession and acting to improve its longer-term competitiveness. Ford and General Motors, being much larger, faced a greater problem of the time lags between recognizing a major issue, deciding what action to take and actually being able to make a major shift in the behaviour of the company. The major issues facing them were in both the shorter and longer term. In the short term, the major issue was how to deal with the impact of the developing recession. In the longer term, the elephant issue was what to do to make a major shift in the company's competitiveness. Inevitably, this would mean major reductions in numbers employed, major changes in organization and moving more rapidly towards cars designed and produced on a global basis.

Focusing now on Jaguar, in 1990 what were the issues which both Ford and Jaguar faced? One was concerned with how to respond to the recession. A second, again similar to that facing Ford as a whole, was to do with rapidly improving longer-term performance.

Prior to the takeover, there were already signs that Jaguar as an independent company was headed for long-term decline. For example, it was not generating enough profit to provide the cash flow to enable it to develop and launch the necessary new models. It needed a 'parent' company with strong financial resources. Its productivity was not good enough. To improve its profitability it needed not only a good new model and good production but also to be tighter on costs; in other words, it needed better financial controls. What other extra 'value' could Ford give to Jaguar in areas like production, financial control and perhaps purchasing, and in what areas would it be better for Ford to leave Jaguar largely autonomous? Probably one of the reasons for Jaguar's poor performance in the late 1970s and early 1980s, when it was part of British Leyland, was that its then parent was not adding the value it should have done. In my view, British Leyland did not distinguish between those areas in which it should integrate Jaguar heavily with other parts of that group and those where Jaguar should be left largely autonomous (and more free to decide and be accountable for its own performance!).

The first moves by Ford were to bring into Jaguar the Ford expertise in financial control, so as to deal with the effects of the recession as well as to give Jaguar better control over the longer term. Ford worked with Jaguar to develop a programme of new models, including considering the development and launch of a smaller Jaguar in parallel with the existing model and its development.

Ford took the view that Jaguar's purchasing activity could be significantly improved by using the skills developed within Ford and by taking advantage of any possible economies of scale. Conversely, it was aware of the importance of the Jaguar image and the need to retain the motivation of all of the Jaguar employees and their pride in its success. So, for example, on the sales side Jaguar would be kept separate, by operating through outlets different from those used by other parts of Ford.

Thus Ford provided the finance for the launch of the new, larger Jaguar, the new XJS series, in September 1994 and for the replacement for the XJS whose launch is expected late in 1996. The smaller Jaguar is being developed with a view to launch in about 1998. The total sales by Jaguar are then expected to be some 100,000 cars, with the smaller Jaguar providing about 60% of the total.

Significant investments have been made in production. Output is now over 5 cars per man per annum in spite of the recession having forced total output to a level some 40% lower than when Ford bought Jaguar.

As part of the change to global production, Jaguar is beginning to benefit from developments in Ford's production strategy. Future power-train (engine and transmission) and platform developments are being co-ordinated. For the smaller Jaguar, this co-ordination will be with developments in the range currently known in the UK as the Scorpio. For the current, larger Jaguar, this co-ordination will be with the Lincoln luxury brand. The XJS will have its V8 engine built in the Ford plant at Bridgend, thus benefiting from economies of scale in that part of its costs.

Purchasing by Jaguar has improved by learning from Ford.

What have been the overall effects of Ford's parentage to date? Ford paid some 2.6 billion US dollars for Jaguar. Since then the costs of reducing the labour force (restructuring) during the recession and in investing in both better production and new model development have totalled a further US$ 1 billion or so.

Sales are increasing. In the final quarter of 1994, Jaguar moved into the black and continued to be profitable in the first quarter of 1995. Jaguar is healthier and the future looks brighter.

8.3   Diversification to Reduce the Impact of Possible Decline in the Core Business

8.3.1   A Route for the Larger Firm

Small businesses heavily dependent on a single product, like Hancock and Lane, the narrowboat building company discussed in section 5.4.3, do not normally have the management capabilities or the financial resources to spread the risk by diversifying by taking over other companies. Larger companies in similar positions do have the financial resources, but if performance is to be improved and risk reduced by such takeovers, care needs to be taken in the choice of the target company and in its integration and management.

8.3.2   Example: Dobson Park Industries

Dobson Park Industries plc is an example of a company which, faced with a potential decline in its core business, diversified to reduce this risk. This was in the 1980s when its turnover was of the order of £200 million p.a.

The technological background   The company had its origins in metal, particularly in foundry and forging activities. During the

1960s and 1970s, it grew rapidly, mainly around the development of powered roof supports for the coal-mining industry. These supports are used at the coal face in the longwall method of mining. Other than opencast mining (mining by opening up the surface above a coal seam), there are two main methods of mining coal, 'room and pillar', and 'longwall'. The longwall method involves driving two tunnels some 200 yards apart and then, between these two underground roadways, taking a slice of coal perhaps one yard in horizontal depth across the whole 200 yards. Previously, when using this method of working, wooden or steel pit props were used to support the roof where the coal had recently been extracted. As subsequent one-yard slices were taken out, these props were either slowly crushed or withdrawn, allowing the roof to lower to the floor. Partly because of the nature of coal seams in the UK, longwall mining methods are more common in the UK than elsewhere.

The production of coal is subject to global competition. To meet this threat, the technology of longwall mining has been, and is, advancing rapidly. Mechanization of coal-face working methods has led to telescopic roof supports which can be automatically advanced as the coal face advances. These involve hydraulic movement and electronic controls in complete coal-face support systems, integrated with the coal-face cutting and coal transport systems.

The competitive environment   In the 1960s, two UK companies led this development of coal-face powered roof support systems: Dobson Park Industries and Dowty. The main customer was British Coal, with the two companies sharing the total orders roughly equally.

Not only were Dobson Park and Dowty the leaders in powered roof support manufacture in the UK, but with longwall coal-mining methods spreading to other countries, they also became world leaders in this area of business.

The issues facing the company   For Dobson Park Industries, success in powered roof supports during the 1960s and 1970s faced it in the 1980s with several issues to be addressed. These included:

- the trend towards more total coal-face systems covering not only better roof support systems but also coal cutting and coal transport systems at the coal face;

- the continual need for investment in technological development;
- the risk associated with the company's future depending heavily on one product area and one customer;
- probable long-term decline in UK coal output;
- how to change the focus of the company without passing through a phase of such poor performance that the company would be exposed to takeover when performance was beginning to improve.

The strategic response   The company's response in the 1980s was:

- to maintain its global position in powered roof supports;
- given the falling total market, to reduce the proportion of resources going into the manufacture of equipment related to coal mining;
- to widen the scope of the coal-mining related activities to offer a more complete system, including coal transport along the coal face;
- to change the balance of sales effort on mining equipment towards export markets;
- to diversify into other non-mining areas (toys and plastics, power tools, industrial electronics).

Diversification always carries risks, and some of Dobson Park's diversification moves were likely to be not very successful. The company was learning how to make takeovers and how to succeed in these new areas. But it was also rationalizing or selling off activities which were not giving the performance or prospects sought.

Did it work?   Looking first at Dobson Park's actions in the area of mining equipment, one has to consider a wider field than just powered roof supports. In 1989, Dowty sold its mining machinery business, which comprised powered roof supports and conveyors, to a management buy-out called Meco International. In pursuit of its overall strategy as described above, in 1993 Dobson Park formed a joint venture with Meco in which Dobson Park's mining machinery business was merged with Meco International Ltd, its major competitor, to form Longwall International Ltd. In 1993, Dobson Park increased its shareholding in this associated company and early in 1995 purchased the balance of the shares to convert Longwall International Ltd into a wholly owned subsidiary of Dobson Park. With total sales in this subsidiary of some £225 million per year this gave Dobson Park market leadership in both powered roof supports and face conveyors in each of the principal markets of the USA, Australia and the UK. The non-UK sales accounted for some 78% of total Dobson Park sales of mining equipment. These moves strengthened Dobson Park's position globally in mining equipment. With good management this should have led to improved profit margins compared to the then 5% or so of sales.

Looking now at the various areas of diversification, Dobson Park divested the power tools division.

At the time of the first edition of this book, the thrust into selected segments of industrial electronics was going fastest and appeared to me to be the most promising. The emphasis in that division shifted to concentrating on a smaller number of segments where significant market positions could be maintained. This was reinforced by modest-sized acquisitions offering significant synergy with existing businesses. Turnover of this division in 1995 was some £70 million per year with good organic growth and 6% profit on sales.

The toys and plastics division had a turnover of some £20 million per year and 8% profit on sales.

Overall, profits of Dobson Park hit a low in 1984. By 1989, profits had more than doubled. But then the company, like its competitors, was hit by the global recession of the early 1990s. Its mining equipment division also had to cope with the rapid reduction in the size of the UK coal-mining industry and, in 1994, the privatization of all of the then few remaining collieries. After a second low in 1993, there was a significant improvement in 1994, with some 50% of profits coming from non-mining activities. Turnover in 1995 was running at some £325 million per year and profits some 5% of sales.

While the diversifications which Dobson Park made did prevent a severe decline in the short term, the longer-term question in the summer of 1995 was whether performance would be improved by greater focus of the company's use of resources. Does mining globally have a good future and, if so, are there sufficient opportunities to warrant Dobson Park withdrawing from both the remaining areas of diversification and concentrating totally on mining

149

equipment? Conversely, is the future in mining equipment still too uncertain and, if so, which of its present areas of diversification offers the best opportunities?

The 1995 takeover of Dobson Park   In the summer of 1995 Dobson Park was subject to a hostile takeover bid from Harnischfeger Industries of the USA, a Milwaukee-based maker of coal-cutting equipment. Strong defence, based on the good and improving performance of Dobson Park's subsidiary, Longwall International, eventually caused the offer to be raised to a level at which the Dobson Park board were able to recommend it to shareholders. At that stage the chairman and chief executive of Harnischfeger said that Longwall would be integrated with Joy Mining Machinery, its mine equipment business, to 'provide our global customers with the world's most advanced longwall mining system'. He also said that they would push ahead with Dobson Park's plans to sell its non-core toys business and were likely to scale back the industrial electronics division.

8.3.3   Shifting the Company Core: a Pictorial Representation

The pattern of businesses within a group can be pictorially summarized in diagrams such as those in figure 8.3(a)–(e). These give the proportions of the group's activities at the core and at different distances away from the core, each column representing a separate business. In contrast to the diversification matrix of marketing versus technology/production shown in figure 5.4, this method compresses all diversification on to a single linear scale.

Figure 8.3(a) represents the single-business company, whether it be small or large, with 100% of its activities in its core business. Unless the company's competitive position is very secure, perhaps because of a patent or clear market leadership in a growing market, this is a vulnerable position to be in.

Figure 8.3(b) is of a company with some diversification, all of which is related to the core. This degree of diversification offers the possibility of reaping synergies between the various businesses as well as making the company less vulnerable to falling performance in its core.

150

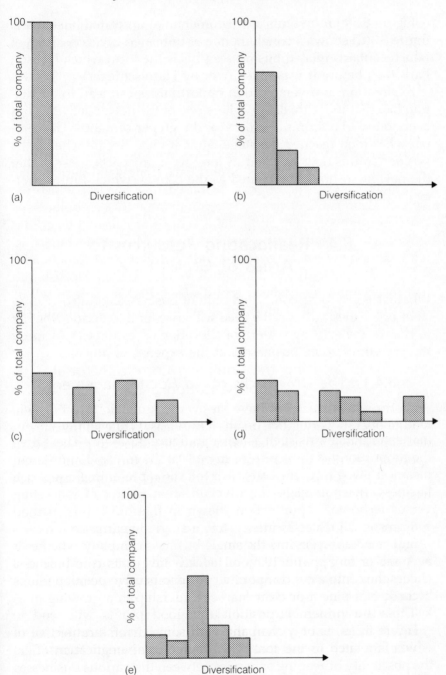

Figure 8.3 Patterns of diversification over time.

Figure 8.3(c) represents a conglomerate of unrelated businesses; figure 8.3(d) shows a conglomerate of unrelated divisions, each of which contains related businesses (this is the form which Dobson Park took before it was taken over by Harnischfeger).

Exploration of diversification opportunities can lead to a situation like that in figure 8.3(e), where one of the newer activities has been found to offer rapid growth and high performance. The company has then reached the stage when it must decide whether its position in this new area and its long-term prospects are such that the new area should be treated as the core on which future strategy will be based.

8.4 Reallocating Resources to Areas of Growth

Whether a group be composed only of businesses or also of divisions or business groups, the need will arise for it to decide whether to change the existing pattern of allocation of resources – to speed the growth of some businesses at the expense of others.

8.4.1 The Drawbacks of *Ad Hoc* Management

A group which does not have an overall strategic direction will tend to operate very much on an *ad hoc* basis. While all investment decisions above a particular value may be subject to group board approval, smaller investments would be on the basis of 'if you have got the funds, you decide.' This largely hands-off approach has three disadvantages:

- There is a greater tendency towards over-optimistic forecasts and hence unwise investment.
- A series of apparently good *ad hoc* investments can lead a company into a cul-de-sac of a poor competitive position where further decline is inevitable.
- Those businesses already making good profits will tend to invest more heavily than those which are not, irrespective of whether such investment is warranted in strategic terms.

Those businesses producing less good profit figures can be in one of three situations:

152

- in an area of business in decline and from which the company should withdraw;
- in a good area of business but with poor management;
- in an area of business offering fast growth for which substantial investment now (perhaps at the price of poor short-term performance) is necessary if good profits are to be reaped later.

Similarly, those businesses which are producing good profits may be in static or declining markets, where high investment is unnecessary and wasteful.

8.4.2 Strategic Preparation for Investment Decisions

A group which is strategically directed will determine its overall strategy before approving individual major investments. When investment proposals are received by the board, the first check to be made is whether the proposal is in line with the approved strategy for the group. This strategic preparation should help it to distinguish between those businesses which should be disposed of and those where poor management needs to be corrected.

The 'Boston matrix'   In response to this need to establish a more effective group strategy across a variety of businesses, in the 1970s General Electric of the USA introduced, and the Boston Consulting Group popularized and further developed, a matrix. This matrix looks at a group of businesses as a portfolio and classifies them into:

- *'stars'* – businesses with a substantial market share in a rapidly growing market; such businesses should continue to receive all the resources they need to remain in the lead;
- *'question marks'* – businesses with a small market share in rapid growth markets; some of these businesses might be allocated resources to help them to gain market share and move into the star category, with advantage to the whole group;
- *'cash cows'* – businesses that are profitable and enjoy high shares of their markets, but in markets which are mature and either slowly growing or declining; investment in these businesses should be limited to that required to maintain capacity in line

with total market needs; the aim of the business should be to generate as much cash as possible for use elsewhere in the group;

* *'dogs'* – usually loss-making businesses with low market shares in mature or declining markets; these businesses should probably be divested or closed.

As with all conceptual frameworks, this matrix requires both skill and care if used as a practical technique. For example, it does not automatically follow that all 'dogs' are making losses and should be eliminated. Some may be extremely well managed on a day-to-day basis and making a small profit in spite of being badly placed. Others, modestly refocused and reinvigorated, may be able to move out of the dog category. Even some of those dogs which are making losses might warrant being retained if their removal would adversely affect other businesses in the group.

Nevertheless, in spite of these difficulties, the Boston approach has been widely accepted as a useful concept; some of the companies which use it extensively have adapted the original technique to suit their particular situations.

Using the Boston matrix   Putting into practical effect the strategy choices which stem from the thinking related to the Boston matrix inevitably raises questions of:

* organization;
* attitude change;
* financial control.

On financial control, any group has to ensure that the cash cow businesses do produce and give up the cash needed elsewhere in the group. Group level also needs to ensure that, after the raising of any additional finance, funds for the development of growth businesses are allocated in accordance with the steps needed to secure the longer-term aims and that performance is checked against set 'milestones' of achievement. Inevitably, not all businesses capable of growth will succeed; so progress against the plan must be reviewed and the plan revised appropriately where necessary.

Organizationally, growth businesses need greater freedom to grow vigorously and more direct access links to the main board.

Some mistakes may be made along the way, but provided that the general direction of their development is broadly in line with the plan, entrepreneurial enthusiasm should not be discouraged by overzealous criticism during what is essentially a period of learning.

After the Boston matrix   For a complex group which is under-performing, looking at its businesses as a portfolio containing important differences has two main effects. The first is to distinguish the more promising businesses from the less promising. The second benefit is to cause questions to be asked about the degree of autonomy which each of the businesses has. A few will have benefited from the added value which the group had given them over and above the group overhead costs and delays which such a relationship caused. Others, and often most, will find that the parent group was interfering too much; it should only do those things which clearly add value and leave these businesses with more autonomy, accountability and motivation. In total this means that not only are some businesses sold and a few bought but also that group headquarters staffing is reduced, leaving it with a more focused and valuable role.

But this then raises different and more 'chunky' issues. For example, do some of the sets of businesses have an interest in working more closely together, perhaps by forming a business grouping of these businesses below the overall group level, with all the disadvantages that this might cause; or can the benefits be achieved by better informal collaboration but without the formality of setting up a business group? Is one of the businesses in the position where real success can only be achieved by developing a strategic alliance with a similar part of another large group? This is why GEC formed alliances with various other groups in the 1980s, for example with Siemens on telecommunications and with Alcatel to form GEC Alsthom in power systems.

This recognition of different relationships between businesses within a group, and of the differing roles which a group should play as a parent to individual businesses, can also raise a different elephant issue. This is whether performance of the group could be significantly improved by splitting it up into two or three entirely separate companies. During the 1980s, the recognition of this issue resulted in Courtauld's demerging its textile operations and Racal demerging Vodafone. Both moves appear to have been successful in terms of performance and increasing shareholder value.

8.4.3 Example: ICI's Strategic Redirection Since 1980

ICI is a large chemical group which illustrates well this series of issues. Its performance relative to competitors had been slipping. In 1980, losses in two quarters added urgency to the need to sort out its portfolio of businesses and the relationship between them and group level. As this process unfolded, it later led to the decision in 1993 to split the group into two companies, ICI and Zeneca. So let us look separately at the issues facing ICI in 1980 and 1993.

With increasing competition, groups like ICI originally, and now Zeneca and ICI, need to be, and usually are, led strategically.

Groups of the size and complexity of ICI normally have several corporate planners, their number and role changing with the needs of the company. In 1980, not only did the senior management spend a considerable amount of time on strategy of the group, its divisions and businesses but it also had a Planning Department; this department had a graduate strength of some 30 to assist this strategic thrust. In ICI (excluding Zeneca) the Planning Department now has 11 graduates.

ICI in 1980 ICI was a large, chemistry-based group which prior to the 1980s was organized on the basis of nine divisions, each containing several related businesses. In 1980, when ICI declared losses in two quarters, the UK was entering a deep recession. Like most of its competitors, it was caught with excess capacity, but in addition its heavy dependence on the UK and the then high value of the pound sterling made things worse.

The situation which ICI faced required a major review of strategy. A modified version of the Boston approach was one of the approaches which the corporate planners used to help the senior executives to address the various issues which the company faced during the early 1980s (Pink, 1988).

In terms of reallocating resources and restructuring, the divisional structure was changed into what may be described as a side-by-side mixture of divisions and international business groups.

Those parts of the previous divisions which were in commodity chemicals – where the market is particularly subject to economic cycles and tends to be tight, and long-term prospects are moderate – were put together in one major division. This division was required to run to contribute long-term cash for the remainder of the group, with limited selective investment directed at increasing the efficiency of existing operations and for expansion only in areas where competitive or differential positions could be built.

The international business groups, which were separated from this and were encouraged to develop, included those focused on pharmaceuticals, agrochemicals, seeds, advanced materials, electronics, polyurethanes, films, explosives, colours and speciality chemicals. These were all in growing, good-quality markets. They were freed from the previous constraints of the divisional structure and were encouraged to grow and to improve their competitive positions in largely global markets. Examples of actions taken included the takeover of various overseas-based companies operating in seeds (e.g. Garst and SES), speciality chemicals (e.g. Beatrice) and paints (e.g. Glidden) businesses.

So this was a period when those businesses which were considered to be in the top half of the Boston matrix (either stars or question marks) were encouraged to show whether they could increase their success, the implication being that the position would be reviewed later, the real winners could then seek more resources, while the others would be treated as cash cows or sold.

These changes led to more decentralization of responsibility to businesses and a reduction in group staff in London from some 1,500 in 1980 to about 500 by 1990. Some staff were transferred to individual businesses while others left ICI or took early retirement. The increased focus on the financial success of individual businesses led to some improvement but this process needed to be taken further.

ICI in the early 1990s: the pressures for change   There were several factors which led to the decision in 1993 to split the company into ICI and Zeneca. These included:

- increasingly global and increasingly intense competition;
- the effects of the deep recession of the early 1990s;
- the experience of the changing performances of the various businesses;
- the realization that the 'cement' binding the group together was

157

fairly strong between certain sets of businesses but not across the group as a whole;
- the relatively poor performance of the company's shares, due at least in part to the fact that it was judged as a broadly based chemical company rather than a chemical company containing a significant pharmaceutical business;
- the threat of a takeover and splitting up implied by Hanson Group purchasing 2.8% of the shares of ICI.

ICI responded. In 1993, it split itself into 'chemicals' and 'biosciences'. Zeneca, the bioscience part, contains pharmaceuticals, agrochemicals and speciality chemicals, while the ICI that remains contains chemicals and polymers, tioxide, explosives and materials. Share prices after the separation of Zeneca clearly showed the stock market's approval of this change and its belief that the other changes associated with this split would lead to performance improving more rapidly. Total headquarters staff of ICI and Zeneca is now down to some 350 and in ICI, in my view, is likely to reduce to perhaps some 200 in total.

In line with this greater focus on the success of individual businesses (and sets of businesses, where appropriate), in 1993 ICI swapped its nylon business for Du Pont's acrylics business, thus giving each a stronger position in one business, in place of weaker positions in two businesses. The range of businesses and their subsidiaries has been tidied up to give greater focus. For example, Soda Ash and Polypropylene have been sold. Others, such as the 50% share in Louisiana Pigments Tioxide plant, have been bought to strengthen the position of existing businesses. There is favourable comment in the financial press for the good timing of the purchase in 1995 by ICI of the Grow Group in the USA, a purchase which significantly strengthens ICI's paints business there.

However, the main thrust in 1995 shifted to investing in organic growth. Investments include those in Klea (CFC replacements) in Japan and the USA, a new US 'Melinar' plant, an MDI plant in Holland for polyurethanes, a paint factory in Indonesia, etc.

Similar strengthening of focus and performance has been occurring in Zeneca.

What have been the benefits? Overall, it will be some years before the full effects of all these changes show but early indications are good (Owen and Harrison, 1995).

Perhaps the biggest issue to be addressed in the not too distant future faces Zeneca. The sector is being restructured. For example, SmithKline French merged with Beecham. Glaxo has just taken over Wellcome. Fisons entered into negotiations with Medeva in an attempt to strengthen its pharmaceutical business but these collapsed and there are still doubts about its long-term success and independence. Since it was established, Zeneca has tightened its costs and strengthened its focus. For example, it has disposed of its Garden and Professional Products business. However, the major issue facing Zeneca is what to do to increase its share of the global pharmaceutical business and thereby strengthen its long-term success. The takeover of another pharmaceutical company is an option to achieve this but there are other alternatives.

8.5 The Dynamics of Strategy and Organization Change

The above examples of the histories of companies, each over several years, clearly show the following.

- At any one time, the elephant issues which a company and its businesses need to address are largely unique to that company.
- Over periods of several years, these issues change. What was 'right' at one time is not likely to be so a few years later. The world of competition is dynamic. To be successful, any company must try to foresee possible changes in the competitive environment and must adapt.
- At times some academics argue about whether strategy choice precedes organizational change (including changing structure, recruitment, training, style, culture, etc.) or vice versa. In my view, that is a sterile argument. Every major strategy change requires organizational change. Every major organizational change will lead to different attitudes to strategy choice. So the two are so heavily interdependent that it is up to those who take the lead in causing change to choose where to focus first. For example, the purchase of a company clearly affects attitudes and can well cause a change in what management feels it must do, and hence a change in strategy. Yes, strategy and organization

159

are heavily dependent on each other – hence the use of the term 'strategic management' by leading business schools.

8.6 Buying and Selling Companies and Forming Strategic Alliances

In all of the examples chosen as illustrations in this chapter, the strategy path has included the buying or the selling of companies or a combination of the two. This is because corporate strategy is not only about how each individual business within the group should pursue strategy, it is also about whether some businesses should be added and others removed and how the whole should be organized and run for maximum overall success. In the case of Powergen, and earlier in the reference to GEC, strategic alliances have also been pursued for certain businesses within the group.

As with buy-outs and buy-ins for single independent businesses, so these changes in ownership within a group can significantly improve performance. But making these changes is also risky, the greatest mistakes being made by those who do not plan well, who lack previous experience in making such deals and who fail to take advantage of external expertise. Expertise is necessary either from internal or external resources on the legal and financial aspects, including both the taxation aspects and the method of financing the deal. These areas are outside the scope of this book. But what can be said about the strategic aspects of making such deals and about the actions which must follow them?

Listed below are some of the points (McLean, 1985; Clarke, 1987; Devlin and Bleackley, 1988; Ohmae, 1989; Lorange, Roos and Bron, 1992) which should be borne in mind.

- Any such deal should be well planned and include a search for the best company with which to make the deal.
- The decision should be based on a well-thought-through strategy to increase long-term success and should include what actions are to be pursued after the deal has been completed. (Without thinking through these actions and their benefits, what justification is there for the price which might be agreed?)
- Timing is important. Because the thinking which has led to the desire to make a deal has been done now, it does not follow that

now is the best time to make the deal. It may already be too late or a deal may be better delayed, to await better circumstances.

- Price is important. Before making a takeover, it is important to decide the maximum level of price which can lead to added, rather than reduced, value for the group as a whole. In the absence of important new information which would significantly change the value expected, this maximum price should not be exceeded. Before making an unwelcome bid, it is important to consider the possible reactions of the bid-for company and any possible competitors and to have responses ready. If the bidding company does do this planning prior to its first bid, it can keep the whole process shorter and thus increase its chances of success. Delays during a sequence of bids can increase both the danger of the bid failing and the ultimate price.
- The success of takeovers or alliances is very dependent not only on the strategic 'fit' in terms of products/markets but also on the behavioural aspects of combining two companies, often with different organizational philosophies, cultures, information and control systems, etc. The planning before the deal must include careful consideration of these behavioural aspects.
- The success of an alliance depends not only on what each gets out of the deal but also on what each contributes. Over time and with the changing competitive environment, the balance between the perceived costs and benefits to each side can change, putting the future of the alliance at risk. Periodic review of the success of the alliance will help to avoid such breakdown.

PART IV

IMPROVING YOUR COMPANY'S STRATEGIC CAPABILITY

KEY POINTS

- What is meant by a company's strategic management capability?
- What contribution can corporate planning processes make to improving this capability?
- How does corporate planning relate to budgeting?
- What benefits does it aim to achieve?
- From the first introduction to effective corporate strategic planning
- What contribution can internal and external strategy consultants make to improving strategic management capability?
- Developing your personal ability

Chapter 9

A Company's Strategic Management Capability

9.1 Different Company Attitudes to Strategy
9.2 How Does Your Company Score on Strategic Capability?

By this stage of the book you should have a good understanding of both business strategy and group strategy. You will have a grasp of several of the concepts which may be useful in your particular company. You will also be developing the variety of ways of looking at a particular company situation which are so necessary if you are to generate the ideas needed to find the best strategy for your company. You will also be developing your ability to appraise critically articles on management, to question the value of corporate strategic planning systems and of strategy consultants.

This chapter, and the two which follow it, look at how you can further develop your own strategic abilities and those of your company, and what part a corporate strategic planning system and strategy consultants can play in this process of development.

165

9.1 Different Company Attitudes to Strategy

To perform well, a company must not only be well run on a day-to-day basis, it must also be pursuing an effective strategy.

Studies of a wide variety of companies have shown major differences in the effectiveness with which strategy is determined and implemented. At one extreme, there are those companies which have no strategy at all. Typically such companies spend much of their time 'fire-fighting', their futures being determined by a series of *ad hoc* decisions. They appear not to realize that if they could only create more time to stand back and consider what is causing this behaviour, they might well be able to make strategic changes which would remove the need for some of it. At the other extreme, there are some companies – typically, but not always, the larger ones – which not only devote sufficient time and quality of effort to making good strategy choices, but also implement strategies effectively.

Between these two extremes, capabilities and behaviours vary. For example, some companies claim to be pursuing sound strategies which outsiders can easily show to be flawed: the senior executives do not have a sufficiently sound basis for formulating strategy.

9.2 How Does Your Company Score on Strategic Capability?

What are the features which indicate whether a company has a well-developed strategic management capability? In my view, those companies which do have such a capability show all of the following features:

- an awareness of the nature and importance of company strategy and a good understanding of its relationship to the management and control of day-to-day operations;
- the conscious allocation of time by top executives, both individually and as a group (e.g. as a board or management committee), to strategy consideration and its implementation;
- vigorous leadership of strategy by the chief executive (and by the top executives of the individual divisions, business groups

and businesses where these exist), discarding unnecessary detail and avoiding unnecessary delay;

- a creative approach to strategic issues (where strategic thinking has lost this creativity, the choice of options is unnecessarily restricted and a good opportunity might be missed, only to be taken up by competitors);
- an ability to assess the company's performance and to focus on the time horizon for strategic thinking;
- the possession by top executives of a good diagnostic ability to recognize strategic issues;
- the possession by top executives of a sound conceptual basis for grappling with strategic issues (without this it is all too easy for top executives to be persuaded by advisers, who sometimes will base their advice on faulty foundations);
- lively awareness of the environment and appropriate sensors of it to pinpoint and assist consideration of strategic issues;
- good knowledge of which are the key competitors, what their strategies are and how they are performing;
- appreciation of the importance to competitiveness of having a lean organisation (including tight control of group and divisional costs, delayering, delegation of power etc.);
- an understanding of the keys to success in the areas in which the company aims to compete;
- a good sense of timing of when to take action (e.g. timing of takeover bids or divestments);
- an effective and not too cumbersome corporate strategic planning process, which assists in the development of strategy and produces the milestones for review and for checking its implementation;
- a readiness by top executives to face up to the issues and, where necessary, to decide to change the strategy;
- the motivation and the ability in top executives to implement these changes effectively, including changes in personnel and organization, to check that the results are as intended and, if not, to make the necessary adjustments;
- simple and effective information systems for strategy planning and feedback of performance against plan.

Pause for a moment and consider how many of these features apply to your company.

Chapter 10

Corporate Strategic Planning Processes and Their Contribution to Effective Strategy

10.1   Systematic Corporate Strategic Planning

10.1.1   When a More Formal Framework is Needed

Planning is concerned with thinking and deciding about the future. Planning may still be effective even when it is not committed to paper (this is particularly often the case in those small single-business companies where the owner is also the managing director). But for companies which are larger and complex, group, divisional and business planning involve a variety of senior executives and cannot be effective without some of the thinking and data being recorded.

When a company decides to introduce a more systematic process of assembling data with a view to deciding its strategy, this process is normally described as corporate strategic planning. Chapter 11 will consider the contribution which internal or external consultants can make to setting up and running corporate planning processes and in providing additional advice on strategy. Before we go on to this, there are several features of corporate strategic planning which need to be understood, whether or not consultants are to be employed.

10.1.2 The Need for Involvement at the Highest Levels

A company's future is a major responsibility of its chief executive. Corporate strategic planning can be effective only if the chief executive and the managing directors at divisional and business levels maintain a leading role in its use in deciding strategy and in ensuring implementation of the chosen plan (Lorenz, 1988).

10.1.3 Designing an Effective System: Common Pitfalls

It is not easy to design and run an effective corporate planning system. The greatest danger is that over time it will become too complex and will fail to diagnose and address the main issues facing the company. Following the recession of the early 1980s, many companies questioned the effectiveness of their corporate planning systems; in most cases major changes were made to simplify the process, to focus more on key issues and to make the process more line-driven.

10.1.4 Different Companies Need Different Systems

Corporate planning systems should, and do, vary among companies. Large, complex groups inevitably have larger sums of money at risk; they need systems which embrace the planning of individual businesses, divisions, business groups (where they exist) and the group as a whole. The greater the autonomy of the individual businesses, the simpler the information which needs to flow to higher levels of the organization.

For the small to medium-sized company wishing to introduce systematic corporate planning for the first time, the set of manuals by John Argenti (1987) gives a detailed description of what needs to be done. While more is now known about designing an effective corporate planning system, there is still a need to review and if necessary modify any system after the first year or two of experience.

10.1.5 Strategic Planning is not Budgeting!

In some of the companies where corporate strategic planning is not effective, this is because it has been confused with corporate budgeting. Typically in such companies, documents received by the board (or planning committee) contain many sheets of numbers and little if any description of the company's competitive position or of its strategy options. Any request to see a summary of the chosen corporate plan is met only by tables of year-by-year financial objectives.

Effective corporate planning is about improving the company's strategic position and its shape and capability for the future. To determine this, logic is more important than numbers. A description of the market and of the sub-sectors within it, of the competitors and their positions and strategies, of the position of the company itself and the options open to it, are essential to a good choice of strategy. If there is a fault in any part of this description, no juggling with numbers can overcome the fact that the basis for strategy choice is seriously defective. This is why up to now this book has concentrated mainly on the logic of strategic situations.

The first purpose of corporate planning is to assist the company in choosing the main thrust of its strategy. Only when that is clear is it necessary to put numbers to the growth in turnover, the profits and to the additional investments required. Where these figures refer to several years ahead, they are coarse estimates indicating magnitudes. The figures within the first year of the plan should be more detailed and accurate; these can then be developed to form the basis of the first year's budget. But treating the figures for years beyond the first year as longer-term budgets to be rigidly controlled is dangerous (Argenti, 1978). Where the oversight of a company's corporate planning procedures lies within the responsibility of the finance and accounting function, it is important that the difference between corporate strategic planning and budgetary control is clearly understood.

10.2 The Benefits Sought from Introducing Corporate Strategic Planning

Introducing corporate planning requires a company to change its behaviour. The introduction of a corporate planning system is vindicated only when the company's performance improves to more than repay the cost and disturbance incurred. Corporate planning seeks to 'pay its way' through performing the following functions:

- Discouraging complacency. Often, before the introduction of corporate planning, companies show little concern if their performance is only moderate. However, good corporate planning involves first setting targets for performance levels which will maintain or improve competitiveness and then searching for strategies to achieve these levels.
- Causing the company to give more weight to longer-term considerations than previously: in other words, causing the company to counterbalance its emphasis on controlling short-term operational performance by also devoting sufficient effort to deciding and directing its longer-term strategic thrust.
- Ensuring that all of the relevant and important information (both descriptive and numerical) is assembled before important strategic decisions are made. Equally, spending more time to obtain information which is less than essential, and thus delaying a decision which is urgent, must be avoided.
- Opening up more alternatives. Without a corporate planning approach, an idea such as a major capital investment proposal tends to be regarded as a choice merely between acceptance or rejection. However, wider thinking will usually expose other alternatives which should be considered. Systematic corporate planning will also include a check as to whether the particular proposal is consistent, or in conflict, with the wider and longer-term corporate plan.

171

- Acting as a focus for the whole company. Initially, developing a plan for a single business brings the functions together, forcing them to see the need for balance between their respective inputs and to exchange their viewpoints for the benefit of the business as a whole. When a plan has been chosen and implementation starts, it provides a base from which communication and motivation should occur to enable the whole business to pull in the same direction. In a group, similar benefits are sought across the businesses and divisions.
- Recording the information in areas on which decisions are being made, so that once the plan has been implemented, actual performance can be compared with forecasts. (Dealing with errors effectively, to improve the company's own understanding of the factors affecting its performance and the value of planning in the future, will be discussed in section 10.3 below.)

10.3   Data, Uncertainty and Risk

Uncertainty is a fact of life in planning (Houlden, 1980; Beck, 1982). But some of the uncertainty can be removed before strategy decisions have to be taken. Rigorous thinking about a situation will usually unearth most of the main factors involved, with the result that unexpected events are less likely to occur and the possibility of their doing so is built into the forecasts themselves. It is important first to describe fully the logic of the situation and to ensure that all the relevant factors have been included, before attempting to improve the accuracy of the numbers involved.

If, as is usually the case, early experience with corporate planning exposes substantial errors in projected data (such as expected sales volume or prices) critical to strategy choice, it is usually worthwhile to make the effort to locate at least some of the causes of these errors, so that they can be reduced in future planning. It is not good use of effort, however, to continue this 'fine tuning' to the point of apparent perfection. Once a reasonable degree of accuracy in the basic data is achieved, strategy decisions must be taken in the face of the remaining uncertainties surrounding the data. Tests can be carried out to ensure that the strategy chosen is not too sensitive to errors in the forecasts; that is, that a more 'robust' strategy is chosen.

In situations when the future becomes even more uncertain, for example when the economy is entering a severe recession, the flexibility of the chosen strategy may be very important. If the choice is between two strategies which at first sight offer fairly equal returns, and the future looks particularly uncertain, the strategy which leaves more options open later is the better choice.

Once a particular strategy appears promising, before it is chosen in preference to another it is wise to ask the question: 'Under what conditions will this strategy yield poor results?' Besides testing its robustness against serious if unlikely events, this question will help to generate plans which could be put into effect in an emergency.

In some cases the risks associated with a particular strategy are such that if things go wrong the company's very survival would be threatened. For example, this could be the case for a company undertaking a sizeable contract in an overseas country where there is a risk of sharp changes in exchange rates, political upheaval or even war. In such circumstances it is reasonable to seek ways of reducing the risk, even if this also reduces the maximum level of profit which could occur if everything were to go right. In this example, the higher-risk parts of the contract could be sub-contracted, currency changes could be hedged against, and so on.

Controlling the level of risk while trying to gain from opportunities is a major part of good strategy choice.

10.4　Short-, Medium- and Long-Term Planning and the Use of Scenarios

10.4.1　How Far Ahead Should the Plans Stretch?

The range of plans that will be needed varies considerably depending on the kind of business involved, the way the company is organized, how large it is and how closely related are its parts.

In some large, integrated companies there are three main types of plan referred to as short, medium and long term. For example, one of the airline companies produces long-term plans covering periods up to ten years ahead, the plans then being broken down into individual years of that period. In this company, long-term plans as far ahead as this are required to guide the company's decisions on replacing its fleet of aircraft. Except for buying second-hand aircraft or in times of severe recession, when new aircraft may become available at shorter notice, acquiring replacement or additional aircraft involves a time-lag of over five years between order and receipt.

10.4.2 How Long is the Long Term?

A long-term plan of this period ahead is necessary for decisions whose lead time and associated effects reach that far ahead. However, these plans do not extend, say, 20 years or more ahead to cover the whole life of the new aircraft. This is because the effects on the company of the new aircraft can easily be assessed by looking at the period of a year or two after the new aircraft are operating normally. Also, no plans are produced now for the next replacement of these new aircraft, because that decision does not have to be taken now and will be of better quality if delayed for several years when better information will be available.

10.4.3 The Use of Scenarios

In drawing up this ten-year plan, a view has to be formed of the environment around that time and how it is likely to change beyond it. For example, if aircraft technology is likely to undergo major change some 12 years ahead, it may be better to keep the present aircraft in operation longer (bearing in mind the associated costs of maintenance, repairs and safety standards) and await the more efficient aircraft.

A scenario of the longer term is a description of the future, taking a view on all its uncertainties. There is a need for alternative scenarios describing the environment over the period up to ten years ahead before the long-term plan can be chosen. These will reflect possible alternative growths in passenger traffic, alternative levels of the price of aircraft fuel, etc. Scenarios are an essential part of the planning process. They give a much sounder foundation for the choice of plan than would a single forecast of the future.

10.4.4 The Medium Term and the Short Term

Continuing with this airline example, there are two other times ahead for which decisions have to be taken now, each involving a cluster of decisions with similar lead times. These two clusters cover such decisions as negotiating for new routes, training of new aircrew, revising timetables, increasing engine overhaul and maintenance facilities, etc. To cover these types of decisions, this particular airline has a medium-term plan for up to five years ahead, broken down into quarters, and a short-term plan of up to about 18 months ahead, broken down into months.

Each of these different plans rolls forward: each year the first year of the long-term plan disappears and a further year is added at the end.

The short-term plan provides the basis of the yearly budget for control purposes.

10.4.5 Different Horizons for Different Situations

In other companies only a short- and long-term plan may be regarded as necessary. Sometimes the long-term plan reaches only five years ahead; in other companies other periods are involved. The number of different plans, the periods covered by them and the units into which they break will depend on the type of business. Normally the content of the plans also differs according to the period under consideration.

- A short-term plan is like looking through a microscope, in that it contains a lot of fine detail;
- a medium-term plan is like looking in the distance with the naked eye;
- a long-term plan is like looking through a telescope, giving only a more overall view.

Each gives a different view of the future.

Sometimes the different views ahead can appear to be in conflict. For example, the apparently best short-term plan can involve closing a subsidiary which the apparently best long-term plan sees as important. If the company is in a survival crisis then the long-term plan is irrelevant; the decision must be based on a very short-term view and even the later parts of the short-term plan may have to be ignored. As survival becomes more assured and the future becomes clearer, so greater weight can be put on the longer term; the short-term plan is then constrained by the need to stay within the broad aims of the long-term plan. When the recession of the early 1990s started to develop, many of those companies which had corporate planning processes not unexpectedly cut out a lot of the effort put into longer-term plans and focused more on up to a year or two ahead. As the recession eased and the future became clearer, so the horizon for planning was extended again.

10.5 From the First Introduction of Corporate Planning to its Effective Operation

Good corporate planning is difficult to establish and difficult to maintain. Its effective management requires review of its processes and of the effort it demands; it also requires considerable input in terms of the ability, skill and judgement of top executives. A company's need for corporate planning will change as its environment, shape and performance change and as the strategic ability of the top executives changes. Not only does it need to be brought up to a good level of effectiveness soon after its first introduction. It also needs to be reviewed and adapted as the company's situation changes (Houlden, 1995).

It is interesting to note that some of the large international companies, whose performance was poor in the early 1990s, had planning processes which had not changed for many years. This was a symptom of the fossilization of their strategic thinking. Replacing the chief executive and major changes in organization were necessary to improve performance.

10.5.1 Introducing the Process: the Need for a Considered Approach

Some companies have introduced corporate planning at one time but have not developed it to an effective state and, being disillusioned, have subsequently removed it. Later, when it has again been realized that the company's performance has suffered as a result of lack of strategic direction, perhaps after a change in the chief executive, it has been introduced again, but in a different form.

Rushing in with insufficient thought and insufficient follow-through is bound to lead to loss of confidence. Take an example.

The chief executive of a large insurance broking company decided to introduce medium-term corporate planning in the group for the first time. External specialist advice was not sought. He issued a directive to the executives responsible for each of the businesses, requiring five-year plans to be submitted within a few weeks. Included within the directive was a centrally set growth target for each of the businesses. Guidance on what effective planning involved was not given. What happened?

The executives submitted plans as required. Then, as the first few months of the first year of the plan passed, it began to emerge that most of the businesses and the group as a whole were failing, by a wide margin, to achieve the planned growth in turnover and profits. Why?

There were several reasons.

Targets must be challenging but realistic First, the targets set by the chief executive were unrealistic. What he had done was to set targets based on the actual growth over the previous few years. But the previous few years had been in the 1980s when inflation was high; he had not allowed for the recent fall in inflation nor for the fact that this fall was likely to continue. A very elementary mistake; but quite common at that time.

- Targets need to discourage complacency but must also be achievable.

Input from executives must be encouraged A second, related, problem was that the directive was interpreted by some of the executives of businesses as just that. They saw no freedom to present more realistic plans (or even to put forward plans which contained a clear statement that their figures assumed that inflation would stay at the rate averaged over the recent years!).

- Effective planning normally involves iteration.

It is often the case that group level gives some guidance on such matters as the need to improve performance, guidance on the likely future economic environment in general, and so on. But plans are then developed by the businesses and put forward for critical appraisal/approval by the group; they may then be returned for revision, once or more often. This progressive adjustment and bargaining is part of effective planning; it stimulates discussions of alternatives, of how performance can be raised further, of how the capability of the business in the longer term can be improved, of the reliability of the forecasts, etc.

Taking a balanced view   Across several small to medium-sized companies where I have been able to observe attempts to introduce corporate planning, there has been initially too strong a belief in the value of corporate planning. This has been followed by cynicism before a more realistic position has been arrived at. Corporate planning is not automatically good. But if it is worked at to make it effective in the light of experiences gained in its use, it can be very valuable.

It is a fairly common experience that whether the targets are set at group level or left to individual businesses, the first attempt to plan results in unwarranted optimism, because formulation of the plans has not been sufficiently rigorous. As a result, those accountable are then criticized for not achieving their targets. So next time round they are more cautious and are in danger of being too pessimistic. It is only when both sides realize that planning involves bargaining between different levels, that healthy proposals and constructive criticism result in better-quality planning.

Committing sufficient time and thought   Besides setting realistic targets, good planning is mainly about *how* a company can improve its competitive position and hence its performance. It is also about converting this understanding into detailed actions to ensure that the expected benefits do occur. Good planning takes significant amounts of time and hard thinking. Plucking ideas and figures out of thin air without thoroughly thinking them through is a waste of time.

10.5.2   The Time Horizon for the First Plan

When corporate planning is introduced for the first time, it is probably best to start with medium-term planning – say, up to three or five years ahead. Once this is established and beginning to be useful, it will be seen to tie in well with one-year budgeting. It will then also provide a good basis for extending to longer-term planning if this is appropriate.

A company introducing corporate planning for the first time

could well save time and effort in getting to effective operation by seeking advice, probably from consultants. We will look at this option in the next chapter. Even so, perfection should not be expected the first time round. The first run should be regarded as mainly for the staff involved to learn that:

- it will probably take longer than expected (next time round sufficient time can be allowed; also, it should be possible to gain from the previous experience and take the process through somewhat more quickly);
- planning is about how to improve the strategy and capability of the company in a changing environment;
- corporate planning is also about bargaining and learning from constructive criticism and discussion between senior executives in different parts of the company;
- some of the information required for good planning is not available and that processes have to be established to make such information available in future;
- some of the data contains such large errors that the first plan is of doubtful value. Before the next planning cycle occurs, effort must be put into improving the quality of the data.

10.5.3 Improving the Process

In small companies which have not involved consultants in the introduction of corporate planning, these experiences will probably cause a shift in emphasis more towards penetrative thinking and hence more effort. Later, the process may need simplification.

In those larger companies where corporate planning is well established, and where it has been progressively improved over several years, the main changes have been:

- the corporate planning process is more line-driven;
- the process has been simplified;
- increased attention in now given to sensing the environment and in particular being more aware of the key competitors;
- there is a stronger focus on the most important issues;
- greater emphasis is given to implementation.

Graham Turner (1984) describes how corporate planning has been developed to a very effective level at ICI.

179

10.6 How Does Your Company Measure Up?

Consider, now, the state of corporate planning in your company.

- Does the process involve description on paper?
- If not, should there not be some movement in that direction to increase its rigour and reliability?

If such a process is in operation, how effective is it and does it need attention to make it more effective? Try the checklist below.

- With hindsight, at group and business levels, did the process fail to diagnose and address any of the elephant issues?
- Are company strategy decisions (at business, division or group level) being made largely independently of the planning process?
- Is contact between those running the process and top executives rare?
- Is strategy largely history extrapolated into the future (rather than outward-looking towards opportunities)?
- Is the process almost entirely top-down or bottom-up (rather than iterative)?
- Does the process contain a large (and excessive) amount of data of spurious accuracy?
- Are planning documents almost entirely in the form of tables (rather than description and logic supported by a very limited amount of key data)?
- Is there no statement of assumptions, serious risks, or levels of uncertainty?
- Are the forecasts being produced by the staff, without strong line backing?
- Are plans limited to financial plans (omitting equipment, materials, supplies and services plans)?
- Is there no communication of the strategy chosen to other parts of the company?
- Is there a lack of checkback on the accuracy of forecasts?
- Do unforeseen events often occur, thus questioning the whole foundation of the existing plans?
- Has the planning process been in its present form, without review, for several years?

If the answer to any of these questions is yes, then there is probably a need to improve your planning process. If yes is the answer to several of these questions, planning in its present form could well be costing more than the value it gives; it urgently needs a complete overhaul!

Chapter 11

Internal and External Consultants and Their Contribution

11.1 Introduction: 'Going it Alone', Consultants and Corporate Planners

A company can take any one of three alternative routes towards improving its strategic management:

- without help from internal or external consultants, gradually develop its existing processes and management;
- employ external strategy consultants;
- recruit a corporate planner and establish an internal corporate strategic planning unit.

The smaller the company, the lower the amount of money at risk and the greater the likelihood that it will gradually develop its

182

own approach without the help of consultants. The larger the company, the greater the likelihood that the best path will include establishing its own corporate planning unit or units. However, the three paths are not necessarily mutually exclusive. For example, some of those companies with sizeable corporate strategic planning units also employ external strategy consultants from time to time. But for our purposes here it is convenient to consider these approaches separately. We will consider them in reverse order, beginning with those situations in which companies have set up their own internal corporate planning units.

In the remainder of this chapter, the term 'corporate planners' is used to describe those who are professional staff, normally graduates, operating within units (often with only one such professional) and whose full-time role is to assist those making strategy decisions on whole-company direction at the single-business, division or group level. A 'corporate planning unit' is defined as containing at least one corporate planner.

11.2   Internal Corporate Planning Units

It is probable that some 400 UK companies now have corporate planning units. The professional body that most corporate planners join is the Strategic Planning Society, whose members also include main board directors with responsibility for corporate planning in companies where no internal corporate planning unit exists.

11.2.1   The Current Presence of Corporate Planning Units in UK Firms

In both 1984 and 1992 I carried out surveys of the members of the Society to which companies with corporate planning units responded (for greater detail please see Houlden, 1985, 1995). The overall pattern of the existence of corporate planning units is summarized in figure 11.1. The turnover figures from the 1984 survey have been increased to allow for inflation and to bring them to the 1992 value of the pound sterling. In both parts of the figure, the dotted part of the line reflects less certainty as to the exact position of the line (in figure 11.1(a) because the information is based on a

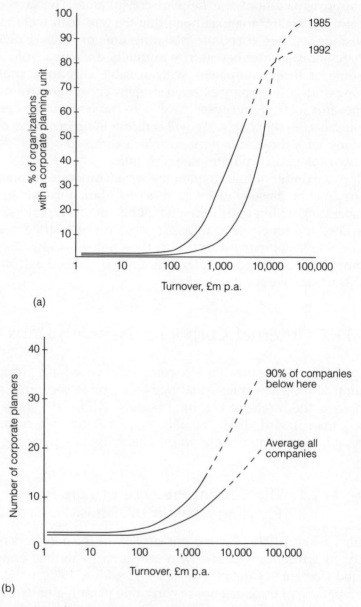

Figure 11.1 (a) The existence of corporate planning units and the size of companies; (b) the number of corporate planners in 1992 and the size of companies.

small sample and in figure 11.1(b) because of the scatter in the number of corporate planners across companies of similar size).

These figures exclude financial institutions. In those banks and building societies where there is a corporate planning unit, there is an average of one corporate planner per £1,500 million of net assets.

Some of the largest companies which were also divisionalized had corporate planning units at both group and divisional levels.

11.2.2 What Determines the Presence or Absence of a Corporate Planning Unit?

Clearly the size of a company does have an important effect on the need for corporate planners. But why do some companies with a turnover of less than £10 million p.a. have their own corporate planner? And at the other end of the scale, why is it that some of the largest companies (for example, GEC) do not?

The surveys concluded that there were three other important factors besides size. These were:

- complexity and level of risk;
- style and organizational structure;
- turbulence in the company's environment.

For example, a group composed of many largely unrelated autonomous businesses is less likely to have a corporate planner than is a more complex group of the same size, in which the businesses are more closely related and less autonomous.

At the other end of the scale, some of the companies with a turnover of less than £10 million p.a. do have a corporate planner, clearly indicating a strong belief by the chief executive in the need for strategic direction. Whether in these companies there is still a need for a corporate planner after an effective corporate planning process has been established and once the top executives have become more strategically capable, probably then depends on whether the company has grown significantly larger in the meantime.

11.2.3 How Corporate Planning Units Evolve

In those companies where one or more corporate planning units have been in operation for several years, it is interesting to note

185

the changes which have occurred as the units learn how to be more effective and in tune with the needs of the company.

It is not uncommon for corporate planning activity to begin as part of the finance function. However, as it broadens its abilities and comes to be seen as more central to the future of the company as a whole, it is more common for the head of the corporate strategic planning unit to report to the chief executive. Including those corporate planning units which had only recently been established, my survey in 1992 showed that 66% of the heads of corporate planning units reported direct to the chief executive (executive chairman, managing director or general manager), 22% to the (group) finance director and 12% to another board director.

Of the professionals within corporate planning units, 93% were graduates, each unit of any size embracing a variety of degree subjects and experiences. The remaining 7% were professionally qualified accountants, company secretaries, actuaries or bankers.

The mixture of people within a unit helps the unit as a whole to view strategy from different points of view; it also causes each member to broaden his or her interests and expertise from interaction with the others. This broadening process was reinforced by the fact that 21% of the corporate planners had taken higher degrees in management (MBA or MSc). Some of the companies with larger corporate planning units saw a period in the unit as a useful stage in the development of management ability in some of its promising young executives.

In those corporate planning units which have successfully developed over several years, the role of the unit has changed over time through a spectrum roughly as follows:

- acting as an agent of change or catalyst – stimulating top executives to think about the future of the company; changing attitudes to give due weight to longer-term considerations;
- designing, establishing and running the corporate planning process; providing guidelines on inflation rates, exchange rates, etc; monitoring performance against plan; improving forecasting methods; monitoring competitors' performance;
- developing abilities – assisting senior functional staff and those responsible for divisions and individual businesses to develop their strategic and planning abilities;

186

- co-ordinating – ensuring that major resource decisions are not taken in isolation from consideration of their impact on other parts of the company, both in the short and the longer term; developing a clear and internally consistent statement of company strategy;
- providing a project-based service to the chief executive – studying businesses in difficulty; assisting with acquisitions and disposals; developing draft plans for new activities; critically appraising the plans of individual businesses/divisions; assisting in presentations to city institutions;
- helping top executives to make judgements on the strategic direction of the whole company; providing alternative scenarios of the future environment; stimulating creative thinking; standing back from the company's planning behaviour and making proposals for its improvement (that is, taking a major responsibility for the quality of planning as an activity right through to implementation); making contributions to the thinking on organizational change and information/communication processes, including board-level information.

The role of the corporate planning units tended to start at the top of this list but, as the strategic management capability of senior executives developed, to shift more towards the activities in the second half of the list. As this role developed, so some of its earlier activities were taken over by the training or accounting departments.

Compare this list of roles with the list, given on pages 166–7, of features which a company with a well-developed strategic management capability shows. An effective corporate planning unit will bring about development of the strategic abilities of the senior executives (Houlden, 1986). As these executives develop their strategic abilities down the list on pages 166–7, so it is appropriate that the role of the corporate planners should also move down the list given above.

This change in the role of corporate planning units from first introduction to maturity and from an early strong emphasis on the use of techniques to a more streamlined planning process has resulted in a reduction in the size of such units, with a concomitant rise in the quality of the planners involved. The corporate planning processes have become simpler and more line-driven.

187

11.2.4 Checking the Value of a Corporate Planning Unit

In some organizations, while a corporate planning unit has existed for many years, its role has not changed. Neither its head nor the chief executive has questioned whether the unit is still giving good value or whether, in line with the changing competitive environment and the changing strategic abilities of the top executives, the unit's composition and role should be changed. The lack of attention to this question spells danger for the company's future and for the future viability of the corporate planning unit.

The head of the corporate planning unit should see the unit as providing an internal strategy consultancy service to the chief executive. He/she should aim to give the maximum added value – not growth of the unit for its own sake. A checklist which he/she might use for both the unit and for any corporate planning process which the company uses is as follows.

- Has the unit (and the process) helped in diagnosing the elephant issues which the company has recently faced and is it likely to continue to help to do this in the future?
- Has the unit (and the process) helped the top executives to analyse these elephant issues and, thereby, to select and implement the right strategy?
- If the unit has existed for more than a couple of years, has its role been reviewed and is it still appropriate?
- Is the main part of its activities now broken down into clearly defined projects with objectives, time scales, costs and expected benefits?
- Is the overall programme of the unit's work reviewed periodically, with both the director to whom it reports and the chief executive? (These, and other suitable occasions, should be used to bring the value given by individual projects to the notice of the CEO and other top executives and directors.)

If the answer to any of these questions is 'no', early action should be taken to remove the weaknesses.

The CEO must see strategy choice personally as a core responsibility. He/she has responsibility for the quality of strategy decisions and the effectiveness with which they are implemented. This requires that periodically he/she must check the answers to the first two questions in the list above. If the answer to either question is 'no' and no action is being taken to correct the position, he/she must act.

11.3 External Strategy Consultants

There is a wide variety of sources from which corporate strategy consultants can be employed.

11.3.1 The Main Types of Strategy Consultant

The larger corporate strategy consultancy activities fall broadly into three main categories:

- the consultancy groups such as McKinsey, Bain, Boston Consulting Group, SRI International, Booz Allen and Hamilton, LEK, etc. whose core activity is corporate strategy consultancy;
- the broadly based consultancy groups such as PA and PE-Inbucon, which include corporate strategy as one of their main areas of activity;
- the management consultancy parts of the larger chartered accountancy partnerships, which in some cases include corporate strategy as one of their main areas of activity; for example, Braxton is the corporate strategy activity within the management consultancy division of Touche Ross.

In addition, there is a whole range of smaller consultancies and even individuals who specialize in particular parts of corporate strategy, or in offering a broadly based corporate strategy service to a particular sector of industry.

For example, Oasis (Organisation and System Innovations Limited) is a medium-sized consultancy group focusing on the organization and system needs of companies, including those which relate to corporate strategy. Wallace Smith Trust Company Ltd, much of whose work is for financial institutions, also offers particular skills in managing divestments.

John Argenti, whose published work I have mentioned earlier, is a good example of an independent corporate strategy consultant.

He specializes in helping small to medium-sized companies to introduce systematic corporate planning.

11.3.2 The Cost of Employing a Consultant

Consultancy fees may range from in the region of £500 to over £3,000 per consultant day, including back-up secretarial and analytical help as appropriate, with the result that consultancy contracts can range from perhaps £4,000 through to over £1 million. A cheaper alternative, which may be more attractive for the smaller company, is to employ an MBA student, supervised by a member of the business school's staff, on a project as part of the requirements for the degree programme itself. The cost of this could be around £3,000 for a three-month study.

11.3.3 The Services Offered by Consultants

Examples of the services which consultants can provide include the following:

- for a company developing its global competitiveness, analysis of competition in a particular sector and the presentation of a strategy of takeover/merger/strategic alliance to establish a strong global position;
- for a company whose performance is regarded as unsatisfactory, a diagnosis of the causes, with a view to reshaping the company's strategy and changing the organization and processes as necessary to pursue the new strategy;
- for a multi-business company, a detailed analysis of the scope for gain by collaboration between subsidiaries (for example, joint distribution, joint purchasing, etc.) and how these benefits can be achieved while still maintaining motivation and accountability of these separate subsidiaries;
- detailed analysis of the parts and the whole of a possible takeover target, both to guide the takeover itself and to define the strategies to be followed, including any divestments to be made, after the takeover;
- assistance in making more successful divestments;
- helping with the introduction of systematic corporate planning

– developing the abilities of senior executives and advising on the design of the process;

• reviewing the design and effectiveness of the company's corporate planning processes in the light of changes in the company and its environment since they were first introduced;
• reviewing existing and likely developments in an area of technology and assisting a company's thrust in relation to these developments, defining how it could be more successful;
• carrying out an urgent review of the performance and prospects of a major part of a company.

11.4 Concepts and Techniques Consultants Use

Because strategy consultants, whether internal or external, may occasionally use specific techniques to assist the development of company strategy, it is important for executives to understand how techniques relate to good decisions at this level.

11.4.1 The Post-war Proliferation of Management Techniques

Particularly since World War II, there have been considerable developments in management techniques, many of them allied to the use of computers. At the functional operational level, managers have learnt how to use techniques such as critical path networks/PERT, stock control systems, etc. Such techniques can be valuable provided that their logics are understood, that modifications are made where necessary to meet the needs of individual businesses and that the manager responsible understands the limits to the scope and value of the techniques.

11.4.2 Operational Techniques and Strategic Techniques

A management technique is an imperfect attempt to describe reality. How fully it describes reality varies between techniques and particularly between:

• those techniques that are of value at the operational level and
• those designed for use at the corporate strategy level.

To illustrate this difference between the use of techniques at the operational level, of which most executives will have had some experience, and the use of techniques at the corporate strategy level, consider first an example of the former.

Example: fleet renewal   Many companies have their own road transport fleets. A fairly common problem is how often these vehicles should be replaced. There is a technique that seeks to address this and other types of replacement problem. It uses historical data concerning the currently and recently used vehicles (information on loads carried, mileage, repairs, fuel, insurance, tax, purchase and sale prices, etc.) and seeks to balance the increase in maintenance costs as vehicles get older against the falling value of the vehicles on resale.

For a company with, say, a large fleet of lorries of the same type, it is possible from the analysis of good historical data to produce in this way a policy, for example of the form: 'From the sixth year after purchase of a new lorry, keep maintenance costs under review. When maintenance and repair costs exceed, or are expected to shortly exceed, £x per year, replace the lorry. Sell all remaining lorries in the tenth year'.

This is an example where a large part of the problem can be analysed and therefore the policy coming out of the analysis is quite good; but it is not perfect and should be improved. Why is it not perfect? Because there are other factors which have not been considered but which may be important. Most techniques of value at the operational management level cover a large proportion of the total problem being addressed – say, 90%. This may be sufficient to give a significant improvement. But to be more effective and to reduce risks it is always the case that management judgement should be applied before action is taken. The 10% not covered by the technique is worth cutting down and in some cases there is a risk that more than this is still at stake!

For example, even if any new lorry to replace an existing lorry comes from the same manufacturer, the detailed design will have changed somewhat since the existing lorries were bought. What effect will these changes have? The quantity and types of goods to be carried in the future may well be different from those in the past. Maintenance procedures may have changed. And so on. The manager responsible for decisions on replacement must add his judgement on these other factors if he is to reach a better-quality decision than that which the analysis alone suggests.

The importance of judgement in applying techniques At the corporate strategy level, the proportions are largely reversed, with the technique only dealing with a small part of the problem and management judgement covering the larger part. Why is this?

There are three main reasons.

First, company strategy situations are more complex than operational questions and it is all too easy to describe only part of any situation, failing to recognize, and therefore leaving out of the analysis other, important factors. This is why it is safer to look at a strategic situation from various points of view rather than just one.

Secondly, the behaviour of executives in competing companies is an important element in strategy choice; it is often difficult to forecast their behaviour – it may even be irrational!

Thirdly, even for those factors which are recognized and included in a technique, errors in the data available are usually much greater than for situations at the operational level.

Techniques are consequently less frequently of value in corporate strategy analysis and much greater care must be exercised in their use to assist decisions at that level as compared to the operational level.

11.4.3 Concept, Coarse Technique, Refined Technique

It is important to distinguish between concept, coarse technique and the refined use of a technique.

A concept is one way of looking at a situation; there may be others. Most of the so-called techniques for use in deciding company strategy are very coarse, or generalized ways of looking at certain types of strategy situations. I regard the point at which a concept becomes a technique as being when some of the factors are quantified. If this quantification is roughly of the right magnitude and not too much is read into the exact figures, then the concept has become a coarse technique. If used with understanding and care, a coarse technique may well be of value at the corporate strategy level.

However, some analysts, not of the best quality, are tempted to push the use of techniques too far. They will put all their confidence in the technique's ability exactly to represent the company situation, when in fact that is impossible. They will then push for greater and greater accuracy in the factors which need to be quantified, with the aim of using the technique in a more refined way. If taken to extremes, the result is a nonsense.

11.4.4 Understanding How to Use Techniques

So any analyst of quality using a concept/technique must understand what it can and, more importantly, what it cannot, do. He/she must understand that while it may give some insight into a strategy situation, this will necessarily only be a partial insight. He/she must also decide how far along the sequence from concept through coarse technique to refined technique it is safe to go. He/she must also attempt to cross-check by looking at the situation from points of view other than that of just one concept/technique.

11.4.5 Example: the 'Boston Matrix' in Action

Consider for example the matrix (Hedley, 1977) referred to earlier on page 153 and best known by the terms 'stars', 'question marks', 'cash cows' and 'dogs'. This matrix is shown in figure 11.2. It aims to classify the various businesses within a larger company, for the purpose of considering how best to allocate group resources. The positions of the lines dividing the four categories are defined by the technique.

What happens when this technique is used in practice?

Difficulties in correctly positioning business It is not easy to put a business in the correct position on the matrix. In some cases, getting information on the size of the total market proves difficult and a rough estimate has to be accepted. So there can be some error in the position of the business on the horizontal scale. A similar difficulty may occur with estimating the rate of growth of the total market. So any business whose position is close to one of the dividing lines between categories could be in danger of being wrongly categorized. Especial care needs to be exercised with drawing conclusions from such cases.

Figure 11.2   The business portfolio ('Boston matrix').

A more serious error can arise from wrongly defining the area of business, in terms of either its sphere or its geographical radius of competition. For example, now that Jaguar is part of Ford, which is a multi-business group, one could apply this technique for guidance on what should happen to its share of group resources. If, in doing this, Jaguar were related to the whole car industry throughout the world, this would mean that the market share recorded would be very small indeed. But it does not compete with large parts of the world car industry. Its competitors are in a particular segment, companies like Mercedes Benz and BMW. So *this segment* is the market to which reference should be made if Jaguar is to be correctly placed on the matrix. Use of this technique requires very careful thought for each subsidiary business on the question 'exactly which business or businesses is this subsidiary in?'

What if the day-to-day operational management of a business is particularly poor or particularly effective? This could result in, say, a cash cow business making a loss while a competing company apparently in a dog position is making a profit.

What about a situation where elimination of a business in the

195

dog category would adversely affect the performance of another business in the group that has not been placed in that category?

Care needed with inherent assumptions The technique does depend heavily on the assumption that large market share gives higher profit margins than does low market share, or at least can be managed so as to give this benefit. While this is the case in many areas of business, where there are significant economies of scale, it is not universally true.

The analyst needs to have a good understanding of, and exercise care in using, this technique.

Modifications to the technique There are developments of the technique aimed at avoiding some of these difficulties in meeting the needs of particular types of situation. For example, Shell has developed the 'directional policy matrix' (Robinson, Hichens and Wade, 1978) with slightly different axes, for use particularly in analysing businesses which are partly interdependent. Their matrix also has two dividing lines in each direction rather than one, giving a total of nine instead of four categories. The extra middle categories encourage caution in areas which would be close to the dividing lines in the original Boston matrix. Other matrices have been developed by other consultants.

The value of the matrix What, then, is the value of the Boston and related matrices?

At the level of a concept, a very high value. Displaying to top executives in this way the variety of businesses within a group, clearly and concisely exposes the issue of appropriate allocation of funds among businesses in various market positions. But it does not tell the company what it must do. Detailed discussions on the competitive and financial repercussions of what may seem to be the suggested reallocation are still necessary. Also, there are questions of how to organize and manage the group as reallocation and its effects take place. There will be situations where changing allocations may stir competitors into behaviour which will eliminate some of the expected benefits.

And there are questions not directly related to the products and markets of a business. For example, one fairly common problem which needs to be resolved is that few executives, used to being judged on growth and profits, will relish being required to manage a business which is to be run as a cash cow. Will they not lose out on promotion prospects compared to others who do well with growth businesses?

A matrix of this type, then, is very useful as a concept in analysing and presenting many group situations. Used at the level of a coarse technique by an analyst who understands it but who will use it as only one of several ways of looking at a situation, it can also be of help, particularly in exposing issues worthy of more consideration. But these issues must then be given wider consideration and considerable discussion with executives who have an understanding of the technique and neither automatically reject it nor accept it without question.

11.4.6 Other Techniques and Their Use

Similar points arise from examination of the use in practice of other techniques that are of some help in strategy analysis. Appendix D lists the main concepts/techniques which you might come across and briefly explains them.

Chapter 12

Towards Better Strategic Management of Your Company

12.1 Recognizing the Need

To be successful, a company needs to be effective not only in day-to-day operational management but also in deciding and implementing company strategy.

A company with poor strategic management is one where the top executives do not give enough attention to strategic issues and almost certainly have not had the experience necessary to develop the ability to address strategic issues, to choose strategies and to implement them. Such companies will tend to underperform.

Conversely, the company with good strategic management is one where appropriate time is given to strategic issues and where effective processes exist for addressing them and implementing the strategies chosen.

Different companies, and their senior executives, are at different points along the spectrum between these two extremes of capability. The problem is to recognize how far your company's capabilities have been developed already, and then to initiate an appropriate programme to bring the senior executives to an effective level within a reasonably short period of time.

12.2 Calling on Appropriate Assistance

Time will be saved and fewer mistakes made by those companies which progress by drawing on the lessons learnt elsewhere. Reading and attending conferences or courses may help, but for many companies this also means employing internal or external consultants. 'Bringing in a consultant', however, is no automatic panacea. As in any other area, not all consultants are of the best quality. They range from those who are very helpful and do excellent work to the other extreme of those who do more harm than good. Good strategy consultants do not come cheap, for they are in very great demand. So how can you find consultants you can trust and who will give good value to your particular company? What kind of remit should they be given, to ensure that transfer of strategic capability to your executives does occur?

12.3 The Starting Remit for a Consultant

12.3.1 Introducing a Corporate Planning Unit

It is common for medium-sized and large companies which introduce a corporate planning unit to be motivated by a perceived need for a corporate planning process to improve the company's strategy decisions. In other words, referring back to the changing role of a corporate planning unit as given earlier (see pages 185–7), it usually wants to jump straight into the second stage – that is, 'designing, establishing and running a corporate planning process'.

In my view that initial remit by itself is not the best. I believe that a better definition of the remit for the head of a new corporate planning unit is possible if one bears in mind the need to develop the abilities of senior executives and the need to develop *quickly* a more effective corporate planning process (de Geus, 1988).

To accelerate the process of development, I would define the initial remit as follows:

- Audit the company's present strategic management capability.
- Plan to improve the strategic management capability substantially within the first two years of operation. To assist this process:
  - design a *simple* medium-term planning process (perhaps up to three or five years ahead) and assist with its introduction;
  - help senior executives to learn how to diagnose and address the most important strategic issues facing the company.
- Once the abilities of the senior executives have been significantly advanced and the process becomes more line-driven:
  - if necessary, help to extend the planning process into the longer term;
  - consider reducing the size of the corporate planning unit;
  - shift the role of the unit to those listed below 'co-ordinating...' in the list given on pages 186–7.

12.3.2 External Consultants: Designing a Process or Addressing an Issue

Where a company is not of the size, complexity or style to warrant the setting-up of an internal corporate planning unit, the process of development is different.

In a few cases, the company may invite consultants to help design and introduce a corporate planning process. If so, then the need to keep it simple and to develop the strategic management abilities of the senior executives should be included in the remit. There should also be a follow-up review stage a year or so after the process has been introduced, to check whether any further development of the staff or modification to the design of the process is necessary.

However, in most such cases external consultants are not brought in to design the process; the more common remit is to address a particular strategic issue that is causing serious concern.

If this is all that the remit covers, again, in my view this is not enough. While consultants will have to explain the reasons behind their recommendations on this particular issue, and hence transfer some understanding of company strategy, there will still be a long way to go before the senior executives have developed their own abilities to think and act strategically in the future, when different issues arise. The consultants may also not think to comment on the existing corporate planning process. So opportunities to benefit by the transfer of strategic management skills from consultants to senior executives will have been missed.

To cover this need, without introducing the dangers of a lack of focus or a substantial increase in fee, I would add, after the specific remit, a paragraph of roughly this form:

> In carrying out this remit, I imagine that you will need to summarize the events leading up to the present position and the stage which we have reached in addressing this issue. You will also be meeting several of our senior executives. We are aware of the need to develop our own strategic abilities and planning processes to cope better with strategic issues. Any observations on how we might develop these abilities and processes will be welcome. However, this does not mean an expansion or diversion of the remit itself.

Any observations made in the consultants' report can then be explored further at the oral presentation of their recommendations.

Of course, consultants like to be able to maintain links with companies and generate a stream of projects over time. Your interest is in trying to transfer some of their skills to your own staff, so that in the future you will only need to employ consultants when more advanced skills are required or when your own staff do not have sufficient time available.

12.4 Developing Your Personal Strategic Ability

It is to be hoped that this book will have started the development of your own strategic ability. You now need to build on this foundation by using and developing in practice the understanding you have gained.

12.4.1 Assessing Consultants and What They Are Offering to Do

For example, you should now be better able to judge whether a strategy consultant is of good quality or not. Any good consultant should be able to explain what he can offer in simple English; if he cannot, he does not sufficiently understand his subject, or that in the end good strategy is good common sense. Before employing a new internal or external consultant, ask him/her to give you the names of, say, three top executives of other companies for whom he/she has previously worked. You should check with at least one of these.

Besides taking care in defining any remit for external consultants, you should require them to produce a plan for the proposed remit. You need to know who is going to be actually carrying out and managing the project. The plan should be more detailed for the early parts and probably coarser for the later stages. It needs to include periodic reporting back to you on how the work is progressing and what the indications are. This will help you to ensure that it is really addressing the issue which caused your concern. At an appropriate stage in the work, perhaps a quarter of the way into the remit, it is usually worthwhile to carry out a thorough review with the consultant. This acts as a good chaser to keep consultants on target; it also allows you the opportunity to consider whether you wish to modify the remit, accelerate it or terminate the contract.

12.4.2 Discussing Strategy with Colleagues

Your personal development will also be assisted by other actions. You should now be more likely to discuss strategic issues with your colleagues. This might well lead to a shift towards more discussion of company strategy at meetings of the top executives. It may also result in the development of company processes to assist strategy choice.

12.4.3 Further Reading

All these developments will create an environment in which you can develop your abilities. However, particularly if you are employed in a medium-sized or large company, you may feel that now having a broad introduction to company strategy, you also wish to go further than the short articles to which I have made reference. You may wish to read more deeply on specific topics. If so, I would refer you to the references Baker, 1987; Cecchini, 1989; Donaldson and Lorsch, 1983; Hill, 1985; Majaro, 1988; Ohmae 1982 and 1985; Peters and Waterman, 1982; and Porter, 1985. These are some of the books which I regularly strongly recommend to those who already have a good understanding of company strategy and who wish to continue with their personal development.

APPENDICES

Appendix A

Using the TOWS Matrix and Strategies in a Changing Environment: Newprint Ltd

Introduction to the Cases
Using The TOWS Matrix: Newprint (A)
The Changing Environment: Newprint (B)

A.1   Introduction to the Cases

This appendix presents cases at two different stages in a company's history. The main purposes are:

- to illustrate what using the TOWS matrix involves;
- to show how the nature of strategy choice can change dramatically, when the external environment changes.

The cases are based on a real company. However, the company concerned wishes that it and its staff should remain anonymous. The names of the company and of its executives have therefore been changed, as have the figures for turnover, profits and staff levels. But these changes have been chosen so as to retain the key features of the company's situation and the magnitude and effect of the recession on the company's performance. I use both cases regularly in my business school teaching.

The degree of detail given in each case is typical of the kind of information relating to strategy which would be easily recalled by the chief executive and conveyed, in an initial meeting, to anyone being asked to advise on what strategy the company should pursue. Whether additional information, which can reasonably be obtained, is needed, is one of the questions which will be considered as analysis proceeds.

A.2   Using the TOWS Matrix: Newprint (A)

A.2.1   Preparing for and Reading the Case

Now read Newprint (A), putting yourself in the position of the consultant, Tom Bryan, in 1976; for the rest of the discussion of Newprint (A) the tenses used will be based on 1976 being the present. Initially read the case quickly, to get an overall view of how well the company is doing (in 1976!) and what you consider its outlook for the future to be. In doing this, ask yourself how far ahead it is appropriate to look (strategic horizon).

Then consider using the TOWS matrix. Because the main question is how fast to develop and exploit the different markets for the computer typesetting part of Newprint's activities, you should quickly realize that you need to consider the computer typesetting and jobbing printing parts of its activities separately. In other words, you need two matrices, one for each of these two activities.

Take one of these activities first: I suggest the computer typesetting activity.

Separately from the matrix itself, try putting down statements which describe the environment for this and any competitors in this type of activity. Then describe the company in comparison with what you imagine to be its existing and future competitors. Next abbreviate these statements into a few key words and try putting those which appear appropriate into the boxes of the matrix itself. In doing this you should be asking yourself questions such as:

• What are the radius and sphere of competition of this activity?
• Which companies are, or which in the future may be, competitors?

- How large is the market now, and how large is it likely to be in the future?
- What strengths/distinctive advantages does this company have in this activity?
- Bearing in mind that to pursue the computer typesetting activity strongly would mean growth, what time-scale might be involved? Does this raise any questions about the company's weaknesses?

Then move to the jobbing printing activity. Create a separate TOWS matrix for this part of the company. Ask yourself similar questions, plus any others which you feel are appropriate, then again enter into the boxes of the matrix itself the key statements which summarize your initial view of the company and its environment, as far as the jobbing printing activity is concerned.

Next note down separately for each activity what additional questions you would ask if you were to visit the company again to spend more time strengthening this part of the analysis.

Then look at the two matrices and note how they compare to each other.

When you have done all this, you are ready to move on to pages 214 and 215 beyond Newprint (A) to see how your matrices compare with mine and how use of them assists in deciding strategy.

Newprint (A)*

Newprint Ltd is a small, privately owned printing company. It was started in 1955 by the present managing director, John Reynolds, who, after completing his apprenticeship, spent five years as a skilled printer in a large printing company in Newcastle upon Tyne. He then decided to set up on his own there. He began in a small way, buying second-hand equipment cheaply. By working long hours and giving careful attention to quality and prompt delivery he gradually built the business to its present size.

In 1976 Newprint had a turnover of some £300,000 p.a. In a good year it made some £40,000 profits before tax, and even in the slight recession at that time it expected to make £15,000 before tax.

The bulk of this turnover came from the area in which the business started – quality multi-colour jobbing printing. Orders varied in size from

* Copyright © B. T. Houlden 1976.

£50 to some £15,000 with the bulk of the value lying in the £500–£2,000 range. Jobbing printing produced 85% of the turnover and about 90% of the profits. Production was in a spacious, well-lit building with good modern equipment. Over the years, John Reynolds had introduced many ideas of his own into both the production and the office areas and although none of these had by itself been major, in total they had contributed to the good overall level of efficiency.

In 1973 John Reynolds started to develop an interest in computer typesetting. He was excited at the technical possibility that computers offered to printing and had some idea of the areas of the business that in a few years' time might be profitably exploited, once the technology had been mastered.

Tom Bryan runs a management consulting firm and had known John Reynolds socially for several years; he had not, however, undertaken any consultancy work for John. Early in 1976 when the two met, John Reynolds talked more freely than usual about Newprint and the developments in computer typesetting. Apparently, over the last year and a half, he had been undertaking a large printing contract using computer typesetting for a tractor manufacturer. This contract had just been completed, the technical snags had been overcome and a further contract was likely with the same firm. As a result, John Reynolds was full of enthusiasm about the possibility of rapid growth of Newprint to several times its size by exploiting the advantages which computer typesetting offered.

The computer he had been using belonged to the local polytechnic and one of the staff there had been acting as a specialist consultant on programming. Relationships had been good and access to the computer was not expected to present any serious problems over the next few years.

The market which particularly attracted John Reynolds is illustrated by the work for the tractor manufacturer – the printing of operating manuals. The normal method of printing manuals involves starting virtually from scratch each time a new manual is required for a new model of tractor. Setting up the type, checking the proof and making corrections takes several weeks and as a result the cost of producing the manuals is high.

However, if you were to compare the manual of one model with that for the next, you would find that a large proportion of all the wording and illustrations was common to both. This is where computer typesetting and proofs correction scores. Although it is tedious and expensive to get the details of the first manual on to a computer disk, it is then much easier, quicker and cheaper to update the disk to incorporate the changes between the first and second manuals. The result is a much quicker service to customers and a long-term reduction in the costs of producing the manuals (for the particular requirements of the tractor manufacturer this saving has recently been confirmed as being of the order of 30%).

An additional advantage of using the computer is in translation of the manuals into other languages. Newprint had developed translation disks which could be matched with the disks containing the English versions of the manuals to permit rapid printing in French and German.

John Reynolds saw a potential market which included manufacturers of cars, computers, military equipment, etc., all of which use large numbers of manuals; the market also included those large firms operating at home and abroad which have extensive price lists that need to be quickly updated and translated.

He had visited a sample of potential customers and had met with a very encouraging response. Seeing the long-term advantages in printing costs and speed, without exception they had been very enthusiastic not only to start drawing up a contract with Newprint, but also to include in the contract a major contribution towards the cost of development (i.e. getting the first manual or price list on to disk). However, John was well aware that as soon as other firms saw the potential of computer typesetting, competition would rapidly intensify. Speed was essential and this would require considerably greater financial resources than were then available to the company.

He was also very concerned to continue to be a good employer; he would be very much opposed to redundancies unless the continued existence of the company were threatened. The people he had brought on for the computer typesetting work were of a higher calibre than the normal jobbing printing labour and he foresaw some wage-grading problems if he did not more clearly separate the two main lines of business. However, this would cause problems, because at present, after the 'master' had been produced via the computer typesetting operations, the running-off of large numbers of manuals was handled on the normal printing equipment.

In 1976 he was able to handle personally virtually all of the marketing and technical supervision of the computer typesetting work as well as much of the marketing and technical work for the jobbing printing side of the business. One of the people who joined the firm in its early days was his number two, Bill Williams. Bill is also an experienced printer, able to handle the production problems of jobbing printing, but not so lively or enthusiastic as John and therefore not so involved on the computer typesetting work. Bill is quiet, reliable and loyal; very good at keeping an eye on the detail of estimating, scheduling work through the factory, ensuring that customers' work is delivered on time and that debtors are chased up.

Bill owned 5% of the shares in the business; the rest were held by John and John's wife (who did not take an active part in day-to-day management). There were some 40 employees, mainly skilled printers, plus a part-time delivery driver and three secretaries/receptionists.

As he listened to John Reynolds, Tom Bryan felt that here was a situation where not only was there a real need for the kind of consultancy which he could offer, but also an opportunity to help a friend to be really successful financially as well as establish himself as an innovator in the printing field.

A.2.2 TOWS Matrix for the Computer Typesetting Activity

At the time of this case, Newprint was exploring the value of technology likely to be used by some other jobbing printing companies in the future.

The advantage which computer typesetting offered was that small differences in customer requirements from one printing order to another at a later date could be incorporated more quickly and more cheaply than would be the case with the then standard method of typesetting. Operating manuals and owners' handbooks for tractors, cars, lorries, etc. all offered this prospect of relatively large orders with relatively minor changes in detailed content over time. Because of the much smaller value of orders, price lists, while offering some extra volume, could not be the main focus in the market.

At the time there was no obvious existing competitor elsewhere in the UK but it was likely that a few other jobbing printing companies were also exploring this possibility.

The development of this capability in association with the tractor manufacturer would not have been worthwhile without the potential of a series of relatively large orders. In contrast to the jobbing printing activity, which (as we shall see later) involves a relatively local radius of competition, the larger size of orders for computer typesetting work means that Newprint could be competitive over a much wider radius, as also could any future competitors. It is difficult to be certain as to what the radius of competition is. If over time the works were to change over completely to this type of business and invest in equipment dedicated to this type of work, the radius of competition could certainly be the whole of the UK. With some of the vehicle manufacturers shifting their strategies towards producing models on a European basis, the radius of competition might even become as wide as Europe itself.

So what is the size of the potential market? A very rough estimate can be produced by taking the number of tractors, cars, lorries, etc. produced yearly in the UK and multiplying this by a rough estimate of the average price per manual/handbook. This leads to a figure of the order of several million pounds p.a. for the whole of the UK and tens of millions of pounds p.a. for the whole of Europe.

This opportunity therefore offers significant growth possibilities for Newprint.

Newprint has a lead. It is likely that any company which had not started developing computer typesetting by the time of the case would take about 12 months to reach the stage which Newprint has already reached. This means that Newprint can either take some risk and go for rapid growth to a company some two or three times its present size, or limit its rate of growth, its ultimate size and the medium-term risk.

The main risk is that another company will go for more rapid growth and attempt to become more dominant in the UK for this type of work. If so, it might gain from economies of scale and so weaken the competitive position of Newprint. For the present tractor manufacturing customer, ownership of the disk gives Newprint a competitive advantage of being able to quote quicker and cheaper delivery compared to other printers. Whether any other new customers would give Newprint the same advantage is doubtful.

If it is to grow rapidly, Newprint will need substantial extra finance. It would probably have to accept external equity participation and if growth was very fast this might lead to John losing his majority holding.

Rapid growth would also require management abilities of a type which John Reynolds and Bill Williams may not be able to develop quickly enough. On the other hand, the development of computer typesetting relies heavily on John Reynolds and if he were to die, this could well endanger this part of the company.

These and other similar thoughts lead to a rough initial TOWS matrix for the computer typesetting activity as shown in figure A.1. The case does not give a deep enough understanding of the company to be sure that the entries in this matrix are all correct and that no others are important. More information and more thought would be necessary before confirming this matrix. For example, how serious would it be if the consultant from the local polytechnic were not able to continue? How good are the records of exactly what he has done?

Ultimately the matrix should give a simple summary of all of the important factors which would have a bearing on success, if the company were to decide to put enough resources behind the computer typesetting activity to make it the most successful such activity in the UK; that is, if it were to choose as its mission to become the UK leader in this type of activity.

Opportunities	Threats
Rapidly growing markets. Total market of the order of several £m p.a.	Possible new aggressive competitor
	Further technology change

Strengths	Weaknesses
Lead (? 12 months)	Limited financial resources
Ownership of disks (?)	Dependence on John Reynolds
	The abilities of John Reynolds and Bill Williams to manage rapid growth and a much larger company later

Figure A.1 Newprint: a TOWS matrix for the computer typesetting activity.

A.2.3 TOWS Matrix for the Jobbing Printing Activity

The radius of competition for this part of the company is of the order of 25 miles or so. Why so small? There are two reasons. The first concerns marketing. The order size is much smaller than with the typesetting work and does not justify visiting widely scattered customers. The customer also requires continued close contact with the company while an order is being processed: he/she usually has only a rough idea of what he/she wants and relies on the printer to provide the further ideas and artwork necessary to arrive at a product meeting the customer's needs. The customer may therefore wish to see more than one mock-up and then to see the final proof before printing. When he/she has cleared the proof he/she usually requires delivery within a few days. The second reason concerns the problem of controlling production. For such a large number of small to medium-sized orders going through the plant at any one time, there is a size level above which it would be more efficient to have two separate production activities rather than one.

You might think that both of these problems could be avoided by not taking small orders. Certainly most jobbing printers avoid the lower quality black-and-white printing and customers whose requirements are all for very small quantities. Nevertheless, most companies with bigger orders to place require that the printing company which does this work also meets its needs on smaller jobs.

Within this radius of 25 miles or so there will probably be some ten main competitors, some smaller but growing, others larger. Their profit/sales figures will probably range between 3% and 12% in normal times.

On the basis of these and similar thoughts, by a similar process to that described in more detail for the computer typesetting activity, a draft matrix for the jobbing printing activity can be drawn up as shown in figure A.2. Again, further information, beyond that given in the case, and further thought are required before the matrix can be confirmed as a fair summary. For example, the company would know who its main competitors were. A visit to Companies House would produce the microfiches of the audited accounts of most of these competitors over the last few years. A look at these would confirm the range of their performance and indicate which of them had been most successful.

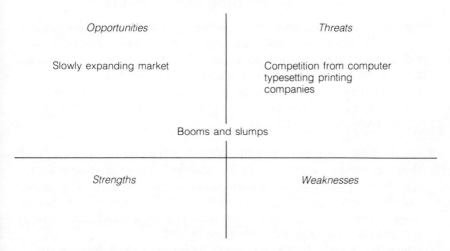

Figure A.2 Newprint: a TOWS matrix for the jobbing printing activity.

The matrix shown in figure A.2 illustrates five aspects of using the TOWS type of analysis:

- Because this matrix is looking solely at the jobbing printing part of Newprint's activities, its computer typesetting side is rightly seen as a threat, even though Newprint runs both types of activity in the same company.
- When using the matrix, it is sometimes difficult to decide whether a particular important feature in the environment is an opportunity or

a threat. In such a situation it is best initially to put it on the boundary of the two boxes, to indicate this uncertainty and to make sure that the factor is not overlooked.

- Under strengths and weaknesses, it is important to only record *distinctive* strengths and weaknesses that mark the company out compared to its competitors.
- The balance between strengths and weaknesses should be checked against the company's performance. With a company outperforming its competitors we would expect mainly strengths, and vice versa.
- Most people, when they start using the TOWS matrix, tend to put some items in the wrong boxes and to include far too many statements in each box. Only the key factors should be recorded; it is usually not appropriate to have more than five in any box. If a company has no distinctive strength or weakness then, as in this case, those boxes should be left empty.

A.2.4 Beyond the TOWS Matrix

After the evidence has been cross-checked and the matrix strengthened, there is still the need to use that analysis to assist in making choices between alternative business strategies. The matrix is also useful in deciding on the best programme of actions to put the strategy into effect.

For Newprint (A), consider the main alternative strategic directions which the company could pursue over the next few years. Then compare your list with mine, as follows:

- Go for maximum growth of the computer typesetting business, with the appropriate programme of investment in equipment both for the typesetting itself and for printing after setting the type. This means deciding on a time in the future after which the company will take in jobbing printing orders only when there is a lull in work generated by the company's computer typesetting operation.
- Specialize in providing a computer typesetting service for other printing companies and pull out of all printing.
- Reduce the risks associated with attempting to grow rapidly by pursuing a mixed strategy of both jobbing printing and computer typesetting with printing.
- Pull out of (perhaps sell) the computer typesetting activity and revert to a jobbing printing company.
- Sell the company.

To assess each of these strategies more fully it is necessary to set down a programme of actions for its implementation and a statement of the likely financial effects as the strategy unfolds.

Let us as an example see how we might explore further the first strategy on my list. To expand the computer typesetting activity requires new customers. It has taken some six months to progress from the stage of starting an association with a company to having the completed disk ready for the first production run. Which customer targets is John Reynolds going for next? Can the development time be cut to four months? Can he and the company safely manage development for two different companies in parallel? When will these developments be likely to require additional capital expenditure? How about recruitment/conversion training of existing staff? How soon will extra financial resources be needed? In what sequence and over what time-scale should the jobbing printing work be run down?

This process could be carried out for each of the other alternatives listed. Subject to any additional views about the feasibility of following these plans and the perceived accuracy of the forecasts, a detached executive could then make a judgement as to which alternative strategy offered the best balance between success and risk along the way. However, in this case the person who is faced with the ultimate decision is John Reynolds. He may be very cautious or he may be willing and able to take some risk to go for a bigger opportunity. So his purpose must be explored.

As explained earlier, it may well take such a person several weeks to get himself in a position to clearly understand his purpose, when faced with a choice of strategies such as this. His purpose is not only concerned with the likely financial consequences of a given strategy move; he is also concerned as to the kind of life he has with the company.

In the real situation, John Reynolds was tempted to consider selling the company, but in the end rejected this option. The following scripted conversation summarizes what in fact took place through a series of discussions over a longer period of time. Read through this, and as you do, ask yourself what it tells you about John Reynolds's purpose in owning this company.

A Discussion between the Times of the Newprint (A) and Newprint (B) Cases*

This note reports part of the discussion between John Reynolds and Tom Bryan which led to the decision to limit growth.

During this time another printing company made an offer to buy Newprint. After several bargaining sessions, during which John Reynolds was able to present his company's plans for growth in such a way that an offer worth twice the original bid was made, he decided not to sell.

The discussions between John Reynolds and Tom Bryan, which extended over two or three weeks, are briefly summarized as follows:

Tom: You will not be able to raise the offer price any more. What do you think about it?

John: First, my daughter is not interested in running the business when I retire and as I have no other children it is really a question of whether I sell now or delay selling until I retire. Secondly, I'm getting absolutely fed up with these continual battles with the unions. Finally, I will be glad to be free of all the other worries and problems. Yes, I might accept the offer.

Tom: What will you do with your time if you do accept?

John: I'll take a long holiday and do plenty of fishing.

Tom: And after the holiday?

John: I'll take it easy, fish in the local river and do some painting.

Tom: All right, supposing you had been free of the business for six months – what would you be doing?

John: Still the same. Why change?

Tom: Suppose you had been fishing for most days when the weather permits for two years, what would you do then?

Long pause, and then:

John: I'd be bored stiff with fishing.

Tom: So what would you do then?

John: I would start another business.

Tom: What kind of business?

John: Printing, I guess.

Tom: So why sell now?

John: Oh. I see what you mean.

A.2.5 John Reynolds's Purpose and the Strategy Chosen

The answers to these questions, together with the information in the case, tell us, as they told John Reynolds, what his purpose was in owning the company. The main points are:

- his main interest in the company now is in the technology and in discussing ideas (artwork and method of production) for particularly interesting customer requirements;
- he wants to maintain at least his present standard of living and would not trade high opportunity/high risk for the present balance of the company;
- he wants to retain family control of the company;
- he justly has pride in his achievements in starting and building up the company over the years;
- he would prefer not to be so involved with day-to-day management (estimating, production, industrial relations, debtor chasing and accounts generally). He prefers to spend more time on the things which interest him in the company and on his leisure interests.

In this particular company, these factors caused him to pursue the mixed, limited growth strategy of computer typesetting plus jobbing printing, and to delegate the day-to-day management increasingly to Bill Williams.

A.3 The Changing Environment: Newprint (B)

A.3.1 Preparing for and Reading the Case

Consider the same company some four years later, after the chosen strategy had evolved further.

Read Newprint (B). Ask yourself what tentative conclusions you draw from the case, particularly from the two tables. How has the situation changed since the time of the Newprint (A) case? If there is further information which you consider important before confirming your view, how urgently would you need it and from what source would you seek to get it? If your initial view is confirmed, how do the time horizon for strategy choice and the choice of strategy now (in late 1980) facing John Reynolds compare with those facing him at the time of Newprint (A)?

Newprint (B)*

The previous case, 'Newprint (A)', described the company and its situation in 1976. This case describes what has happened between then and December 1980 when the UK was in deep recession.

In 1977, when Tom Bryan finished his analysis of the company's strategy alternatives, it was clear from John Reynolds's reactions that the alternative of rapid growth in the computer typesetting business was not acceptable: John Reynolds wanted to keep his majority shareholding and limit growth to that possible from internally generated funds.

Although the computer typesetting activity has since then expanded to about a third of the company's turnover, most of this is still for the tractor manufacturer. Word processing has begun to be available to others operating in this part of the market and John has seen little merit in pushing this type of work any more than the ordinary jobbing printing.

Tables A.1 and A.2 summarize the growth of the business since 1976.

Table A.1   Newprint Ltd: Performance, 1976–80

Year ending April:	Turnover £000	Profits before tax £000
1976	314	17
1977	401	24
1978	560	38
1979	770	12
1980	1,123	42

Table A.2   Newprint Ltd: Monthly Performance, 1980

Month	Turnover £000	Profit before tax[a] £000
January	121	11
February	130	39
March	68	(26)
April	138	48
May	53	(10)
June	144	18
July	80	(5)
August	105	4
September	71	(13)
October	96	(8)
November	63	(14)
December	61	(16)

[a] Figures in brackets denote a loss.

In 1978 growth began to be restricted by the physical limitations of the existing works. At about that time a more modern factory nearby with about twice the floor space became available on a freehold basis at what then was a very reasonable price. John Reynolds decided to buy it, the whole company was transferred to the new building and the remaining lease of the original premises was satisfactorily disposed of.

The company continued to grow and in 1979/80 achieved its highest ever turnover and profits. Partly as a result of this but also because of deteriorating health, John Reynolds decided to hand over the running of the business to his deputy, Bill Williams. During the early part of 1980 John Reynolds made himself available for advice whenever Bill Williams required it, but later that year John decided that Bill had developed sufficiently to take full responsibility. He therefore retired more completely, saying: 'I don't want to be contacted unless an emergency occurs – it is time you took full responsibility and stopped leaning on me.'

During 1980, because demand increased, John and Bill decided to put the three main printing machines on to double-shift working and, to support this higher planned level of activity, they increased the number of employees from 60 to 74. (Double-shift working involved paying all the men on the three printing machines and their assistants $1\frac{1}{4}$ times their normal wages.)

To support this increase in capacity the company also took on its first sales representative. His role was defined as keeping in close touch with existing customers to ensure that the company secured the bulk of their orders, that the company understood their needs and that a prompt response could be made to any criticisms of the work done.

This increased manning included three supervisors reporting to the works manager and covering each of the three main parts of the works: photography/artwork; typesetting; and printing and guillotine/binding.

At that time, when skilled labour was hard to recruit, the company took on five apprentices, hoping that they would be able to retain them three years later when they were fully trained. For similar reasons they also introduced a non-contributory sickness insurance scheme for all employees with more than one year's service.

Another innovation was a bonus scheme in the works to reward operatives whose work was completed in less than the estimated time, subject of course to maintaining quality and keeping paper wastage within certain limits. During the later part of 1980 Bill Williams decided to withdraw this bonus scheme because, although work was being completed ahead of the planned time, there was insufficient work available to allow the company to benefit from efficient working.

221

Just before Christmas 1980 John Reynolds wrote again to his old friend Tom Bryan:

I'm a little worried about Newprint Ltd. The last two monthly accounts have shown large losses. Small losses are not unusual at this time of the year but these are much larger than usual and I am not sure that all is well. Please pop in to see Bill Williams and if necessary help him to analyse what changes he should make to avoid the worst effects of the recession. If you find that the volume of business is not sufficient to maintain profitable operations, I suggest you look into the government's special short-time working scheme. I hear that for days not worked the government will refund 75% of the wages plus the national insurance contribution. I prefer not to declare redundancies, so that when the market picks up again we will have the people we need.

A.3.2 Analysis of the Newprint (B) Situation

The company's strategy in the years leading up to the time of the case has been based on increasing capacity within a growing market.

Care has to be exercised in interpreting the figures for turnover year by year in table A.1; these were the years when inflation in the UK was increasing to a peak of over 20%. However, even after detailed corrections to allow for inflation, there is still growth in volume. Further analysis would be needed to show whether the company has kept pace with a growing market or improved its market share. While national statistics would give a first indicator of this, a definite view would have to be based on analysing sales within Newprint's radius of competition, that is, within and near Newcastle. For all but the immediately previous year, this would require that copies of competitors' audited accounts be obtained from Companies House.

Table A.1 shows that in the earlier years the company had been performing reasonably well (6–7% profit/sales) but probably not as well as some of its competitors. The fall to less than 2% profit/sales in 1978/9 is worrying. There has been some recovery in 1979/80 but not to a satisfactory level. Probably the move to new premises and the computer typesetting developments have eaten into profits but, if these developments are to be beneficial, much greater improvements in performance need to be seen soon.

Moving on to table A.2 which covers some months in the year 1979/80 and further months after April in the current year, you should quickly pick up two patterns. The first is the big oscillation month by month in both turnover and profits. The second is the trend from good profits in the early months to losses in the second half of the year. You should be considering whether the company is in a survival crisis.

As far as the oscillation month by month is concerned, you should also quickly realize that, because turnover is probably recorded after the goods have been despatched and when the invoices have been sent out, the oscillations are probably caused by some combination of:

- bunching of large orders being completed;
- statutory holidays;
- works holidays;
- bunching of preparation and posting of invoices.

Provided that invoicing is not unduly delayed, the oscillation should not cause any worry. But to get a clearer picture it is better to look at a moving average covering three or four months. This will show up the marked decline in the second half of the year. With hindsight, of course, it is easy to see the coincidence with the start of the deep UK recession of the early 1980s.

With the possibility of a survival crisis looming, urgent checks must be made. What about the bank overdraft? Is there usually a decline in turnover and a period of losses before Christmas? What were the figures for the months in the second half of last year?

In the real situation on which this case is based, the answers to these questions were available within a few minutes. Turnover does tend to decline before Christmas but the decline this year is much worse than normal. The bank overdraft limit has been a problem. It was breached some weeks ago but action on debtors brought the level back within the limit. Since then the limit has been breached again on more than one occasion and it is becoming increasingly difficult to keep within it. In short, the company does have a survival crisis on its hands.

So, in contrast to Newprint (A), when things were going well and the company could look to the medium term and choose between several strategies, in Newprint (B) the time horizon is very short and there is only one strategy that can be contemplated – a survival strategy.

The next question is whether the crisis has been brought about by the company's own actions, perhaps the efforts on computer typesetting and staff increases, or whether it is the environment which has changed, with the result that competitors are also having the same problems.

Again, this is a question which can be, and was, quickly answered. Given the small radius of competition and the closely knit nature of the printing industry, employees who meet socially with printers from other companies will quickly know of any short-time working nearby. Within a few further minutes the answer from the print room was that some competitors were already on short-time working.

So the core of Newprint's problems at the time of this case is that it has been pursuing a strategy of growth and increasing capacity in a growing market and is now faced with a significant market downturn and excess capacity. Unless the market recovers again within a few weeks, the company must cut its wages costs to prevent collapse. But how much excess capacity is there, and how much will wages and other costs have to be reduced to stem the outflow of cash? Will the company be able to deal with the industrial relations problems quickly enough, and if so, how? How soon will it be before the bank manager wakes up to the dangers? Will the company need a temporary increase in the overdraft limit? Should a request be made to see the bank manager, rather than wait for him to call the managing director in? These and other problems had to be urgently addressed and to be followed by actions within the next few days.

A.3.3 Remedial Actions Taken

One of the directors became sufficiently concerned to cause a meeting of the available directors the following morning. During that morning an outline strategy addressing the crisis was agreed and actions were started to pursue it.

The two core problems which the chosen strategy addressed were:

- the uncertainty as to how far the market had actually fallen and how much further it would fall;
- how to gain co-operation from the employees rather than run into a strike which could quickly put the company into the hands of the receiver.

It was agreed that one of the directors should address all the employees that afternoon to alert them to the crisis and to the actions which the board proposed to take. Employees' questions would be welcomed but this was not a negotiating meeting. The employees should then consult their shop stewards with a view to a meeting between the directors and union officials later the same week.

The directors also agreed at the morning meeting that an appointment be made to see the bank manager the next day, to alert him to the situation and the actions proposed.

The board agreed that if the government's special scheme for short-time working was as it appeared at first sight, then the company should seek to register under the scheme, to cut its costs and give it more time to understand what was happening in the market.

The message to be put to the employees, and to the union representatives later the same week, was clear. The interests of the company and of the employees alike lay in ensuring that as much of the company as possible survived. Pulling together for this end was essential and any ideas would be welcomed. Subject to certain conditions the company proposed to register under the government's short-time working scheme. This required that redundancy notices be issued and that they then be withdrawn by agreement between the company and the unions as one of the conditions for entering the scheme. The company would have full freedom to vary the numbers of days worked per week but this was expected to be either three or four days for most employees and occasionally five days for some to clear bottlenecks. For the other days, pay would be no more than that received from the scheme. During the period of six months during which the company would be in the scheme, every attempt would be made to improve the company's position and save jobs. Nevertheless it was almost inevitable that several redundancies would follow at the end of that period. The number of redundancies in each of the parts of the company would be for the company to decide, but which individuals this would affect would be matter for negotiation. Redundancy payments would be no more than the minimum required under the legislation.

The directors had already offered to share the 'pain', accepting a 10% reduction in their pay.

It was made clear that without this agreement the only alternatives were immediate redundancies or the company closing.

The employees were concerned that they should not listen to the directors without consulting the unions first. However, once it was made clear that the meeting was only for information and understanding on their part, they agreed to attend.

The bank manager was seen the following day. He had not realized that there was a crisis. He was impressed with the company's speed of action and, subject to the employees and their unions agreeing to the company's plan, was prepared to agree a short-term increase in the overdraft limit.

Later that week the officials of the unions concerned met the directors and agreed to go ahead on the basis proposed.

Other actions taken, and agreed with the employees where necessary, were:

- Withdrawal of the second shift and the return of the supervisors to machine operation.
- Withdrawal of the sickness scheme in return for a small increase in wage levels at the normal yearly review.

- Renewed efforts by the accounts clerk to chase up debtors, backed up where necessary with direct telephone calls by the managing director or visits by the sales representative.
- Individual attention by the managing director to all estimates for large orders. In an environment where capacity utilization is critical, the battle for survival is mainly about winning a better share of large orders. The salesman's knowledge of competitors and indications of their prices for a particular job was critical to a decision on whether to drop the price to get an order. For such potential orders the paper supplier was in a similar position and so a deal could be struck for the paper price for that particular estimate to be dropped in parallel with a larger reduction of the estimate by the company.
- Detailed line-by-line reduction in the budget, including no recruitment, no new commitments on training, no entertainment without the express approval of the managing director beforehand, etc.
- A change in the remit of the salesman, requiring him also to chase new business.
- A temporary addition to the sales effort, by putting one of the more suitable craft printers out on the road in a territory not well covered previously.
- Efforts to reduce waste, discussions being held with the employees to find ways of reducing the levels of waste of paper and electricity (machine operation, lighting and heating).

The results were encouraging. A co-operative working mood developed. Cash flow held and then began slowly to recover. A few of the employees decided to leave and take up jobs elsewhere (presumably where the industry crisis had not been recognized!). At the end of the six months, fewer redundancies were necessary than had been feared. These went ahead quickly and in line with the agreement. The climate within the company had changed from one of 'us and them' to one of easier communication and greater collaboration.

The only important problem during this crisis period was that, because of the short-time working, the larger orders took a noticeably longer time to complete. In one case this soured client relationships, which had to be carefully nurtured back to health.

A.3.4 Lessons from the Case

The executives and directors of Newprint have learnt from this experience. They are now more careful when considering increases in capacity and prefer making such expansion in several small steps rather than one large jump. They are also much more cost- and profit-conscious. The company performed better in the mid- to late 1980s than over the five years prior to its survival crisis of 1980–1. It coped better with the deeper recession of the early 1990s and is now in a good position to perform well in the second half of the 1990s. Reflecting his motivation as discussed earlier, in 1995, John Reynolds, who by then had passed normal retirement age, sold the company via a management buy-out to Bill Williams and the other two executive directors.

Now look back on this case. In the real situation, why did it take several weeks for the company to realize that a crisis was developing?

First, because not even the figures given in table A.2 were available to them. All they had was total sales in the company year to date, so good sales in the spring/early summer period obscured the downturn later in the year. And even if they were to separate out the figures month by month as in table A.2, it was difficult to see the underlying pattern without smoothing the oscillations. Also, they did not have last year's figures handy for comparison.

When action did occur it was already three or four months too late, with the result that significant haemorrhage of funds had already occurred. What else could have been done to recognize the problem earlier and so reduce this outflow of funds?

The underlying cause of the problem was the start in the UK of the deep world recession of the early 1980s. The market in which Newprint was operating had suddenly collapsed. The company had to recognize the signals and then the causes. But sales figures in the accounts reflect market conditions about three months previously. The accounts record completed orders despatched to customers. Some of the delay in realizing that the market had collapsed could have been reduced if the directors had been receiving monthly or even weekly totals of orders received. An even earlier signal would have been information on the totals of the quotations being sent out.

The directors now do receive regular information on both sales and total order intake, month by month. If these figures cause concern they can also quickly obtain information on the totals of the quotations being sent out.

With hindsight, one can also look at what has happened to computer typesetting. Newprint and most leading printing companies now use bought-in standard computer typesetting equipment. Computer typesetting turns out to have been a core technology development for the industry. Did Newprint err by investing in leading this development or gain by being experienced when standard equipment became available? In analysing the 1976 position, we were right to separate the computer typesetting TOWS matrix from that for jobbing printing. However, computer typesetting is now involved in the production to meet most of the company's orders and of those of its main competitors. If we were wanting to analyse the strategy forwards from now it would be appropriate to use just one TOWS matrix for which computer typesetting equipment would be part of the equipment of each of the competitors.

Appendix B

Using the More Detailed Framework: Weston Hydraulics Ltd

Introduction to the Case
Analysis of Weston's Situation
The Recommendations from the Project
What has Happened since this Project was Carried Out?

B.1 Introduction to the Case

The purpose of this appendix is to illustrate the use of the more detailed general framework for analysing the strategy of a business, as described on pages 48–53.

The case of Weston Hydraulics Ltd is one I use in my teaching as the starting-point for a progressive experience of what this type of analysis involves in practice. The progression moves through different steps in the analysis and reveals how the picture of the company and its strategic issues builds up as the study proceeds. So, in the teaching environment, extra information beyond that given in the case itself is supplied as the teaching progresses. This is what will also be done here. The view of the 'iceberg' which gradually develops will also be described here, together with the normal uncertainties about the accuracy of the view that is being developed.

Appendix B

Weston Hydraulics Ltd is the actual name of the company, which was located in Birmingham at the time of the case but has since moved to Redditch. The data given and the names of some of the people involved are factual; this has been possible with the agreement of the people concerned, so as to expose as much as possible of the reality of the situation.

Norman Gidney, the Chairman of Warwick Engineering Investments Ltd, contacted me just after his group had bought Weston. Before that stage he obviously had a view of the actions which were intended to be taken once Weston was acquired. After the takeover he had developed these views further. To make more sure that no important fact had been overlooked and to open up other ideas, he asked me to carry out an independent analysis of Weston.

Specifically, my remit was to recommend:

- what short-term actions should be taken to improve the performance of Weston;
- what longer-term strategy should be pursued;
- what the relationship, if any, should be between Weston and another company in the group, Mechanical Tools and Gauges (MTG).

The whole study was to be carried out quickly and in fact took just two weeks over Christmas 1983. Norman Gidney contacted the managing directors of Weston and MTG to explain my remit and to ask them to give me the necessary assistance.

This appendix describes how I used the framework to analyse this particular situation. Strategic thinking and strategy decisions do not suddenly happen, they evolve. Both Norman Gidney's thoughts and mine led to the actions which followed, and subsequent developments in the competitive environment also influenced the sequence of decisions in the following years. To show how the picture developed in this early period relates to later actions and events, the last section of this appendix is devoted to a description of what has happened to Weston and associated activities since the time described in the case.

The case itself gives the information available to me at the start of the remit. When you have read it through, you will be in the same position as I was at the start of the consultancy project.

Weston Hydraulics Ltd (A)*

Weston Hydraulics Ltd manufactures hydraulic cylinders (often known as 'rams'). The case is set in December 1983, only a few days after Weston had been sold by its parent company, Butterfield Harvey plc, to Warwick Engineering Investments Ltd.

The Hydraulic Cylinder (or Ram) Industry

Figure B.1 shows the parts of a typical hydraulic cylinder or ram. Rams are telescopic components of the moving parts of many types of mechanical equipment. They operate by valve-based control of a fluid (oil or grease).

There are well over 200 equipment manufacturers in the UK that use rams in the construction of a wide variety of equipment. There is little import or export of rams. The total import value is thought to be about £6 million per year, often from other companies within the same engineering groups as the equipment manufacturer. The value of rams manufactured in the UK is about £100 million per year. Of this total, about three quarters are manufactured in-house by the equipment makers themselves – most of the larger companies which use more than £1 million per year of rams, manufacture in-house. These equipment manufacturers who manufacture most of their own rams do, however, buy in some rams, particularly at times of sudden increases in demand. For these requirements they and the other (usually smaller) equipment manufacturers purchase some £22 million worth per year of rams from independent sources. Table B.1 summarizes the usage of rams (both bought in and made in-house) by UK equipment manufacturers.

Table B.1 Rams used by UK equipment manufacturers

Type of equipment	% by value of total ram usage
Earth moving and agricultural	40
Mining (mainly roof supports)	27
Fork-lift trucks	13
Vehicles, trailers and attachments	12
Aircraft	1
Cranes, hoists, presses and miscellaneous	7

Rams vary in size from small rams (2 inches in diameter and 1 foot in length) right through to those large rams (24 inches in diameter and 40 feet in length) used in, for example, large construction equipment.

* Copyright © B. T. Houlden 1984.
(The 'B' case is not reproduced here.)

231

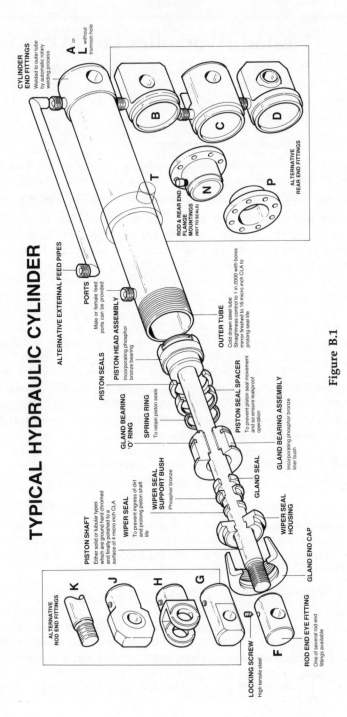

TYPICAL HYDRAULIC CYLINDER

CYLINDER END FITTINGS
Welded to outer tube by automatic rotary welding process

A or **L** without trunnion hole

ALTERNATIVE EXTERNAL FEED PIPES

PORTS
Male or female feed ports can be provided

PISTON SEALS

PISTON HEAD ASSEMBLY
Incorporating phosphor bronze bearing

GLAND BEARING 'O' RING

SPRING RING
To retain piston seals

WIPER SEAL SUPPORT BUSH
Phosphor bronze

WIPER SEAL
To prevent ingress of dirt and prolong piston shaft life

PISTON SHAFT
Either solid or tubular types which are ground hard chromed and finally polished to a surface of 4 micro inch CLA

ALTERNATIVE ROD END FITTINGS

LOCKING SCREW
High tensile steel

ROD END EYE FITTING
One of several rod end fittings available

GLAND END CAP

WIPER SEAL HOUSING

GLAND SEAL

GLAND BEARING ASSEMBLY
Incorporating phosphor bronze liner bush

PISTON SEAL SPACER
To prevent piston seal movement and so ensure leakproof operation

OUTER TUBE
Cold drawn steel tube
Straightness control to 1 in 2000 with bores mirror finished to 16 micro inch CLA to prolong seal life

ROD & REAR END FLANGE MOUNTINGS
(NOT TO SCALE)

ALTERNATIVE REAR END FITTINGS

Figure B.1

232

The recession of the early 1980s took its toll on both equipment manufacturers and ram manufacturers. There are now probably some 80 'free-market' manufacturers of rams, ranging from companies like Parker Hannifin, Edbro, Cascade UK, Chamberlain Industries and Cessna Fluid Power (each of which, among other activities, manufactures over £1 million worth of small to medium-sized rams per year), right through to the smallest engineering companies, with total turnover in all products of less than £100,000 per year, which also manufacture small rams in smaller quantities.

Warwick Engineering Investments Ltd (WEI)

Gidney Securities is the ultimate holding company for WEI. Gidney Securities is wholly owned by its founder Norman Gidney and his wife. Norman Gidney is also chairman of WEI.

WEI is a group with a turnover of some £25 million per year embracing eight wholly owned subsidiary engineering companies operating in various areas of the metal processing and mechanical engineering sectors. Only one of these companies, Mechanical Tools and Gauges (MTG) Ltd, is involved in the hydraulic engineering business. It specializes in the honing (that is, the internal polishing) of the steel tubes used in the manufacture of rams. It has a turnover of about £3 million per year and is a well-managed company with a good record of growth and profitability.

Norman Gidney is a successful entrepreneur, now 52 years of age. He was born dyslexic. This hampered his schooling and left an ambition frustrated by lack of educational achievement. On leaving school, like many of his contemporaries he joined an engineering company as an apprentice. In 1950 he joined the Army and rapidly rose to the rank of major in the Military Police. This career gave him the insight into human behaviour and confidence in his own ability so necessary to his eventual success in business.

After leaving the Army he and a colleague decided to start in business on their own by buying a small engineering firm. Since then Norman Gidney's path has not been all plain sailing: on his own admission he has made major mistakes – but both these and his successes have developed him into the successful businessman he is today.

As with many manufacturing businesses. WEI was badly hit by the recession which began in 1980. The slow recovery since then has in most cases left its subsidiaries facing markets where the demand is still well below the peaks reached in the 1970s. For example, even though it has competed well and gained market share, MTG in 1983 had a turnover some 10% in value below the pre-recession level. On the plus side, the recession saw a determined effort, stimulated by Norman Gidney himself throughout the companies in the WEI group, to make them leaner and more competitive.

Before the recession, WEI had a group office staff of eight professionals, including two joint managing directors, plus eight secretaries, with Norman Gidney as chairman. As a result of the economies made during the recession, Norman Gidney is now more closely in touch with all of the subsidiaries and the group staff has been reduced to Norman Gidney himself plus two accountants and two secretaries.

The group's performance has recovered from the worst effects of the recession. The purchase of Weston Hydraulics represents one of a small number of recent purchases of companies still in the recovery stage, these purchases having being made at lower prices than would have been possible before the recession. Approximately £600,000 was paid for Weston.

Weston Hydraulics: History and Current Performance

Founded in 1943 to manufacture and supply industrial hydraulics, Weston was taken over in 1971 by Butterfield Harvey plc, a public company with subsidiaries in engineering, furniture manufacture, plastic moulding and the factoring of marine equipment and clothing. In 1983–4 Butterfield Harvey had a turnover of £45 million p.a. and had experienced losses before tax over a period of four years ranging from 7% to 1% of turnover.

Weston Hydraulics manufactures medium-sized to large rams; the largest share of its output goes to UK crane manufacturers.

Over the period 1973–8, when UK demand for rams first dropped slightly and then recovered to its initial level in volume terms, Weston performed only moderately. It lost about a sixth of its share of the total ram market and its profits before tax averaged about 4% of turnover.

The pattern then changed. In 1978 a new managing director was appointed; he stayed until early 1983 when he was replaced. Over this period performance was as shown in table B.2.

Table B.2 Performance of Weston Hydraulics, 1978–1983

Year to April:	Sales £m	Profit before tax/sales %
1978	2.4	+3
1979	2.5	−15
1980	2.2	−5
1981	2.5	−2
1982	3.1	−5
1983	2.2	−7

By late 1983, the position of the company was as follows:

- losses were continuing;
- the four executive directors saw no sign of an upturn in the market for rams;
- the budget agreed only a month or so previously was being revised downwards;
- some of the spare space was being rented out to an importer of equipment but, with factory space generally in excess of demand, the rental income was poor;
- an activity producing special leg fittings for handicapped children which had been introduced a year or so previously to take up some of the spare machining capacity was producing sales of the order of £50,000 p.a. with moderate profits;
- the former marketing director, appointed from outside the company about two years previously, had been managing director for about a year;
- morale was low.

B.2 Analysis of Weston's Situation

B.2.1 Preparatory Work before Visiting the Companies

It was necessary first to be clear as to how the supply of steel tubes, the honing of the interior surface of these tubes, ram manufacture and the manufacture of equipment related to each other. Figure B.2 (overleaf) summarizes the relationship between these stages and the companies involved in the UK. Some three quarters of the rams required by equipment manufacturers are manufactured by the equipment manufacturers themselves, some of whom also do their own honing. Some of the independent ram manufacturers also do their own honing; they supply roughly a quarter of the rams required by the equipment manufacturers, usually those with insufficient output to warrant in-house manufacture of rams. This overview leads to two conclusions:

- honing and ram manufacture at this time were too dependent on supply from British Steel. With the opening up of the market to European competition, companies in both honing and ram manufacture would be vulnerable to imports from Europe as exchange rates and steel prices outside the UK changed.
- the degree to which equipment manufacturers manufactured their own rams (and the degree to which ram manufacturers did their own

Steel tube supply	Honing	Ram manufacture	Equipment manufacture
Mainly British Steel	British Steel	Some of the equipment manufacturers	Equipment manufacturers
Some imports	Some of the equipment manufacturers	Independent ram manufacturers	
	Some of the independent ram manufacturers		
	Independent honing companies including MTG		

Figure B.2 Ram manufacturing and its relationship to tube and equipment manufacture.

honing) would change not only as demand changed but also as competition increased and companies were forced to focus more sharply to remain competitive.

The second preparatory stage was to find out whether there were any national statistics on ram manufacture or on the level of output of the main sectors of equipment manufacture in which rams are used.

Table B.3 gives the sales of rams by the independent UK ram manufacturers. The information in the second column is taken from the HMSO publication *Business Monitor*, which surveys all manufacturers above a particular size. You will notice that there are two figures for 1980. In that year the basis of the statistics was changed. Prior to 1980, all companies with 25 or more employees were covered. From 1980 onwards, only those with 35 or more employees were covered. When using statistical summaries such as these, it is important to check the wording to ensure that the statistical base is understood, to find out if it has been changed during

The More Detailed Framework

Table B.3 Sales of Rams by UK Manufacturers, 1972–1983

Year	Sales £m[a]	Calculated % change on previous year
1972	6.5	
1973	12.1	+87
1974	14.6	+21
1975	17.5	+20
1976	19.2	+10
1977	25.9	+35
1978	31.6	+22
1979	30.8	−3
1980	32.2	+6
1980	31.6	+6
1981	28.8	−9
1982	26.8	−7
1983	20.6	−23

[a] *Source: Business Monitor* (London, HMSO, various years)

the sequence and to establish what proportion of the total of all employees this sample covers. In this particular case, the survey has covered 92% of the total, and the change in the cut-off point has only marginally affected the total sales figure. We can conclude that in 1983 the total free market for rams was of the order of £22 million p.a.

What do these figures show? There is a need to be cautious because inflation was at high levels during the 1970s, when, for example, steel tube prices increased five-fold and labour costs four-fold. Without detailed correction for inflation, we can probably safely say that the market increased overall up to about 1978, with booms in 1973 and 1978, but that certainly from 1979 to 1983 there was a substantial fall in the total market, probably to less than half its 1978 volume.

Thus we may come to understand how the market decline, which must have begun earlier in this industry than the main UK recession, which started in 1980, has affected companies such as Weston. Weston has been in an environment where many ram manufacturers have been going under.

Figure B.3(a)–(e) summarizes similar information, from other issues of *Business Monitor*, for the levels of activity in the customer industries – the equipment manufacturers. In each of these figures the line marked 'Actual £' is based on *Business Monitor* data. The line marked '1982 £' is my attempt to correct these data for inflation. To do this I have developed my own inflation index, using other national statistics on steel tube prices and wage rates in the mechanical engineering industry. The correction made is therefore a coarse correction.

237

Appendix B

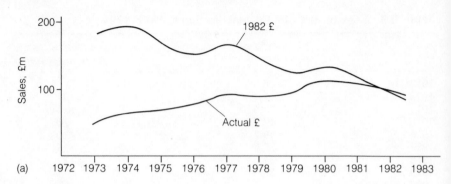

(a)

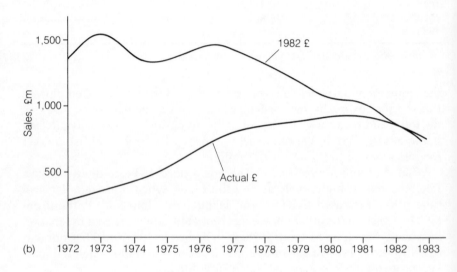

(b)

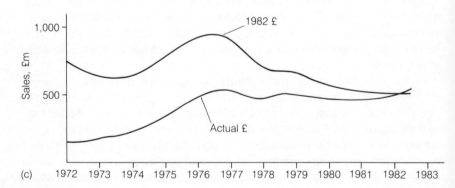

(c)

238

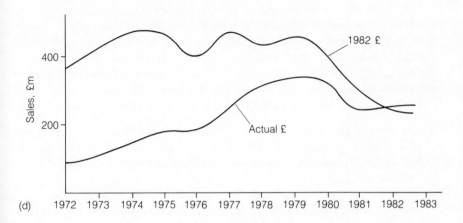

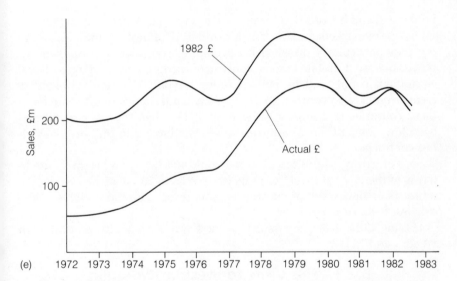

Figure B.3 Sales of equipment using hydraulic cylinders, by UK manufacturers, 1972–1983: (a) power-operated mobile cranes; (b) earth-moving and construction equipment (and parts); (c) wheeled tractors; (d) fork-lift trucks; (e) mining roof supports.

239

What picture do these figures give us? Taken together, they broadly confirm the overall conclusion from table B.3 – that is, that over the latter part of this period companies in the ram manufacturing industry were fighting for survival in a depressed market. The figures also tell us, not unexpectedly, that these various markets are subject to boom and slump, the times for each varying among the different sectors.

Looking at the sectors individually, the main conclusions are:

- the market for larger rams, on which Weston is focused and which is heavily dependent on the power-operated mobile cranes sector, has declined more than most and has been in long-term decline since 1973–4;
- of all the sectors represented, that for fork-life trucks collapsed most rapidly with the start of the 1980 recession; it may have already reached its lowest level by 1983 and be ready to start recovery, although probably at a slow rate.

Looking ahead beyond 1983, we can also say that, dependent as they are on overseas markets for construction and agricultural equipment, and in the past particularly on oil-rich developing countries, the markets for power-operated mobile cranes, construction equipment and agricultural equipment could well be still declining beyond 1983 and unlikely to recover quickly. In contrast to the 1970s when the price of oil soared and these countries had money to burn, in 1983, when the price of oil had been low, some of these countries were even having to pull out of existing contracts.

So, at the time of the case, Weston could not look to a bright future in terms of the level of turnover in its present focus. It either had to change its focus or find ways of cutting its costs to become more viable at the existing level of the markets.

Having done this preparatory work I was then ready to visit both Weston and MTG.

B.2.2   The Visits to Weston Hydraulics

Having experienced five years of losses and having now been taken over by another group, it was to be expected that the senior executives of Weston would be anticipating a further period of redundancies, perhaps including themselves. My role had to be to focus on the future of the company and to encourage them to talk while I would mainly listen.

The main conclusions I drew from what I heard were:

- not unexpectedly, morale was low;
- the senior executives of the company had few ideas on how to make it more successful;
- the way in which prices were calculated appeared to contain flaws;

- pricing policy appeared to be inflexible;
- the company's knowledge of the total free market for rams contained major errors;
- the company appeared to have a distinctive strength in its design function;
- the leg-fittings business appeared to be occupying much more of the time of the senior executives than its size warranted, possibly to the detriment of its ram business.

I then looked around the works and talked with some of the employees as I did so. The low level of morale extended to the work force on the shop floor. During the tour I noted the following:

- not unexpectedly, there was plenty of spare space and a low labour density across the equipment;
- most of the equipment was old (again, not surprising, given the five years of losses).

I asked about the purchase of honed tube from the independent honing companies. Weston did not do any honing itself. Most honed tube came straight from British Steel. Approximately £14,000 p.a. of honing was done by MTG and some £28,000 p.a. by other independent honing companies. My conclusion from this was that while some relationship between Weston and MTG might be appropriate, a very close linkage between the two in production was inappropriate.

The Managing Director of Weston gave me audited copies of the previous year's accounts, shown here in tables B.4 and B.5. We discussed the accounts of the previous years and in particular the levels of numbers employed in the works and the offices. It was clear that considerable efforts had been made to reduce direct costs, but that office staffing was static and, with the falling level of demand, had increased significantly as a proportion of the total and hence of total costs.

Table B.4 Weston Hydraulics Ltd: Profit and Loss Account for year ending 2 April 1983

	1983	1982
Turnover	£2,216,729	£3,121,047
Trading loss before exceptional item	(£98,940)	(£121,901)
Exceptional item: redundancy payments	(73,229)	(£20,000)
	(£172,169)	(£141,901)
Taxation	(£104,400)	(£60,303)
Loss after taxation	(£67,769)	(£81,598)
Depreciation of building written back on revaluation	£64,089	–
Loss for the year	(£3,680)	(£81,598)

Appendix B

Table B.5 Weston Hydraulics Ltd: Balance Sheet for year ending 2 April 1983

	2 April 1983		3 April 1982
ASSETS EMPLOYED			
Current Assets			
Stock and work in progress	£619,039		£944,336
Debtors	£603,790		£981,599
Bank balance and cash in hand	£591		£1,605
Amount due from fellow subsidiaries	–		£4,932
		£1,223,420	£1,932,472
Current liabilities			
Creditors	£321,492		£1,132,359
Amount due to fellow subsidiaries	£24,585		£15,101
Bank overdraft (secured)	£40		£1,520
		£346,117	£1,148,980
Net current assets		£877,303	£783,492
Fixed assets		£490,104	£532,031
		£1,367,407	£1,315,523
CAPITAL EMPLOYED			
Share capital		£63,300	£63,300
Reserves		£146,509	£212,483
Shareholders' funds		£209,809	£275,783
Unsecured loan stock 2001		£750,000	£750,000
Amount due to parent company		407,598	£289,740
		£1,367,407	£1,315,523

My conclusion from this and from the view of the market's future was that office costs had to be cut to bring them more into line with the levels of the market.

I also asked for information on competitors and customers.

Although those ram manufacturers who concentrate in the production of medium-sized rams occasionally make some larger rams, surprisingly there was only one competitor of importance: Spenborough Ltd. It was important that I should obtain copies of their accounts from Companies House.

Table B.6 summarizes Weston's pattern of customers in 1983. With one customer, Coles Cranes, taking such a high proportion of total sales, it was important also to get this company's accounts.

Table B.6 Weston's Customer Profile

Customer company or sector	% of Weston's total sales
Coles Cranes	45
Coventry Climax and other fork-lift truck manufacturers	15
Babcock and other mining equipment manufacturers	13
Truck and vehicle manufacturers, excavator manufacturers and miscellaneous	27

B.2.3 The Visit to Companies House

The next stage in the analysis was to visit Companies House to obtain copies of the accounts of Spenborough and Coles Cranes. A summary of these accounts is reproduced in tables B.7 and B.8.

Table B.7 Performance of Spenborough, 1978–1984

Year	Turnover £m	Profit (loss) before tax/turnover %
1978	1.4	+8
1979	1.5	+10
1980	1.4	+8
1981	1.3	−3
1982	1.0	−7
1983	1.0	−7
1984	1.0	−7

Table B.8 Performance of Coles Cranes, 1972–1983

Year	Turnover £m	Profit (loss) before tax/sales %
1972	23	+7
1973	17	−7
1974	23	−1
1975	31	+6
1976	49	+8
1977	53	+8
1978	69	+5
1979	73	+5
1980	69	+4
1981	69	−1
1982	83	−2
1983	72	−14

Appendix B

Comparing Spenborough's performance with that of Weston (see pages 241 and 242), it is clear that before the UK recession began in 1980, Spenborough was performing better than Weston. Since then the performance of the two companies has been similar. Weston has a larger share of the market and has maintained this through the period 1980–3. Because Spenborough is a private company and did not have a larger group to protect it, it could well go into receivership soon if its performance did not recover. But could Weston rely on this?

The information on Coles Cranes, summarized in table B.8, caused immediate concern. Could Weston's main customer be about to go into receivership? It was part of the Acrow Group, so that group's accounts were also obtained. In the year ending 1983, the group as a whole incurred losses of the order of £10 million, virtually all arising from Coles Cranes, which was a major part of the group. Could the group as a whole go into receivership shortly?

B.2.4   The Visit to MTG

The purposes of the visit to MTG were:

- to understand its business and how well it was doing;
- to get the Managing Director's view of the state of the hydraulic equipment business and its future.

Similar ground was covered to that in my visit to Weston. I walked around the works to see the production process and also discussed the purchasing of steel tube and the marketing of the honing activity. The view I had developed on the industry in general was largely confirmed, thus strengthening the foundation for any recommendations.

The main conclusions from my visit to MTG were:

- although MTG had suffered from the recession, being the leading independent honing company with a turnover of some £3 million p.a., it was in a stronger position than its competitors and was still marginally profitable;
- the rest of the independent honing industry was probably making losses;
- the second largest independent honing company, Honing and Tubes, which had a turnover of some £2 million p.a. and had been fighting for market share against MTG, was in trouble. It had recently lost some £3/4 million of orders and would therefore be making heavy losses. I made an estimate of the effect of this loss of business on its financial performance. It was vulnerable to takeover and might be

bought cheaply with the result that rationalization could lead to price recovery and more viable levels of operation for all the independent honing companies.

B.3 The Recommendations from the Project

My report on the project presented the above information together with other relevant details collected during the study. This information, together with the knowledge already in the group, meant that the group then had a stronger basis for its future strategy in this area of activity.

The recommendations, often confirming Norman Gidney's own views, were as follows.

In the short term:

- Cut the number of directors at Weston and the level of staff and other overheads to reflect the new level of the market.
- Take a view on the leg-fittings business. Decide whether it can be expanded to a turnover of the order of £$^1/_4$ million p.a. within two years with a good level of profit or not. If it can, then it needs someone to 'run fast' with it. If not, it should be sold to a company with other products and a sales activity in the health field.
- Be wary of Coles Cranes possibly passing into receivership. They are too important a customer to ditch but care is needed to keep deliveries not yet paid for within reasonable limits.
- Buy Honing and Tubes, then rationalize the MTG and Honing and Tubes activities and bring prices to a more viable level.

With plenty of spare factory space elsewhere, thanks to the recession, I considered it better to retain the spare space at Weston until either it was needed again or industrial property prices recovered.

On the relationship between Weston and MTG, I concluded that, while there were some common interests, they should remain as separate largely autonomous profit centres but have a common top executive. Let me explain the reasoning behind this. Their production processes were entirely different and even if all the honing done by other independent honers were brought into the group, this was nowhere near sufficient to warrant physically moving one of the two companies to be next to the other. Weston sells to equipment manufacturers whereas MTG sells to ram manufacturers and to those equipment manufacturers who make their own rams. So the marketing activities are different. But both marketing activities need to develop a view on what is happening in the total market: they could therefore benefit from a periodic exchange of views. The only major opportunity for synergy was considered to be in purchasing, where MTG had a strength and, for a larger volume, could provide a better service for the two companies jointly.

Over the medium to long term, Weston would have to seek growth from some combination of increased exports to Europe and expansion into medium-sized rams. The ram manufacturing industry could be divided into three segments, roughly as in figure B.4.

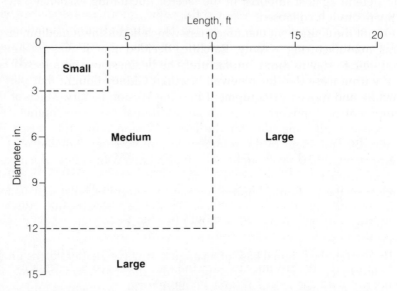

Figure B.4 The segment of the ram manufacturing industry.

The volume segment, producing medium-sized rams, contains most of the larger companies and appears to offer more growth in the medium term than does the large rams segment. The segment in which Weston was operating requires larger equipment and overhead cranes suitable for moving large rams around the works. The small rams segment is not an attractive segment for Weston to enter; it contains most of the smaller companies including small general engineering companies which enter and leave it from time to time. Entry and exit costs are lower in the small ram segment than for the other two segments.

B.4 What has Happened since this Project was Carried Out?

All except one of the directors left Weston. Non-direct labour and other overhead expenses were cut. Honing and Tubes was bought and both it and MTG became reasonably profitable.

Acrow did pass into receivership. This was a difficult time for Weston. The international crane group, Groves Cranes, bought Coles from the receiver and integrated it into its European operations. Weston was able to maintain its position in the large rams business but, as with any activity where the radius of customers' activities increased, so the radius of competition for Weston increased. Both Weston and MTG had to export and defend against imports, in the face of fluctuating exchange rates.

Spenborough collapsed.

One of the equipment manufacturers which had its own medium-sized rams manufacturing activity, Ratcliffe, decided that it was no longer economic to stay in ram manufacture. The business was in a leased factory with a lease due for renewal. Norman Gidney bought that part of Ratcliffe and moved its equipment into the Weston factory. Much of the equipment was modern and with an additional computer numerically controlled (CNC) machine for the larger Weston rams, this raised the quality of equipment in the company to a more competitive level.

Norman Gidney also bought two other related companies which were in some difficulty. These were the ram manufacturer Cattermole, of Redditch, and the hydraulic equipment manufacturer Telehoist, of Cheltenham, which had its own small activity in ram manufacture. Weston, including Ratcliffe, was moved to Redditch and integrated with Cattermole.

Thus, from the original base of an engineering conglomerate, the group was developed around this capability. Hydraulic engineering became one of the main thrusts of the group as a whole. The fragmented ram sector has been rationalized and concentrated.

Before moving on to the next appendix, look again at conglomerate groups on pages 123–4 to see how this action by Norman Gidney also strengthened the competitiveness of the group as a whole.

Recently Norman Gidney sold this group of hydraulic engineering businesses.

Appendix C

Using the Group Strategy Framework: Steel Springs Ltd

Introduction to the Case
Analysis of Steel Springs' Situation

C.1 Introduction to the Case

The case of Steel Springs Ltd concerns not a real company but an artificial company composed of features of different companies. Its origins lie in some consultancy work which I did for the chief executive of a group. He required a fuller understanding of the competitive environment of the group's subsidiary engaged in the manufacture of cold coil wire springs. As part of that project I analysed competition in the whole of the springs 'industry'.

Most real group situations are so complex that a very long case would be necessary to explain the group, before using it as an example to explain group strategy. The Steel Springs case was created to overcome this difficulty in illustrating the use of the group strategy framework.

Now read the case. As you go through it, decide what are the main strategy issues facing the group. Then consider the organization, in terms of the role which the group should play in relation to the individual subsidiaries and whether any of these should be merged.

Steel Springs Ltd*

Springs come in very many shapes and sizes. They can be grouped together under three main sectors:

- *Heavy leaf and laminated springs*, used mainly in the suspension of heavy vehicles plus a few cars. This sector is not involved in this case and therefore will not be described further.
- *Bedding and upholstery springs*. These springs are relatively easy to make. The total UK market is worth about £26 million per year and is dominated by seven relatively large manufacturers, of which the two largest have over 1,000 employees. An order for a particular type of spring is usually worth several thousands of pounds.
- *Light springs used in general engineering*. The total UK market is about £110 million p.a., of which about £60 million is for what is known as cold coil wire springs (i.e. springs made by twisting wire into the required shape at normal temperatures). The other £50 million per year of the light springs market includes spring washers, spring presswork and watch and clock springs.

Steel Springs Ltd consists of four subsidiaries, one making bedding springs and the other three cold coil wire springs.

Most cold coil wire springs cost a few pence each and an order for a particular type of spring varies from, say, £10 up to a few thousands of pounds. The springs vary in the type and thickness of wire used, the shape and overall size of the spring itself and the shaping of the ends of the springs. To meet the variety of springs which customers require, most manufacturers have a range of spring-making machines. These machines coil the wire into the basic form of the spring. Other machines are used to grind the ends of the springs; other end shapes are formed usually by female labour, using various hand tools and jigs.

One of the features of the cold coil wire spring part of the industry is the ease with which skilled operators of the coiling machinery can buy up second-hand machines and set up in business on their own with low overheads, producing the simpler springs of moderate quality at low price. As a result, this part of the industry in the UK contains about 200 manufacturers, some three quarters of whom have less than 50 employees each.

Of the springs produced, about two thirds are bought by vehicle manufacturers or by their component suppliers. Outside the vehicle industry,

* Copyright © B. T. Houlden 1979.

249

there is a wide variety of users of these springs, of which the domestic electrical appliances industry is probably the largest. Roughly 8% of the UK output is exported directly (there are of course many other springs manufactured in the UK which are exported as parts of products). Conversely, roughly 15% of the UK demand for light springs is met by imports.

Steel Springs Ltd is a privately owned company with four subsidiaries. The chairman, George Taylor, has a secretary but there are no other group staff, all the other active directors and any other staff and resources being part of one or other of the four highly autonomous subsidiary companies.

The company began in 1954 as G. Taylor Ltd when George Taylor and a colleague, both of whom were then employed by a cold coil wire spring company in West Bromwich, decided to start up a cold coil wire spring business in West Bromwich on their own. Both were skilled spring coiling machine operators. In contrast to most who start out on their own, George, who had recently won a large dividend on the pools, chose to go for the quality end of the market rather than starting at the low quality end of the business, and to specialize in the springs required by the car industry. His colleague, Gerald Hughes, had no funds to invest but worked long hours to help the company establish itself. With the post-war growth of the car industry and much hard work, the company prospered. By 1974 it had reached a turnover of £½ million p.a. and a profit before tax of £80,000 p.a. In recognition of his support, George Taylor had given 10% of the shares in the company to Gerald Hughes.

As the boom of 1973–4 receded, so some of the competitors of G. Taylor Ltd found the going getting more difficult. In 1976 George Taylor bought Springs Ltd, another spring business based in West Bromwich. Springs Ltd had two factories, one in West Bromwich making cold coil wire springs (mainly for the car industry) and the other located in London and making bedding springs. The following year George Taylor also bought a cold coil wire spring business located at Redditch. It was at this time that he decided to change the name of the parent company to Steel Springs Ltd and to restrict the name G. Taylor Ltd to the original subsidiary in West Bromwich, where the name was well respected for quality cold coil wire springs. He also decided to make the two parts of Springs Ltd into separate subsidiaries.

By 1978 Steel Springs Ltd had expanded to a turnover of £5.4 million, split between its four subsidiaries as shown in table C.1. George Taylor is now 55 years old and Gerald Hughes is 52. George's son John, an Oxford graduate in history, has been trained in the business, has spent some time as marketing director of G. Taylor Ltd and is now managing director of Bedding Springs Ltd. The group board consists of four active directors plus George Graham, the previous owner of Redditch Springs, who is now 75 years of age and retired (except for attending the board meeting once a year when the annual accounts are presented). The other active director is James Weekes, a local chartered accountant who advises the group on accounting and financial matters on a part-time basis.

Table C.1 Breakdown of Steel Springs Ltd by subsidiary, 1978

Subsidiary	Location	Turnover £m	Profits before tax £000	Products
G. Taylor Ltd	West Bromwich	1.1	180	Cold coil springs
Springs (West) Bromwich) Ltd	West Bromwich	0.8	80	Cold coil springs
Bedding Springs Ltd London	London	1.5	120	Bedding springs
Redditch Springs Ltd	Redditch	2.0	60	Cold coil springs

The shares of the business are divided as follows:

George Taylor	(Chairman)	55%
John Taylor	(Director)	15%
George Graham	(Director)	15%
Gerald Hughes	(Director)	5%
Elizabeth Taylor	(George Taylor's wife)	5%
Jean Williams	(Daughters of the original	2½%
Barbara Williams	owner of Springs Ltd)	2½%

C.2 Analysis of Steel Springs' Situation

It is clear from the description of the three sectors at the beginning of the case that, as far as analysing strategy is concerned, there is really no such thing as 'the springs industry'. Although they all have the word 'springs' in their description, these three sectors are entirely different areas of competition, with no significant overlap of customers or technology. They are all in the wide field of metal manufacturing but that is as far as any link exists. Steel Springs is therefore a conglomerate of companies operating in two different areas of activity.

Besides checking that each subsidiary is periodically reviewing its strategy, there are three main issues which this group should address, or cause to be addressed. These are:

- Why is the performance of Redditch Springs so poor, compared to the two other cold coil wire spring companies in the group?

251

- What should the future balance of resources be between the wire springs and bedding springs businesses?
- Should the three wire springs businesses remain independent of each other and largely autonomous or should the group play a more active role?

The description of the three sectors at the start of the case contains information vital for understanding the answers to these questions. We can omit the heavy leaf and laminated springs sector, as this is not involved further in the case.

C.2.1 What is the Nature of Each of the Business Areas?

The description of the bedding and upholstery springs sector clearly indicates that market share and company size are important in this area of business; there are significant economies of scale. Orders are much larger than in the wire springs business, there are fewer customers, some standardization is possible and investment in equipment coupled with high productivity to bring costs down is the route to success.

The wire springs business is different. Entry and exit costs are low. While there are economies of scale which small companies can pursue, there appear to be diseconomies of scale beyond a certain size, for the total turnover of £60 million p.a. is shared among some 200 companies and no company is dominant.

What are these diseconomies of scale, and why do they exist? Think for a moment about the variety of situations in which these wire springs are used. Whether they be destined for vehicle construction, domestic appliances or electric light fittings, these springs are small. Therefore an order for, say, 1,000 may only cost a few pounds. The spring required by the customer has to fit into a particular space, have a particular strength, be of a particular length and coil diameter and have suitable ends (bent, chamfered, etc.) for fitting into the product and performing its role.

So these springs are produced in batches to meet customers' individual requirements. This means that the machines have to be set up separately for each individual order. During running, the machines may slip out of tolerance and need adjustment. So a machine minder will look after a small number of machines, both to set them up between batches and to correct them when necessary during production.

But that machine-based production process only converts a coil of wire into a large number of short wire springs; the ends still have to be formed to suit the particular customer's requirements. Besides its set of spring-making machines, therefore, a wire spring factory has an area where the ends of the springs are formed into the required shapes. This is usually done by women sitting at benches using jigs specially designed by the individual companies.

Economies of scale are clearly limited; diseconomies of scale arise from the problem of controlling production. Think back to Newprint (appendix A), where a similar problem occurred. With wire springs we again have mainly small value orders with batch production. There is a level at which the number of orders going through a wire spring works is excessive, with the result that production planning and control deteriorate, causing unit costs to rise.

At the time of this case this loss of efficiency would appear to occur somewhere in the range of £1 million to £3 million p.a. turnover; taking into account inflation since then, the figures now would be nearer three times these levels.

One of the ways in which it might be possible to get round the problem of diseconomies of scale and grow efficiently to a larger size is to attempt to persuade some of the customers to design their products around standard springs. This would allow longer production runs and greater automation of the equipment of tolerance control, enabling one machine minder to cover a larger number of machines. At the time this case was written, a European company was in fact successfully pursuing this path on a very narrow range of wire springs.

The other way around the difficulty is to set up a group of wire spring businesses, with the group level doing only those few things which add synergy, without destroying the profit accountability and motivation of the individual businesses.

C.2.2 Addressing Steel Springs' Problems

Now we are ready to address the particular issues facing Steel Springs.

The issue of the poor performance of Redditch Springs is mainly a business strategy rather than a group strategy issue. The earlier parts of this book should have given you enough understanding of most of the possible causes, from poor day-to-day management to business strategy, for repetition here to be unnecessary. However, there are two other aspects of this particular case which I should draw to your attention.

- It is possible that the difficulties being met by Redditch arise from its pattern of customers and size of orders. Some costing and comparison with the patterns for the other two wire spring businesses in the group would help in assessing whether a change in market focus and pricing policy is needed.
- Another possibility is that Redditch has already grown to a size when diseconomies of scale begin to be serious. If this is so, breaking the production activity into two would seem the obvious solution.

253

Appendix C

Now let us move on to the other two group strategy issues.

At present the group is half-heartedly backing two horses. The danger with this strategy is that, without considerably greater resources, it will become less competitive on both. The group needs to decide between being a major competitor in the bedding springs business or a group containing a larger set of wire spring businesses. So it needs to look at its financial strength, its current position in both areas of business, the prospects in each and the sequence of takeovers and divestments which would be necessary to achieve a longer-term shape which will give the group greater competitive advantage.

The structure of the group as a whole and the role of the group level itself will depend on the choice of group strategy between bedding springs and wire springs.

Let me illustrate this organizational choice by looking only at the wire springs part of the group. It is all too easy to jump to the conclusion 'merge the three wire spring businesses', but that would risk inefficiency arising from the diseconomies of scale. Alternatively, the subsidiaries could remain separate, with the group taking on staff in production and marketing. This, though, would add to costs and demotivate the individual businesses. So the real question is:

- what limited role should the group level perform which will generate real synergy?

A group chief executive, as at present, with no other managerial staff at group level, plus performance-based incentives for managing directors of individual businesses may be the most effective option; but let us consider other alternatives.

In marketing, should the businesses compete with each other? Given the wide market and the large number of competitors, the crude answer is probably yes. It may be that for the largest potential orders (for which many of the smaller springs businesses would not be able to compete) the businesses within the group could find that they were mainly in competition with each other. If so, then in these few situations perhaps the chief executive should intervene; but that does not require additional group staff.

Small companies find it difficult to gain export orders. Should the group appoint a marketing executive purely to gain export orders for the three businesses? If so, then how can he/she be held accountable and his/her post eliminated if the activity proves not to be worthwhile? Perhaps he/she should be treated as a small separate profit centre with the right to take orders and to sell them at a lower price to individual businesses. If he/she cannot make enough profit between the two to

254

exceed his/her total costs (salary, office, car, etc.) as well as yielding a group profit (synergy), the experiment should be terminated.

Purchasing steel wire may be a similar opportunity, but this would probably not merit a full-time appointment. Would the export executive be able to do both jobs, including buying wire from Europe or the UK as appropriate?

How about production? The businesses could be free to sub-contract to each other in times of over-full order books and delays in delivery. How about production equipment and systems? For example, what about transferring ideas on the jigs for shaping the ends of the springs? This does not merit the appointment of a group production executive. If it is not already occurring, the production managers of the individual businesses only need some encouragement to learn from each other.

The crucial point in this example, as in other group strategy situations, is to think through the opportunities for synergy and for the group level to get involved only in those activities which yield a clear overall benefit.

Appendix D

A Brief Introduction to Some of the Techniques Strategy Consultants Use

The role of concepts/techniques in the analysis of company strategy was discussed in chapter 11 (pages 191–7). The purpose of this appendix is to give a very brief introduction to some of the techniques which internal or external strategy consultants may occasionally use. References are given for those who wish to pursue their interests further.

Wide use will be made by consultants of economic forecasts and of some statistical techniques (Chandler and Cockle, 1982); these fall outside the scope of this book.

The list given below is restricted to those techniques which consultants tell me that they have found useful and require their staff to understand.

Adding value and value chains (Porter, 1985; Bergsma, 1989; Goold, Campbell and Alexander, 1994; Koller, 1994)
Please see pages 111–12.

Benchmarking Please see 'Competitor benchmarking' below.

Business portfolio (Hedley, 1977)
Please see pages 153–6 and 194–7.

Business process re-engineering
Please see 'Core process redesign' on page 257.

Competitor benchmarking (Walleck, O'Halloran and Leader, 1991)
In the 1970s, 'interindustry' and 'intra-industry' comparisons were popular as a means of setting targets for performance improvement (please also see 'Gap analysis' on page 259).

Competitor benchmarking is a development of that thinking into a practical way of setting targets at every level down to the most detailed. For example, in the car industry comparison can be taken right through from profit per car and cars produced per man year, down to the efficiency of, say, the stages of treating the bodywork to prevent corrosion, the efficiency of the transportation of finished cars to the customer, the efficiency of parts of the research laboratory, the efficiency of an activity of the accounting department, or even the efficiency of response to telephone calls to the company. Competitive benchmarking involves comparison by collaboration between companies in the same industry, where possible, but also the exchange of information about activities in different industries, which although involving different products do in fact require a similar task to be achieved.

Aiming to improve to the level of the best and incorporating ideas from elsewhere can lead to more rapid improvement in efficiency than simply studying one's own operations.

Core process redesign (Kaplan and Medlock, 1991; Hagel III, 1993)
Over time and as the needs facing companies change, so the detailed processes tend to be adjusted to meet the new requirements. This process of modification can well lead to situations where the whole set of processes has become very complex and costly, when in fact, if one were to start with a clean slate, a simpler and more effective set of processes would be used. The term 'process re-engineering' can apply to the process of producing a single product or to a major and wider process spanning the company as a whole. To distinguish its use from that at the more detailed level, at the level of company strategy it is usually referred to either as 'core process redesign' or 'business process re-engineering'.

For a single business company there are usually only two or three major processes which determine the company's efficiency.

For example, at Rover, one of these core processes is the one which attracts interest in buying new cars, aims to meet a particular customer's requirement in terms of the exact colour and specification of car required and seeks to supply that car to the customer within a few days. Until a few years ago, stocks of new cars were mainly held at the various dealerships. Except when the particular car which the customer required happened to be in stock, there was a choice of taking not the same but a slightly different car immediately, the dealer getting the required car within a few days by transfer from another dealer or a longer delay while waiting for a car of the precise specification required to be manufactured and delivered. As a result, this type of process was not ideal. Because some customers were persuaded to take a slightly different car, the signals back to the company were not an exact reflection of customer requirements. Because many cars were being moved from one dealer to another, occasionally damage occurred which had to be repaired, causing extra cost and delay in addition to the cost of transport itself. The then fairly long delay between an order being sent into production and a customer receiving delivery was also discouraging.

Standing back from this process and asking some basic questions about its objective, what the customer needs, how to measure the success of the process and how else the process could be designed, led to a major change in the process and in its effectiveness.

The main stock of new cars is now held at just five locations across the UK. A customer's requirement goes straight into the production schedules either to replenish the stockholding because it has quickly met his/her requirement or to meet his/her needs directly.

The results of this major change in process are very significant. Customers are receiving the precise cars they require on average much more quickly than before, production schedules reflect actual customer preferences, damage to cars in transit has been much reduced and there has been a major reduction in the number of cars in stock and hence in capital required.

Directional policy matrix (Robinson, Hichens and Wade, 1978; Hussey, 1978)
This matrix is described briefly on page 196. It is a development by Shell of the business portfolio developed by the Boston Consulting Group. The directional policy matrix has slightly different axes from the business portfolio and each is divided into three rather than two, making a total of nine boxes rather than four.

One of the axes classifies the business sector's prospects across a range from unattractive through average to attractive. The other axis classifies the company's competitive capabilities in relation to that business sector, from weak through average to strong. Several factors are considered before placing a business on either of these axes.

Experience or learning curve (Hedley, 1976)
Time does not automatically cause learning to occur: learning has to be earned.

Studies across a variety of industries have shown that a relationship frequently exists between the total cost of manufacturing, distributing and selling a product and the accumulated experience over the whole period in which it has been produced. Each time the accumulated experience doubles, the total cost in real terms (that is, excluding inflation) can be made to decline by a percentage, depending on the type of product involved but normally in the range of 20–30%. For some products the curves are available in the literature.

This 'law' arises from several causes. There is learning over time from repeatedly producing the same product; and as a company produces more of a product it also tends to grow and therefore to gain economies of scale. Other factors are the move towards greater mechanization/automation and changes in the design to lower the cost.

This experience effect is an important factor in deciding strategy in those businesses involving standard products which can be transported cheaply. For example, in the microchip business, some companies base their plans over several years ahead, on at least getting costs down to those on the experience curve. Advance prices are quoted on this basis and controls introduced to force this rate of learning to occur. The logic behind this is that if the company fails to achieve this rate of learning, it will lose to competitors which do.

Gap analysis (Argenti, 1989)
Gap analysis is a concept and an implied process rather than a mathematical technique. First, the improvement in performance which a company wishes to achieve over a planning period is stated. Next, the likely year-by-year performance is calculated, assuming that no change is made from the existing strategy. The 'gap' is the difference between the targeted performance and the minimum performance implied by the no-change-in-strategy option. Alternative strategies are then considered in attempts to close the gap and ultimately to reach a plan which will meet the target.

What this process does is to combat complacency. Without the setting of a target for improvement, complacency can well lead to poor performance. In practice, it is important to set a target which is difficult to achieve but not obviously impossible. Setting such a target involves considering the current and likely future performance of the most effective competitors. If the company being considered is already in the lead, the target set should be tough compared to its own previous performance – hence the use of the abbreviation BHAG ('big hairy audacious goals' – Collins and Porras, 1995) to describe the behaviour of a sample of leading companies.

PIMS (profit impact of market strategies) (Schoeffler, Buzzell and Heany, 1974)
Based on research started by General Electric of the USA and then developed by other US firms over several years, PIMS is a service now also available in the UK from the Strategic Planning Institute. It involves research relating business success to strategy choice.

Companies joining this research activity pay a fee and are required to provide commercially sensitive information on a confidential basis. This information includes year-by-year details from the profit and loss account and from the balance sheet, for each individual business, right down to such details as R&D expenditure, advertising expenditure, etc.

Suitably modified to protect confidentiality, this information for a large number of businesses from a variety of sectors is fed into a computer.

What this research seeks to do is to explore the relationships between the various factors involved and commercial success, with a view to providing some guidance on strategy choice. Among the many factors whose effect on future success have been analysed are R&D expenditure, product (or service) quality, investment intensity and corporate diversity.

Information from this continuing research is provided to members, who can seek additional analyses from this large, anonymous database.

A major advantage of the PIMS approach compared to many other strategy techniques is that it does not rely on only two or three important factors: it considers over 30 factors and highlights those which are more important in different cases.

My view is that, like any other techniques, PIMS by itself cannot tell a company what strategy to pursue. But used with understanding it can help in several ways. It can produce a statement of the financial perform-ance which a company should be achieving if it is well managed. It can help to generate ideas for different strategies. It can also be used to sift through existing ideas to find those which merit further attention by other means, before a particular strategy is chosen.

Scenario generation (Chandler and Cockle, 1982; Leemhuis, 1985; Wack, 1985; Schnaars, 1987)
The future is uncertain. It is important to have descriptions of the variety of possible future environments which the company may meet, both in generating a shortlist of alternative strategies and in checking out the robustness of the likely best choice.

A single scenario is a description of a possible future in which eco-nomic, technological, political, social and other developments evolve in a consistent way.

Because strategy choice is heavily dependent on the environment, in recent years (particularly for larger companies) considerable efforts have been put into developing methods for generating and using alternative scenarios.

Spreadsheets
To save effort, most strategy consultants use computer programmes for calculating and laying out, as a series of figures over time, the effect of various strategy choices on the company's profit and loss account and balance sheet. Such a spread of numbers is known as a spreadsheet.

Technological forecasting
There have been many attempts to forecast future developments in technology. Among the best known of these is the Delphi method. Given the uncertainty of technological development, it is not surprising that none of these methods can do more than slightly reduce the uncertainty. The article by Twiss (1979) is still a fair summary of the present state of these efforts.

TOWS or SWOT matrix (Weilrich, 1982)
Please see pages 47–8.

References

Argenti, John, 1975. 'Company failure: the tell-tale signs at the top', *The Director*, September, pp. 278–81.

Argenti, John, 1978. 'Long-term budgets can damage your company's health', *Management Accounting*, May, pp. 105–7.

Argenti, John, 1987. *The Argenti System*, a series of three manuals from Argenti Systems Ltd (Pettistree Lodge, Woodbridge, Suffolk).

Argenti, John, 1989. *Practical Corporate Planning* (London: Unwin).

Argenti, John, 1993. *Your Organisation: What Is It For?* (Maidenhead: McGraw Hill).

Ashley, Cedric, 1995. 'Innovation is vital for your long-term success', *The Strategic Planning Society's News*, May, p. 3.

Baker, Michael J. (ed.), 1987. *The Marketing Book* (London: Heinemann for the Institute of Marketing).

Beck, P. W., 1982. 'Corporate planning for an uncertain future', *Long Range Planning*, vol. 15, no. 4, pp. 12–21.

Bergsma, Ennius E., 1989. 'Managing value: the new corporate strategy', *The McKinsey Quarterly*, Winter, pp. 57–72.

Blackburn, Virginia L., 1994. 'The effectiveness of corporate control in the US', *Corporate Governance*, vol. 2, no. 4, pp. 196–202.

British Institute of Management, 1988. *Profile of British Industry: The Manager's View* (London: British Institute of Management).

Cadbury, Sir Adrian, 1992. *Report of the Committee on the Financial Aspects of Corporate Governance* (London: Gee).

Campbell, Andrew, 1995. 'Vertical integration: synergy or seduction?', *Long Range Planning*, vol. 28, no. 2, pp. 126–8.

Cecchini, Paul, 1989. *The European Challenge, 1992: The Benefits of a Single Market* (Aldershot: Wildwood House).

Chandler, John and Cockle, Paul, 1982. *Techniques of Scenario Planning* (New York: McGraw-Hill).

Clarke, Christopher J., 1987. 'Acquisitions: techniques for measuring strategic fit', *Long Range Planning*, vol. 20, no. 3, pp. 12–18.

Collins, James and Porras, Jerry, 1995. 'How the best stay at the top', *Director*, June, pp. 56–64.

References

Copeland, Tom, Koller, Tim and Murrin, Jack, 1989. 'The value manager', *The McKinsey Quarterly*, Autumn, pp. 94–108.

de Geus, Arie P., 1988. 'Planning as learning', *Harvard Business Review*, March–April, pp. 70–74.

Devlin, Godfrey and Bleackley, Mark, 1988. 'Strategic alliances: guidelines for success', *Long Range Planning*, vol. 21, no. 5, pp. 18–23.

Dewhurst, Jim and Burns, Paul, 1983. *Small Business: Finance and Control* (London: Macmillan).

Donaldson, Gordon and Lorsch, Jay W., 1983. *Decision Making at the Top: The Shaping of Strategic Direction* (New York: Basic Books).

Friberg, Eric G., 1988. 'The Challenge of 1992', *The McKinsey Quarterly*, Autumn, pp. 27–40.

Gluck, Frederick W., 1982. 'Meeting the challenge of global competition', *The McKinsey Quarterly*, Autumn, pp. 2–13.

Goold, Michael, Campbell, Andrew and Alexander, Marcus, 1994. *Corporate Level Strategy: Creating Value in the Multi-business Company* (New York: John Wiley).

Hagel III, John, 1993. 'Core process redesign: keeping CPR on track', *The McKinsey Quarterly*, no. 1, pp. 59–77.

Hamel, Gary and Prahalad, C. K., 1980. 'Strategic intent', *The McKinsey Quarterly*, Spring, pp. 36–61.

Hamel, Gary and Prahalad, C. K., 1986. 'Do you really have a global strategy?', *The McKinsey Quarterly*, Summer, pp. 34–50.

Hedley, Barry, 1976. 'A fundamental approach to strategy development', *Long Range Planning*, vol. 10, December, pp. 2–11.

Hedley, Barry, 1977. 'Strategy and the business portfolio', *Long Range Planning*, vol. 10, February, pp. 9–15.

Hill, T., 1983. 'Manufacturing's strategic role', *Journal of the Operational Research Society*, vol. 34, no. 9, pp. 853–60.

Hill, Terry, 1985. *Manufacturing Strategy: The Strategic Management of the Manufacturing Function* (London: Macmillan).

Hill, Terry, 1987. *Small Business: Production/Operations Management* (London: Macmillan).

Houlden, B. T., 1980. 'Data and effective corporate planning', *Long Range Planning*, vol. 13, October, pp. 106–11.

Houlden, Brian, 1985. 'Survival of the corporate planner', *Long Range Planning*, vol. 18, no. 5, pp. 49–54.

Houlden, Brian T., 1986. 'Developing a company's strategic management capability', *Long Range Planning*, vol. 19, no. 5, pp. 89–93.

Houlden, Brian, 1990. 'Buy-outs and beyond: motivations, strategies and ownership changes', *Long Range Planning*, vol. 23, no. 4, pp. 73–7.

Houlden, Brian T., 1994. *The Performance of MBOs: Some Issues for Investors* (London: Touche Ross).

References

Houlden, Brian T., 1995. 'How corporate planning adapts and survives', *Long Range Planning*, vol. 28, no. 4, pp. 99–108.

Houlden, Brian and King, John, 1978. 'Time for professional directors?', *Director*, November, pp. 46–8.

Houlden, Brian and Spurrell, David, 1986. 'Caught in the strategy trap', *Director*, October, pp. 75–6.

Houlden, Brian T. and Woodcock, David J., 1989. 'When production is under stress', *Sundridge Park Management Review*, vol. 2, no. 8, Spring, pp. 3–6.

Houston, Bill, 1989. *Avoiding Adversity* (Newton Abbott: David and Charles).

Hussey, D. E., 1978. 'Practical experience with the directional policy matrix', *Long Range Planning*, vol. 11, August, pp. 2–8.

Kaplan, Robert B. and Medlock, Laura, 1991. 'Rethinking the corporation: core process redesign', *The McKinsey Quarterly*, no. 2, pp. 27–43.

Koller, Timothy, 1994. 'What is value-based management?', *The McKinsey Quarterly*, no. 3, pp. 87–101.

Leemhuis, J. P., 1985. 'Using scenarios to develop strategies', *Long Range Planning*, vol. 18, no. 2, pp. 30–7.

Loose, Peter, 1987. *The Company Director: His Functions, Powers and Duties*, 6th edn (Bristol: Jordan & Sons).

Lorange, Peter, Roos, Johan and Bronn, Peggy Simcic, 1992. 'Building successful business alliances', *Long Range Planning*, vol. 25, no. 6, pp. 10–17.

Lorenz, Christopher, 1988. 'General Electric of the US: Why strategy has been put in the hands of the line managers', *Financial Times*, 18 May.

Macdonald, A. M., 1972. *Chambers Twentieth Century Dictionary* (Edinburgh: W. & R. Chambers).

Majaro, Simon, 1988. *The Creative Gap: Managing Ideas for Profit* (London: Longman).

McLean, Robert J., 1985. 'How to make acquisitions work', *The McKinsey Quarterly*, Autumn, pp. 65–75.

Mintzberg, Henry, 1988. 'Crafting strategy', *The McKinsey Quarterly*, Summer, pp. 71–89.

Mitchell, David, 1989. '1992: the implications for management', *Long Range Planning*, vol. 22, no. 1, pp. 32–40.

Ohmae, Kenichi, 1982. *The Mind of the Strategist: The Art of Japanese Business* (New York: McGraw-Hill).

Ohmae, Kenichi, 1983. 'The strategic triangle and business unit strategy', *The McKinsey Quarterly*, Winter, pp. 9–24.

Ohmae, Kenichi, 1985. *Triad Power: The Coming Shape of Global Competition* (New York: Free Press).

References

Ohmae, Kenichi, 1989. 'The global logic of strategic alliances', *Harvard Business Review*, 67(2), pp. 143–54.

O'Neill, Hugh, 1986. 'Turnaround and recovery: what strategy do you need?', *Long Range Planning*, vol. 19, no. 1, pp. 80–8.

Owen, Geoffrey and Harrison, Trevor, 1995. 'Why ICI chose to demerge', *Harvard Business Review*, March–April, pp. 133–42.

Parker, Hugh, 1978. 'Letters to a new chairman', *Director*, April–December.

Peters, Thomas J. and Waterman, Robert H., 1982. *In Search of Excellence: Lessons from America's Best Run Companies* (New York: Harper and Row).

Pink, Alan I. H., 1988. 'Strategic leadership through corporate planning at ICI', *Long Range Planning*, vol. 21, no. 1, pp. 18–25.

Porter, Michael E., 1979. 'How competitive forces shape strategy', *Harvard Business Review*, March–April, pp. 137–45.

Porter, Michael E., 1985. *Competitive Advantage: Creating and Sustaining Superior Performance* (New York: Free Press).

Porter, Michael E., 1987. 'From competitive advantage to corporate strategy', *Harvard Business Review*, May–June, pp. 43–9; reprinted in *The McKinsey Quarterly*, Spring 1988, pp. 35–66.

Reinton, Sigurd E. and Foote, Nathaniel, 1988. 'Why parents must be more particular', *The McKinsey Quarterly*, Autumn, pp. 46–53.

Robinson, S. J. Q., Hichens, R. E. and Wade, D. P., 1978. 'The directional policy matrix: tool for strategic planning', *Long Range Planning*, vol. 11, June, pp. 8–15.

Schnaars, Steven P., 1987. 'How to develop and use scenarios', *Long Range Planning*, vol. 20, no. 1, pp. 105–14.

Schoeffler, Sidney, Buzzell, Robert D. and Heany, Donald F., 1974. 'Impact of strategic planning on profit performance', *Harvard Business Review*, March–April, pp. 137–44.

Slatter, Stuart, 1984. *Corporate Recovery: A Guide to Turnaround Management* (Harmondsworth: Penguin).

Stone, W. Robert and Heany, Donald F., 1984. 'Dealing with a corporate identity crisis', *Long Range Planning*, vol. 17, no. 1, pp. 10–18.

Turner, Graham, 1984. 'ICI becomes proactive', *Long Range Planning*, vol. 17, no. 6, pp. 12–16.

Twiss, Brian C., 1979. 'Recent trends in long range forecasting for technology-based organisations: a review article', *Long Range Planning*, vol. 12, April, pp. 120–4.

Wack, Pierre, 1985. 'Scenarios: shooting the rapids', *Harvard Business Review*, November–December, pp. 139–50.

Walleck, A. Steven, O'Halloran, J. David and Leader, Charles A., 1991. 'Benchmarking world-class performance', *The McKinsey Quarterly*, no. 1, pp. 3–24.

References

Waterman, Robert H., Jr, Peters, Thomas J. and Phillips, Julien R., 1980. 'Structure is not organization', *Business Horizons*, June (Foundation for the School of Business, Indiana University); reprinted in *The McKinsey Quarterly*, Summer 1980, pp. 2–20.

Waterworth, Derek, 1988. *Small Business: Marketing* (London: Macmillan).

Weilrich, Heinz, 1982. 'The TOWS matrix: a tool for situational analysis', *Long Range Planning*, vol. 15, no. 2, pp. 54–66.

Wilder, Simon, 1985. 'Directing technological development: the role of the board', *Long Range Planning*, vol. 18, no. 4, pp. 44–9.

Wright, Mike, Normand, James and Robbie, Ken, 1990. *Touche Ross's Management Buy-outs* (Cambridge: Woodhead-Faulkner).

References